BEYOND
THE
CLOSED
DOOR

BEYOND THE CLOSED DOOR

*Chinese Culture and the
Creation of T'ai Chi Ch'uan*

ARIEH LEV BRESLOW

ALMOND BLOSSOM PRESS

The Almond Blossom Press, first edition, June 1995
Beyond the Closed Door
Copyright © 1995 by Arieh Lev Breslow

All rights reserved under International and Pan-American
Copyright Conventions, including the right to reproduce
this book or portions thereof in any form whatsoever.
For further information address the Almond Blossom
Press, PO Box 10600, Jerusalem, Israel

ISBN: 0-9644730-0-3

Graphic design and cover by Benjie Herskowitz

Cover artwork courtesy of Jacob Pins Collection
16th-Century landscape, artist unknown

All photography by Debbi Cooper
unless otherwise specified
Photographic model: Anne Breslow

Printed in Israel

Dedicated to my father David (z"l)
and my mother Minnie,
without whose spiritual and material support,
this book could not have been written.

For wisdom is a defense,
Even as wealth is a defense;
But the advantage of wisdom is
that it preserves the life
of the one who has it.

Eccleseastes, 7:12

Landscape, Peach Blossom Spring.
Artist: Yüan Chiang, Dated 1718
Courtesy of the Princeton University Press

CONTENTS

PART 1 – THE CANVAS OF CHINESE CULTURE

PART 2 – THE DEVELOPMENT OF CHINESE RELIGIOUS AND PHILOSOPHICAL THOUGHT

PART 3 – THE CREATION OF T'AI CHI CH'UAN

Acknowledgements

There is a saying in the Jewish tradition that 'you should make for yourself a teacher' and in the Chinese tradition that 'a teacher for a day is like a parent for life.' I was very fortunate to have studied T'ai Chi with three superb teachers. The first was Ken Cohen who introduced me to T'ai Chi and taught me its deep connection to nature and a way of being in the world. My second teacher was Benjamin Pang Jeng Lo. He taught me the meaning of 'the basics' in T'ai Chi and interpreted the words of the masters in way that I could apply to my T'ai Chi practice. Lenzie Williams was my third teacher. He taught me the importance of the link between the basic principles of T'ai Chi and push-hands. What little I know about push-hands comes from him, and, of course, our teacher, Benjamin Lo.

There are others who helped me along the way. Jou, Tsung Hwa gave an important workshop that influenced my understanding of Chi kung. Although I only had the opportunity to take a few lessons with him, William C. C. Chen shared some of his unique insights into the art of relaxing in the form and in push-hands. Baatan and Jane Faigao conducted a wonderful workshop in the Rocky Mountains that pointed me in the right direction. One day during a visit to Israel, Bill Helms took time off to push-hands with me as well as to teach me a set of Chi kung.

In my early years in Israel I was lucky to have three teachers who freely shared their knowledge with me; Mark Green, Ossie Ben Porat, and Nitsan Michaeli.

My longtime students have been an inspiration to me. I am sure that I have learned as much from them as they from me. A few of them are Ellah Cohen, Ora Wiskind, Moishe Shuster, Zak and Elisheva Shavin, Victoria Sureya, Bette Schwietzer, Shalom Perl, Gidion Dilbari, Karni Yishai, Eiphat Covshi, Dina Ritchie, Netta Efroni, Rifka Talmon, Gila Silverman, Telma Gotlieb, Tammy Haas, Al and Norma Potashnik, Nomi Shultz, Sally Oren, Danny Loney, and Shoshana Lederman.

Chava Naeh was helpful with her wide knowledge of healing arts as well as her readiness to help me with the manuscript.

Nellie Klabbers and Marita Wessels organized the workshops of Benjamin Lo in Holland which provided me the opportunity to continue my studies with him. Those retreats in the woods were something very special.

I want to thank my editor, Mordecai Beck, who put this book in order and did his best to get me to write an intelligent sentence. Noga Fisher, one of my students, also read this manuscript and I benefited from her sage advice and corrections.

Many thanks go to Esther Rosenfeld who proofread the manuscript.

Nothing said here could begin to express my appreciation for the help and love I received from my life's partner, Anne. She has been wife, mother, cheerleader, a shoulder to cry on, inspiration, and fellow devotee of T'ai Chi. If T'ai Chi did only one thing for me, it would be enough that it provided a context to meet her. This project has not been easy for her. During the writing of this book when I was often closeted away, she managed the family alone while ensuring that I would have the space to research and write. My love, thanks, and devotion to her are forever.

In the end, in spite of everyone's help, as every author knows; 'the buck stops here.' I am responsible for any and all errors that remain in this text. I only hope that these errors will not prevent you, the reader, from benefiting from the knowledge contained within.

PREFACE

T'AI CHI — WHY A BOOK?

"Cut doors and windows for a room.
It is holes that make it useful."
Tao Te Ching, ch. 11

China is the most populous nation on the face of the earth, yet it's history and culture are surprisingly little known or understood by outsiders. This point was driven home to me recently in a class that I was conducting at the Jerusalem School of T'ai Chi Ch'uan. In the middle of the session, I asked the students if any of them had read the *Tao Te Ching* of Lao Tzu. Out of fifteen students, only two hands were raised. This surprised me. The *Tao Te Ching* is one of the most important books in Chinese literature. It contains many ideas that form the foundation of T'ai Chi, and is an important key to understanding Chinese thought. The *Tao Te Ching* is readily available in many languages, including English and Hebrew. Here was a class of students eager to learn this exotic discipline without the slightest notion of the background from which it grew. When I thought about what had happened in the class, I wondered if I had known much more than my students about Chinese culture when I had begun my T'ai Chi studies.

At that moment a seed had been planted that would grow into this book. Little did I know how much I was to learn about Chinese history and culture as I plunged ever deeper into the vast ocean of Chinese thought. Researching and writing this book has been a humbling and exciting experience, and I hope some of that excitement will rub off on my readers.

One other question occurred to me as a result of my class. If so little is known about T'ai Chi why should outsiders want to learn it? The answers that come to mind are varied — that it is good for one's health, that its meditative style can reduce tension, that it contains a supreme method of self-defense.

Whatever the initial motivation, a serious study of T'ai Chi requires time and perseverance. In this respect a general knowledge of the background of this fascinating discipline can help clarify much unnecessary mystery and misinformation. This present volume is a response to my class, as well as to the many other people in a similar fog about basic concepts concerning China and the Far East. It is also written for those who have studied Oriental thought and would like to know more, and for the general reader who simply loves knowledge and ideas for their own sake. The perspective of this book is that of a Westerner who feels comfortable in his own culture but is also drawn to the wisdom of other cultures. The book highlights the many parallels as well as the contrasts between East and West.

There are many kinds of walls. There are those to keep people out, like the Great Wall of China. There are those to keep people in, like the once notorious Berlin Wall. There are walls of remembrance and prayer like the Western Wall in Jerusalem which, for some, is a gate opening from this world to the Heavens above. Then there are walls with windows and doors built into or chiseled out of them. As the proverb quoted above suggests, a door or window with a view to the East could offer a useful way of understanding not only T'ai Chi in particular but also Chinese culture as a totality. This book is meant to be such a window, which will enable Westerners to better understand the enigma that is China.

Arieh Lev Breslow
Jerusalem 1995

List of Illustrations

DEFINITIONS*

T'ai Chi Ch'uan, also known as T'ai Chi, is a form of Chinese exercise characterized by slow flowing movements that are performed in a relaxed conscious manner. It combines physical exercise, meditation and self-defense with the goal of leading a healthy life through the balance and harmony of mind, body and emotions. T'ai Chi is different from other forms of exercise in that it emphasizes the internal systems of the body (mind, organs and energy) in contrast to the external systems which stress the power generated by the muscles.

Push-hands is a companion exercise to the T'ai Chi form in which the students learn how well they have embodied the principles of the T'ai Chi. It is characterized by the dynamic interplay of two partners who stand across from each other and begin a 'push-hands form,' which gradually flows into spontaneous pushing and yielding.

T'ai Chi form and push-hands are explained in detail in Chapter 8.

TRANSCRIPTION AND PRONUNCIATION

In 1979 the People's Republic of China officially adopted the Pinyin system of romanization. For example, "Peking" became "Beijing." However, the older way called the Wade-Giles system is still widely used. In order to conform to the transcription most commonly used in scholarly literature, I have chosen to employ a modified version of the Wade-Giles system. "Modified" means that I tried to use names and terms that would be easily recognized by the general reading audience.

ch	pronounced	j
ch'		ch
e		short *u* as in *fun*
j		like English *r* in *ready*
k		g
k'		k
p		b
p'		p
t		d (tao is pronounced dao)
t'		t
ts		dz
ts'		ts
hs		sh

PART 1

---

*The Canvas
of
Chinese
Culture*

CHAPTER 1

THE TRANSFORMATION OF CHINESE SOCIETY

Historical Background

Chinese civilization began in the southern part of the Loess Plateau and spread over Shensi province, East Kansu, West Shensi, and West Honan. Gradually it expanded outwards until its growth was limited by the Tibetan Plateau, which was too high and too cold to sustain large numbers of people. Nevertheless, historically the Chinese have laid claim to Tibet as part of its 'manifest destiny,' often sending ethnic Chinese to settle there, despite the harsh conditions. To the north the Gobi desert formed another natural barrier which inhibited expansion. Only to the west and south, in what is now Southeast Asia, Bangladesh and India, could the Chinese hope to expand more easily. At various times the peoples of Southeast Asia were colonized or dominated by their powerful northern cousins. (See map p. xxi)

Because of these geographical barriers and an apparent reticence for social intercourse with outsiders, Chinese civilization remained peculiarly insular for centuries from the rest of the world. H.G. Wells observed that the flowering of ancient Chinese civilization was at one point parallel to that of the Roman Empire

3

in the West and yet the two had no significant contact, as if these two great civilizations existed on different planets.

It would not be until the demand for Chinese silk, in the first and second centuries (CE),* that meaningful trade relations developed with other nations, including India, Persia and the Roman Empire. These encounters were not restricted to commerce along the Old Silk Road. Alongside economic exchange there were also meetings of cultural and religious importance. The most significant of these meetings took place in the first century (CE), with the arrival of Indian Buddhist missionaries whose work would bear fruit with the flowering of Chinese Buddhism. Soon, Chinese Buddhists were traveling to India in order to study at famous Indian centers, to learn Sanskrit, and to translate Buddhist texts into Chinese. Except for Indian Buddhism, however, these initial contacts with other cultures did not substantially influence the course of Chinese civilization.

Due to the wide distances between provinces, poor roads and communication networks, and rugged barriers of terrain, central governments did not dominate the entire area of China, unless they were exceptionally strong. It was only during the dynasties of the Han (206 BCE-220 CE), the T'ang (618-907 CE), the Ch'ing (1644-1911 CE), and the present day Communist regime, that the central government was able to maintain control of the vast area known today as China.

Considering her immense size and population, China is a surprisingly homogeneous nation. Today the population of China is approximately 1 billion, 200 million souls. This means that little less than one person out of every four in the world is Chinese — an astonishing statistic!

---

* *Designating the Common Era of the Western calendar, instead of the more usual Christian Era.*

China is a multi-national country comprising a large number of ethnic and linguistic groups, nearly all of which evolved from Mongoloid stock. Unlike many countries in the West, which contain substantial minorities of different ethnic groups, the Han Chinese constitute approximately 95% of the total Chinese population. This degree of homogeneity can be viewed not only from a racial standpoint, but also from a cultural, traditional, and linguistic one. The most widely spoken language, for example, is Han Chinese. Though many dialects are spoken, rendering various regional groups incomprehensible to each other, the vast majority of Chinese speak and understand Mandarin. There are also pronounced regional differences between the Han. Nonetheless, it is possible to view the Chinese as one large family, whose differences could erupt in familial conflicts on an enormous scale, sometimes leading to a devastating loss of life. Yet, despite these tensions, the Han Chinese were able to forge an impressive history and a common destiny.

The Origins of Chinese Culture

Though their origin may be mythic, three important figures dominate early Chinese history. They are Fu Hsi, Shen Nung and Huang Ti, all of whom were considered wise sages as well as strong rulers.

According to legend Fu Hsi taught the early Chinese the art of hunting while Shen Nung taught the craft of farming, invented the plow and developed the marketplace. Huang Ti, the most revered of the Chou period, established the royal family, invented the boat, cleared the land for raising cattle and, most importantly, developed the principles of medicine. Huang Ti, who is also known as the Yellow Emperor, is said to have ruled from 2696-2598 BCE and authored the *Nei Ching Su Wen* ("The Yellow Emperor's Classic of Internal Medicine"). This medical treatise, on which all Chinese traditional medicine is based, con-

Fu Hsi.
Courtesy of The National Palace Museum Taipei, Taiwan

The Yellow Emperor, Huang Ti.
Courtesy of The National Palace Museum Taipei, Taiwan

sists of a dialogue between The Yellow Emperor and Ch'i Po, his trusted and wise minister. It is impossible to determine exactly when the book was written, or even if The Yellow Emperor was an actual person. What seems fairly certain is that most of the text existed during the Han Dynasty (end of third century, BCE) and that a substantial portion is older, and was probably passed down orally. [1]

The most striking characteristic of Chinese philosophy to be found in this ancient text is the harmony that reigned between mankind and Heaven if the 'ways' of the universe were adhered to. While the Chinese were deeply aware of the unity and mutual interrelation of all things and phenomena, mankind represented the meeting-place of Heaven and earth. Because human beings of old understood their role in the cosmos and thus lived long lives — similar to those like Methuselah in Western tradition — the Chinese often looked to past generations as examples of harmonious living. In *The Yellow Emperor's Classic of Internal Medicine* Huang Ti asks Ch'i Po why the ancient people lived to be old and active while today (in his time) people grow old and decrepit much earlier. Ch'i Po answered:

> "In ancient times those people who understood Tao (the way of self-cultivation) patterned themselves on the Yin and the Yang (the two principles of nature) and they lived with the arts of divination. There was temperance in eating and drinking. Their hours of rising and retiring were regular and not disorderly and wild. By these means the ancients kept their bodies united with their souls, so as to fulfill their allotted span completely, measuring unto a hundred years before they passed away." [2]

In this passage Ch'i Po clearly linked the health of the individual with living harmoniously according to the dynamic forces of Tao and Yin and Yang. We will discuss these ideas at greater length in later chapters. Nevertheless, it can be observed here that ideas like Yin and Yang or Tao originally grew out of an agrarian society rooted in nature rather than in the abstract ideas of intellectuals or the educated elite. Chinese philosophy was practical and down-to-earth. The cycle of the seasons and the ways of nature were experienced by everyone on a day-to-day basis. Before the 20th century, peasants, although generally illiterate, were knowledgeable in the oral tradition and thus the pivotal ideas of their culture through proverbs, tales, wandering theaters and the ancient form of religion. These traditions were shared by the peasantry and the upper classes who expanded on them and shaped them into coherent structures of thought. No matter what one's station in life or intellectual point of view, ideas like Yin and Yang and Tao were the fulcrum on which the Chinese worldview rested.

Ch'i Po also mentioned the "arts of divination." Undoubtedly the most famous book of divination is the *I Ching* or "The Book of Changes" which has been connected to T'ai Chi by many authors. [3] The art of divining a future course of action provided the individual with a powerful tool that enabled him or her, when caught in the jaws of a difficult dilemma, to cope with the unknown vicissitudes of life. The ancient Chinese knew that they walked a fine line between life and death, between success and failure. Living close to nature, or just being on the wrong side of a political struggle, could lead to a false move that meant the loss of social status, wealth, and even death. In these kinds of extreme cases, as well as in the problems of everyday living, divination was a way of mitigating the fear and anxiety associated with the mysterious unknown.

In ancient times, before the *I Ching*, the Chinese had the custom of heating the bones of sacrificed animals or the shells of tortoises for purposes of divination. This custom is not so strange if compared with the divination techniques of Western Eurasia where the entrails of sacrificed animals were examined. For the ancient Chinese, divination was so crucial and pervasive that it had a bearing on almost every activity of their lives, from agricultural planting to worshipping their ancestors to appeasing the gods themselves.

The Changing Image of the Divine Creator

The early canonical books of the Chinese record a divine being who bears a remarkable resemblance to the God of the Western tradition. Apparently he was a creator and preserver of the world and humankind. His name was Tien (sky) or Shan-Tien (supreme sky), or Shan-ti (supreme lord). He was considered to be eternal, unchanging and independent. As the father of all people and the absolute ruler of heaven and earth, he rewarded good and punished evil. He employed the awesome signs of nature, such as earthquakes and famine, to warn mankind of its wicked ways, but if human beings repented, he exercised his compassion and was quick to forgive them.

During the Chou dynasty (from about 1025 BCE), a revolutionary idea began to emerge. The anthropomorphic god was replaced by an impersonal supreme being which revealed itself only "to those who cultivate their virtue (or conduct) and form a harmonious social order." [4] The implication of this idea represented a fundamental and radical change for Chinese culture: *all future notions of man's place in the cosmos would involve some form of personal or spiritual self-cultivation.* Spiritual development became man-centered rather than god-centered. This of course brings us back to Ch'i Po's answer to The Yellow Emperor that the key to a long and healthy life lies in understanding the Tao or the way of self-cultivation. All forms of self-cultivation, including T'ai Chi, owe their origin to this new view of the divine being.

This evolving notion of God as an impersonal force of nature did not imply that people no longer respected or worshipped Shan-ti or the lesser deities. His position, or status, whether out of custom or fear, demanded recognition while his potential anger required appeasement. What had changed was the perception that man's potential for cultivating virtue, divining the future, and living in harmony with nature (Yin and Yang) had replaced the once omnipotent power of the personal God. Tao, which reflected the 'way' or the laws of nature, now came to represent the underlying reality of the world. The common people sought to 'appease' Shan-ti, while the sage sought to 'know' Tao. Taken to its extreme, as it was by the later Taoists, human beings — through the internal alchemy of cultivating their physical and mental faculties — could achieve immortality as well as a balanced social order.

Harmony, in this world and the next, in all strata of society and personal endeavor, was the elusive goal coveted by the sage. Yet this emphasis on harmony may have been a kind of psychological compensation for the disharmony that the seekers of sagehood saw around them.

The Age of the Warring States

From the 8th century to 221 BCE, China experienced a violent process of change which led to the birth of a unified nation. It was a period of brutal wars, political uncertainty, and palace intrigues that dramatically transformed the entire spectrum of society. From the perspective of Chinese thought, these difficult times naturally influenced the ideas of philosophers like Confucius and Lao Tzu — particularly the way they viewed morality, society and the role of human beings.

The feudal system of the Chou State gradually collapsed from the burden of its own weight. A new central authority established itself and reduced the influence of the nobility to the point where they could not easily challenge the central government. The new power structure was hierarchical. Important positions in the government were based on merit and seniority, and not on personal loyalties to a noble who, in the past, could establish his own independent structure and challenge the monarchy. The significance of the new hierarchical power structure was that it heralded the beginning of the professional bureaucracy which would dominate China's government until well into the 20th century.

Nearly all the great philosophers in Chinese history were educated for this bureaucracy in which they often found a position, however minor or temporary. Confucius, the most influential of Chinese philosophers, formulated the basic educational ideas for entrance into the civil service, where he himself held some minor posts. Lao Tzu, too, held a post in the bureaucracy and, according to legend, he was leaving his post in the imperial library when he was stopped by the gatekeeper and asked to record his knowledge for posterity. This resulted in the writing of the *Tao Te Ching*.

Just how badly life had deteriorated in this period is amply illustrated by a passage in a collection of stories called "Strategies of the Warring States:"

"Usurpers set themselves up as lords and kings, states run by pretenders and plotters set up armies to make themselves superpowers. Increasingly they imitated one another in this, and their posterity followed their example. Eventually they engulfed and destroyed each other, colluding with larger territories and annexing smaller territories, passing years in violent military operations, filling the fields with bloodshed. Fathers and sons were not close to each other, brothers were not secure with each other, husbands and wives separated — no one could safeguard his or her life. Virtue disappeared. In later years this grew increasingly extreme, with seven large states and five small contesting each other for power. In general, this was because the Warring States were shamelessly greedy, struggling insatiably to get ahead." [5]

From this bleak description it is clear that warfare had become a way of life, inflicting untold suffering on all strata of Chinese society. New methods of war were introduced which greatly enhanced the ability of armies to destroy one another. In the preceding feudal period, war was a profession of the nobility and, similar to its European counterparts, was based on an elaborate code of chivalry. These warriors of the nobility gradually yielded their role to an army of professional soldiers and mercenaries whose allegiance to the central authorities was more reliable. In the new army a soldier could be born of any class and still achieve distinction and honor on the battlefield. Most military encounters were fought by thousands of foot soldiers with the help of cavalry and war chariots. These foot soldiers were mostly commoners with little or no experience in the military arts. This type of martial system required a professional officer corps who received its position from the central government and whose job it was to train and supervise the continual tide of raw recruits.

The result of this transformation was that it was not unusual for men, officers and conscripts who had served in the army, to return or to retire to their villages and teach what they had learned to their family, friends and neighbors. As a consequence, the art of war gradually spread to the population as a whole. Over time this led to the development of many and varied types of martial combat — such as T'ai Chi, Shaolin Kung Fu, and the use of weapons — geared to the requirements of the individual warrior. Chinese martial arts grew out of a real need for an agrarian population to protect itself from roving bandits as well as rapacious government officials. In fact the first solid evidence for the origins of T'ai Chi is found in the rural setting of the Ch'en family village.

The Warring States Period and its Influence on Chinese Thought

No sane person could help but be appalled by the bloodshed of the Warring States period. This time of troubles provided fertile ground for ideas to grow and flourish. Both Confucius and Lao Tzu lived during this period. Confucius was born in 551 BCE and, though there is a historical question whether Lao Tzu was or was not a real person, most experts agree that his *Tao Te Ching* was written around the time of Confucius. Undoubtedly their philosophy was dramatically influenced by what they saw around them. It compelled them to come to terms with the devastating reality of war and societal conflict.

Lao Tzu was more unequivocal about war than Confucius. In the *Tao Te Ching* we find:

"Good weapons are instruments of fear;
all creatures hate them. Therefore followers of
Tao never use them. The wise man prefers the left.
The man of war prefers the right." [6]

Confucius, on the other hand, also disliked war but saw it as a necessary evil. When asked what was least important for government — food, military equipment or the confidence of the people in their ruler — he answered, "military equipment..." [7] Yet Confucius recognized the need for an army under the strong hand of a "virtuous" leader. What kind of man should lead the army? Confucius replied, "I would not have him to act with me (in a military confrontation), who will unarmed attack a tiger, or cross a river without a boat, dying without any regret. My associate must be a man who proceeds to action full of solicitude, who is fond of adjusting his plans, and then carries them into execution." [8]

This description of Confucius corresponds with the ideas in

Sun Tzu who wrote the famous classic, *The Art of War*. This book became mandatory reading for all military men and martial artists. Sun Tzu was also heavily influenced by Lao Tzu. For practitioners of T'ai Chi, the ideas of Sun Tzu formed the basis of their martial strategy and can be found in the T'ai Chi Classics, which is the 'written' tradition of T'ai Chi. The subtle concept of "listening" — the idea of knowing yourself and your opponent, so crucial in T'ai Chi — finds its source in Sun Tzu. The strategy of Sun Tzu sharpened the blade of a double-edged sword because it could be employed by the general of an army or wielded by the lone martial artist.

Summary

During the Warring States Period, Chinese society was turned on its head. The former class of nobility was impoverished while a new class of soldiers, bureaucrats and intellectuals arose to do the State's bidding and to weave the intellectual fabric of Chinese philosophy. Confucius and Lao Tzu were two of the most notable members of this emerging class of elite scholars. These members of a meritocracy were often in great demand by the various political states as each central authority competed for the most talented from this new class. The competition could be fierce. The intellectuals were enticed by offers of social mobility on a grand scale. Yet their status was perilous and often rocky. Just as easily they could be thrown into a dark dungeon or condemned to an early execution when the waves of political power turned against them.

There is a famous story which illustrates the intelligentsia's reticence to enter government service. This was especially true among followers of Lao Tzu. The Prince of Chu sent two vice-chancellors to invite Chuang Tzu to be Prime Minister. Chuang Tzu, who was fishing in the Pu river, reminded the two ministers of the sacred tortoise that was sacrificed three thousand years ago and, wrapped in silk, was still venerated by the prince on an altar in the Temple. Chuang Tzu asks:

> "What do you think: is it better to give up one's life and leave a sacred shell as an object of cult worship in a cloud of incense for three thousand years, or to live as a plain turtle dragging its tail in the mud?"
> "For the turtle," said the Vice-Chancellor, "it is better to live and drag its tail in the mud!"
> "Go home!" said Chuang Tzu. "Leave me here to drag my tail in the mud!"

Despite Chuang Tzu's refusal, this story points to an underlying fact of Chinese history — namely the recruitment of intellectuals into political life which compelled them to deal with the social and political problems of their day. Many did so out of purely altruistic motives, especially those who counted themselves as disciples of Confucius. Others were not adverse to walking the halls of political power, striving to secure financial and social status for themselves. Whatever their motives, these thinkers were often committed to improving the society in which they lived, through maintaining, developing, and propagating the intellectual and spiritual fabric of their ancient traditions. These scholars studied the wisdom of the past, borrowed ideas from each other, and gradually built the structure that came to house Chinese philosophy. It was in this home that T'ai Chi was born.

T'ai Chi is the child of this unique blend of philosophy and physical movement, of traditional wisdom and martial arts, and literally represents the physical incarnation of its culture's worldview.

THE DYNAMIC UNIVERSE: YIN/YANG AND THE FIVE ELEMENTS

Historical Background

The period of the Warring States drew to a close with the formation of the Chin Empire in 221 BCE. It had been a brilliant and creative time, generating a sparkling array of religious and philosophical ideas that filled the Chinese metaphysical firmament. The most prominent schools of thought were those of Confucianism, and the philosophical Taoism of Lao Tzu and Chuang Tzu (see chapter 3). There were other schools, too — like that of Mo Tzu, who was an opponent of Confucius, and Mencius who was a follower of Confucius — but most others left little trace and are no more than footnotes on the large panorama of Chinese history. Except for Buddhism, the schools of thought that followed Confucius and Lao Tzu were mainly commentary. Confucianism, Taoism, and Buddhism were to serve as the basic philosophical elements that later comprised Neo-Confucianism, which formed the foundation of Chinese thought until the early twentieth century.

The Chin Empire, though lasting a mere fifteen years, left its mark on Chinese society. It was an autocratic state that fell under the influence of the Legalist school of philosophy. The Legalists rejected Confucian morality and extolled the absolute authority of the ruler which they sought to promote in any way possible, including war and political terror. Although exacting a terrible cost, the greatest accomplishment of the Legalists was the complete centralization of power in the person of the monarch.

The first ruler of the Chin Empire, Chin Shih Huang Ti (221-210 BCE) expanded its authority from the Mongolian plateau to the Yangtze river including the area of present-day north Vietnam. In order to create the all-powerful state, the Legalists tried to eliminate any opposition. In 213 BCE, the Emperor ordered the burning of all books except those dealing with medicine, divination, and technology. Among those books saved were The *Yellow Emperor's Classic of Internal Medicine* and the *I Ching* or "Book of Changes," which contain the basic ideas of Yin/Yang and the Five Elements. Hundreds of scholars were burned alive as the Legalist state moved to stamp out its opponents. No philosopher or philosophic school was safe, save that of the Legalists themselves. In addition the Great Wall of China was constructed to keep out the nomadic invaders of the north. In a real sense, the Legalist apparatus strove to build walls around all aspects of Chinese society, including what the intellectuals thought or were thinking, with the only keys held tightly in the hands of the Emperor. This oppressive regime was bound to rouse discontent. In fact, it provoked several peasant revolts, the last of which, led by Liu Pang, resulted in the establishment of the Han dynasty in 202 BCE.

Though of peasant stock, Liu Pang took the name Emperor Kao Tzu as befitting the founder of the Han dynasty. In contrast to the previous Chin dynasty, Pang is seen in a favorable light by most Chinese historians. Regarding the centralization of state power, however, he continued along the path charted by the Legalists. But he was not impervious to the plight of the people from whence he came. The new Emperor acted quickly by reduc-

Chin Warrior (Reminiscent of the posture "shoulder stroke" in T'ai Chi).
From an exhibition of The People's Republic of China

ing taxes and improving agricultural techniques, thereby following Lao Tzu's dictum of "filling bellies" and "strengthening bones." Most draconian methods of harsh punishment were rescinded.

During the early period of Han rule, the ban on philosophical and historical writings was lifted and scholars began the tedious process of reassembling the classical texts that had been burnt during the Chin period. Most importantly, Confucian ethics began to supersede the Legalist system and later Confucianism became the official state doctrine, thus enshrining its role, if not its function, as both a religious and political creed. Theoretically at least this led to the bureaucracy and the government being staffed by men according to merit and not their position in the upper classes. In 124 BCE, the Han established an imperial university for the study of the Confucian Classics and this ensured that a thorough knowledge of Confucianism would provide the most important element in advancing within the governmental bureaucracy. Overall, the Han rule offered a period of relative repose for the people of China and represented a political, social, and economic consolidation and growth that would form the basis of Chinese society for the next two thousand years.

Yin/Yang

As Chinese society gravitated towards centralization during the Han period, many philosophical ideas like Yin/Yang and the Five Elements theories, which lacked a coherent and cogent structure, were systematized and coalesced into a single doctrine. These ideas, which were meant to explain the intricate workings of the universe, were present long before the Han period. Yin and Yang are found as far back as the period of the Yellow Emperor and form the basis of the ideas of Confucius, Lao Tzu, and Chuang Tzu. The Five Elements are also traced back to the time of the ancient dynasties. Interestingly the Five Elements are not explicitly mentioned in the Confucian classics, although later Confucians, including his grandson and Mencius, were reputed to have followed the Five Elements theory. [1] It would be no exaggeration to say that Yin and Yang and the Five Elements exerted a predominating influence on all of Chinese culture, and T'ai Chi was certainly no exception. It is hard to imagine how T'ai Chi could have existed at all in an environment where Yin and Yang, or ideas of a similar nature, were not an integral part of the philosophical milieu. It is therefore not surprising that Yin and Yang and the Five Elements are found in the authoritative writings on T'ai Chi which are collectively called the "T'ai Chi Classics." Two such examples are:

"T'ai Chi
comes from
Wu Chi
and is the mother of Yin and Yang." [2]

or

"Anyone who has spent years of practice (T'ai Chi)
and still cannot neutralize,
and is always controlled by his opponent,
has not apprehended
the fault of double-weightedness.

To avoid this fault
one must know yin and yang.

Yin and yang
mutually aid and change each other." [3]

Although they are mentioned less often, the Five Elements are also woven into the Tai Chi Classics. In a passage purportedly handed down by the founder of Tai Chi, Chang San-feng (13th-14th century CE), he links certain movements in Tai Chi to the Five Elements:

"Step forward, step back,
look left, look right
and central equilibrium
are the Five Elements (which are)
...metal, wood, water, fire and earth." [4]

The five movements mentioned here are considered part of the original thirteen, which are credited to Chang San-feng.

The great modern teacher of T'ai Chi, Cheng Man Ch'ing, elaborated on this theme and imbued certain T'ai Chi postures with qualities of the Five Elements. In this way the postures take on a life of their own, because the T'ai Chi practitioner has something to focus on, an emotion or a feeling to evoke, which is then experienced in the movement itself. This is how Cheng Man Ch'ing explained them: [5]

ELEMENT	QUALITY	POSTURE
Water	soft, round	Turn Body and Sweep Lotus with Leg
Wood	straight, piercing	Separate the Foot (kick)
Fire	terrible	Turn and Strike with heel
Metal	hard	Golden Pheasant Stands on One Leg
Earth	rising power	Squatting Single Whip

The famous T'ai Chi Master, Yang Cheng Fu (d. 1936): "Turn and strike with right heel."

The important fact to grasp is that the masters and teachers of T'ai Chi understood Yin and Yang and the Five Elements as the philosophical underpinning of their art. In this respect they were no different from painters, poets, or physicians.

Until the Han dynasty, Yin and Yang and the Five Elements theories were found in different sources as two distinct and separate theories. By the late Han (2nd century CE), a period of about four or five hundred years, a Confucian scholar, Tung Chung-shu, had combined the two theories:

"When the Ch'i in the universe is condensed, it becomes One. When it is divided, we have Yin and Yang. When it is quartered, we have the four seasons. When it is further divided we have the Five Elements. Each element has its own movement. On account of this difference in movement, we speak of the five movers." [6]

In the Chinese language the word Ch'i can denote "ether" or

"gas" and was often used to signify the "cosmic breath" of the universe. It can also refer to the vital internal energy that flows through the meridians and provides the body with life. In the West we find a similar idea in the book of Genesis when God created man from the dust "...and breathed into his nostrils the breath of life." [7] The idea that the Ch'i condenses can be likened to water being solidified into an ice-cube; once frozen, the water becomes unified and static with only the potential for movement. When it melts, the water divides and is able to flow, thereby becoming more dynamic.

The above passage from the Confucian Tung Chung-shu mirrors the *Tao Te Ching*, and one senses the invisible hand of Lao Tzu who wrote: "The Tao begot one. One begot two. Two begot three. And three begot the ten thousand things." The ideas of Lao Tzu and Tung Chung-shu, the former being the father of Taoism and the latter a Confucian, clearly follow the same line of thought as to how things in the universe divide and create. What appears to be new here is the way Tung, of a later period than Lao Tzu, understands that Yin and Yang and the Five Elements are the primary mechanisms affecting change in the universe. On the other hand, it is possible to conjecture that Lao Tzu understood them in much the same way, though his enigmatic style lent itself to mystery and understatement.

What is important to remember is that there was an ongoing synthesis of ideas between the different schools of thought, and categories, like Confucianism and Taoism, were often blurred by this fact. To complicate things further, there were certain assumptions that everyone in China accepted as true. In the case of Yin and Yang and the Five Elements, they were a starting point for most of the major philosophical and religious trends, which no one challenged, certainly after the Han period, and probably a good deal before. As Westerners interested in understanding Chinese culture, it will serve us well to keep this in mind.

In their endeavors to explain the nature of the universe, the Chinese observed that movement and change were the key elements of a dynamic cosmos. Night follows day, and day returns again. The seasons likewise reflect an eternal cycle of change or the way in which birth and death lead to rebirth in nature. Yet, while the cycles are forever changing, they are also changeless by virtue of process of eternal returning. Within this changelessness ("it becomes one"), the Chinese deduced that there was a dynamic division into opposites — like night and day, winter and summer, woman and man — which they named Yin and Yang, and which accounted for all of the vigorous creativity in the universe. This philosophy provides the basis for the deep-held Chinese belief that there is an innate unity between man and nature, because *everything* in the universe participates in the dynamic flow and the balancing of opposites.

While the theory of Yin and Yang harks back to China's ancient past, it remains an abiding mystery — and an area of scholarly dispute — as to their origins, and to the exact etymological source of the words, Yin and Yang. Joseph Needham, the well-respected scholar of Chinese culture, has suggested that Yin and Yang were originally "connected with darkness (yin) and light (yang) respectively. The character yin...involves graphs for hill (shadows) and clouds; the character yang has slanting sunrays or a flag flittering in the sunshine." [8] Other scholars have averred that Yin and Yang may have been representative of the archetypal female and male. [9]

Yin and Yang do not represent forces of good and evil in a moral sense, nor are they in any way to be construed as material entities. Rather they are fluid ideas that suggest how various energies in the world relate to one another and how the universe is propelled in perpetual motion. For the Chinese, Yin and Yang reveal a rational, scientific theory of creativity in the universe. Value judgements are rarely employed except as to how one must act in relation to Yin and Yang's dynamic motion, that is to say, the individual must seek harmony with the ongoing changes of Yin and Yang. If not, he will be out of sync with the laws of nature, which may result in becoming ill prematurely and ultimately risking death. This is the basis of traditional Chinese medical theory as clearly stated by Ch'i Po to The Yellow Emperor.

Yin and Yang are found in everything that exists in the world and are never separate from one another. They are two sides of the same coin or the cloud with the silver lining. This is what Lao Tzu meant when he wrote that "All can know good as good only because there is evil." [10] Not only is it impossible to separate good and evil, which contradicts much of Western religious thought, but evil is recognized as playing an important and indispensable role in the world. The assumption of Lao Tzu is that evil cannot be eradicated because it shares a reality with its other part, or opposite, good. This idea is difficult to Westerners to accept because it views the world in terms of complementary opposites, and not as separate dualities. When we Westerners think of opposites, generally we image two separate entities such as him and her. The Chinese might understand him and her as two qualities residing in the same person that are needed to create the whole.

Here are a few of the complementary opposites that comprise Yin-Yang:

CATEGORY	YIN	YANG
Time	night	day
Gender	female	male
Season	fall, winter	spring, summer
Temperature	cold	hot
Weight	heavy	light
Motion	downward	upward
	inward	outward
Brightness	dark	light

Yin and Yang theory has been developed and refined over a long period of time in China. Although it may appear as a giant obstacle for Westerners trying to understand Chinese philosophy, this need not be the case. In his excellent book, *The Web That Has No Weaver*, Ted Kaptchuk, a Westerner trained in traditional Chinese medicine, has explained the Yin and Yang theory with five basic principles: [11]

1) "All things have two aspects; a Yin aspect and a Yang aspect." Man and woman or day and night, for example.

2) "Any Yin or Yang aspect can be further divided into Yin and Yang." A man could be divided into his masculine and feminine parts, both of which could be divided *ad infinitum*.

3) "Yin and Yang mutually create each other."
That is to say, the qualities of Yin and Yang
are determined by their relationship to each other.
For example, one can only know tallness if there is
shortness or good if there is evil. The same holds
true in reverse.

4) "Yin and Yang control each other."
This is to speak of the balance between Yin and Yang.
If one is too aggressive (yang) in martial arts, the
passive (yin) or soft side will be overwhelmed and this
will lead to an imbalance. The reverse is also true.
Moreover, when an imbalance occurs, there is a natural
process toward re-establishing balance.

5) "Yin and Yang transform into each other."
This principle indicates that the process of change
remains continuous. For example, during a race, the

marathoner is expending Yang energy, probably reaching
a peak somewhere after the first half of the race.
Afterwards, the runner needs to rest which is a Yin
period. During the rest, the Yang energy is replenished,
so that he or she can run again. There is a constant
interplay between activity and inactivity in our lives
which are dependent on each other.

What is drawn below is the modern diagram for Yin and
Yang. The diagram itself is also known as *T'ai Chi*. Readers who
remember the Olympic games held in Korea in 1988, will recall
that the Tai Chi diagram is part of the Korean flag.

If one examines the T'ai Chi diagram carefully, one notices
that the black (Yin) and the white (Yang) areas, which resemble
two fish, are of equal area and thus are in perfect harmony and
balance. Simultaneously, their differing shapes within the circle
are meant to show that they are in continuous motion, while
maintaining their balance and harmony.

The black dot (Yin) inside the white Yang portion and the
white dot (Yang) inside the black Yin portion, symbolize the im-

portant principle that there is always a little Yin within Yang and a little Yang within Yin. Thus, one can only understand Yin and Yang in the context of their relationship to one another. Moreover, it tells us that there is always the potential of each within the other to grow or diminish, which allows for continual motion and change. There is no such thing as 'absolute' Yang or 'absolute' Yin.

 The changing amount of white area expresses another important idea; the increasing area of white (Yang) is invariably transformed into the small area of black (Yin), like our marathon runner above who needs to rest after the race. Of course, it can work the other way; great Yin will eventually turn into small Yang. Thus, great Yang will create small Yin and great Yin will create small Yang.

Kaptchuk's five principles sum up the meaning of Yin and Yang in a way that makes them clear and accessible to the Western mind. Yet his five principles would have been readily accepted by the likes of Tsou Yen (305-240 BCE), who lived just before the Han period and is credited with unifying the theories of Yin and Yang and the Five Elements into one coherent system. Although none of Tsou Yen's works survive, probably victims of the Chin book-burning edicts of the Legalists, we know about him from the great historian Ssu-ma Ch'ien (about 2nd century BCE) who wrote:

"He therefore probed deeply the increase and decrease of Yin and Yang...He mentioned and cited the fact that ever since the separation of heaven and earth, the Five Powers (Five Agents or Five Elements) have been in rotation. The reign of each power was quite appropriate and how has it corresponded to fact!" [12]

Tsou Yen connected the changes Yin and Yang and the Five Elements with practically every kind of phenomenon imaginable, including the rise and fall of the imperial dynasties. He seems to have been the first thinker to create a philosophical structure out of Yin and Yang and the Five Elements that encompassed all aspects of nature and society.

One of the best descriptions we have of Yin and Yang is found in the Appendices of the *I Ching* which traditionally is attributed to Confucius, but was probably written in the early Han period. Here the triagrams Ch'ien and K'un are explained:

"Therefore the strong and the weak interact and Eight Triagrams activate each other. Things are stimulated by thunder and lightning and enriched by the influence of wind and rain. Sun and moon revolve on their course and cold and hot seasons take their turn. The way of Ch'ien constitutes the male, while the way of K'un constitutes the female...The Master (Confucius) said, "Ch'ien is Yang and K'un is Yin. When Yin and Yang are united in their character, the weak and the strong attain their substance...." [13]

This passage describes the dynamic act of creation; the power and the potential of propagation, the electric interplay of Yin and Yang, and the vital forces of nature serving as a kind of cosmic matchmaker. The Yellow Emperor puts it this way:

"...The principle of Yin and Yang [the male and female elements in nature] is the basic principle of the entire universe. It is the principle of everything in creation. It brings about the transformation to parenthood; it is the root and source of life and death; and it is also found within the temples of the gods." [14]

Practically speaking, if a man or woman could attain perfect harmony between Yin and Yang and then maintain it, he or she could vastly enrich their life with health and longevity; whereas disharmony of Yin and Yang inevitably meant illness and death. This notion of balance and harmony within and without the human organism — that is, in relation to heaven and earth — represents the very foundations of Chinese medicine. Many Taoist sages carried this logic to its ultimate conclusion; that perfect balance of Yin and Yang could lead to immortality through a myriad of self-cultivation techniques — meditation, visualization, breathing, sexual yoga, physical exercise, and other esoteric practices — all employed to discover the elixir of eternal life. Chinese folklore is filled with legends of this search. As Westerners, we would do well to remember that it is a universally human wish to stave off old age and death. One important impetus for Europeans to explore the new world was the search for the fountain of youth.

There were those, of course, who understood Yin and Yang in a more melancholy, earthly sense, like this lament of an anonymous poet from around the Han period:

> "Yin and Yang turn round in ceaseless flow
> spans of years like morning dew
> men's lives go fast like stops overnight
> old age lacks the fixity of iron or stone
>
> eons on end we saw them off
> no saint nor sage that found escape
> some took drugs to find the potions were wrong
>
> better to drink good wine
> and clothe yourself in satins and silks." [15]

The sensitivity expressed here to the cycle of life and death is echoed in poetry from other epochs and other cultures. The great Welsh poet, Dylan Thomas, for example, captured a similar sentiment in the following poem:

"The force that through the green fuse drives the flower
Drives my green age; that blasts the roots of trees
Is my destroyer.

And I am dumb to tell the crooked rose
My youth is bent by the same wintry fever." [16]

Thomas understood that the same force that gives birth to the flower also contains his death, which, according to Chinese thought, is the very essence of Yin and Yang. Another powerful statement of Yin and Yang is found in the Bible:

"To everything there is a season and a time to every
purpose under heaven:
a time to be born, and a time to die;
a time to plant, and a time to pluck up that which is planted;
a time to kill, and a time to heal
a time to break down, and a time to build up;
a time to weep, and a time to laugh;
a time to mourn, and a time to dance...." [17]

The idea that Yin and Yang (not the terms themselves, of course) should influence Western poets or be found in the Bible is not surprising in itself. The theory of Yin and Yang came about in China through the observation of nature which is a process open to all sensitive men and women, whether they be of the East or the West.

What is somewhat surprising is the influence of Yin and Yang in the world of modern physics. Niels Bohr, the famous Danish physicist, developed the important concept of "complementarity" which attempted to give two complementary descriptions of particles and waves. According to Bohr, only in this way could physicists truly understand atomic reality. Significantly, Bohr was a student of Chinese culture and, when he was knighted for his contribution to science and Danish cultural life, he chose the modern symbol of Yin and Yang (T'ai Chi) for the design of his coat of arms with the inscription: "Contraria sunt complementa" (opposites are complementary). [18] Speaking from a Westerner's point of view, Bohr observed that: "Anyone who is not shocked by Quantum Theory has not understood it." We can speculate that Bohr's ideas would be less shocking to a Chinese scientist who has grown up with the ideas of Yin and Yang as an integral part of his culture.

The Five Elements

Like the concept of Yin and Yang, the sources of the Five Elements theory are found deep in the hidden recesses of Chinese antiquity. The Five Elements, too, offer a theory that seeks to explain a universe teeming with dynamic change. They are a way of understanding the mechanism of transformation in a vigorous and creative world. This theory can be traced back to the Chou dynasty of about 1200 BCE and even further in antiquity to the "great Yu" of about 2200 BCE. The clearest expression of these theories emerged just before the Han dynasty, when they were united by Tsou Yen's school of thought.

From the outset, we should clear up a common misconception about the Five Elements; namely, they are not "elements" in the sense of something static. "Elements" is an old translation that became part of common usage. This usage also bears too close a resemblance to the "four elements" of ancient Greek philosophy. As John Blofeld points out, "...the term Wu Hsing has often been incorrectly translated 'the five elements', for wu means 'five' and hsing has the basic meaning 'to walk, to act, to do'. Elements are static, hsing dynamic." [19]

Because the Five Elements suggest change of a dynamic nature, they share a similar meaning with modern physics' understanding of matter. For the physicist, matter is not viewed as something "...passive and inert, but as being in a continuous dancing and vibrating motion whose rhythmic patterns are determined by the molecular, atomic and nuclear structures." [20] Of course the ancient Chinese philosophers did not speak of the Five Elements theory in terms of "molecular, atomic and nuclear structures," but they undoubtedly understood that their "rhythmic patterns" were propelled by something innately catalytic within the nature of the elements themselves. For the Chinese, all matter was energy, dynamic, and alive. This is no small insight on its own, and, had the Chinese been interested in and developed a rigorous scientific methodology to test and prove their insights, they would have jumped light years ahead of anything that occurred in the West.

Each of the elements — water, fire, wood, metal and earth — contain a trait specific to its nature. In the "Book of History," purportedly an ancient Confucian classic — though most modern scholars date its material from around Han times — the theory of the Five Elements is set out in detail:

"The first category is the Five Agents (or Elements): namely, Water, Fire, Wood, Metal, and Earth. The nature of Water is to moisten and descend; of Fire, to burn and ascend; of Wood, to be crooked and straight; of Metal, to yield and to be modified; of Earth, to provide for sowing and reaping. That which moistens and descends produces bitterness; that which is crooked and straight produces sourness; that which yields and is modified produces acridity; that which provides for sowing and reaping produces sweetness." [21]

The above passage contains but one of many categories of the five elements. The combination of Water, Fire, Wood, Metal and Earth is the most well-known. However, there are others including the five musical notes, the five colors, the five legendary emperors and many more. Moreover, a specific kind of relationship exists between the elements themselves in that they can create or destroy one another, which explains the impetus for change. Wood creates fire, fire creates earth (from the ashes), earth creates metal, metal creates water (an idea that metal attracts condensation), and water creates wood. The element that creates another enjoys a special relationship with it like mother and child. The element that destroys another like fire burns wood or water puts out fire represents a conflict in nature, which is also creative because it fosters change. *In essence, the Five Elements theory was the way in which the Chinese explained what caused the universe to be in constant flux. Creation and destruction, within the context of Yin and Yang and the Five Elements, make the world turn on its axis, cause the seasons to come and go, and even, according to Tsou Yen, determine the rise and fall of dynasties.*

A partial list of the physical expressions of the five elements yields the following:

FIVE ELEMENTS	WOOD	FIRE	EARTH	METAL	WATER
Directions	east	south	center	west	north
Seasons	spring	summer	long\ summer	fall	winter
Colors	blue	red	yellow	white	black
Flavors	sour	bitter	sweet	acid	salt
Organs	liver	heart	spleen	lung	kidney
Sense Organs	eye	tongue	mouth	nose	ear

Summary

Inherent in the theories of Yin and Yang and the Five Elements is a strong belief that the universe is both harmonious and logical, that things are always in process and never static, and that each and every phenomenon is connected in a multifaceted way. Long before mass communications made it clear that what happens in one part of the globe affects every other part, the Chinese had intuited the interdependence of all living things. One cannot overestimate the value and significance of Yin and Yang and the Five Elements in the continuing development of Chinese thought. Wing-tsit Chan sums up their importance in this way: "The harmony of Yin and Yang accounts for much of the central emphasis on harmony in Chinese life and thought, and it has reinforced the Doctrine of the Mean common to Confucianism, Taoism, and Buddhism. It (also) formed the backbone of Neo-Confucian metaphysics." [22]

For Westerners to have any notion what T'ai Chi is about, we must first grasp the ways in which the Chinese understood creativity and motion in the universe. This means that we must have at least a basic knowledge of Yin and Yang and the Five Elements. And while the ways of the Chinese are different, it might be helpful to remember that they are not necessarily foreign to our intellectual traditions. Understanding that opposites are complementary, as Neils Bohr did, contains profound implications for the way we view ourselves and the world. But perhaps most importantly, the ideas of Yin and Yang and the Five Elements call out to us to take a wider and more balanced perspective, to look below the surface — that things are not always what they seem.

THREE THINKERS WHO SHAPED THE CHINESE MIND: CONFUCIUS, LAO TZU, CHUANG TZU

Confucius and Lao Tzu were seminal figures in the history of Chinese philosophy and culture. While Lao Tzu appears to have made the greatest impact on T'ai Chi, It could be argued that Confucius contributed at least an equal portion.* Chuang Tzu, the lesser of the two historically, subtly influenced the course of Chinese thought, especially Buddhism and Taoism. It was Chuang Tzu, for example, who fleshed out Lao Tzu's idea of the sage. The three great religious movements — Confucianism, Taoism and Buddhism — would be based, to one degree or another, on their ideas.

CONFUCIUS

The Life of Confucius

Confucius was born in the state of Lu, which is today part of Shantung province, in 551 BCE. His father is variously reported

---

This will be discussed at the end of Chapter 8.

Portrait of Confucius.
Courtesy of The National Palace Museum, Taipei, Taiwan

as a governor or a soldier. Confucius probably came from an aristocratic though impoverished background, perhaps a result of the nobility's decline of status. As was the custom he married early and then by all accounts apparently held some minor posts in the government of his home province. His mother died when he was twenty-four and this loss appears to have been a turning point in his life. He is reported to have observed the rites and customs attached to burying the dead in the manner prescribed in ancient times. This point is emphasized in various chronicles of his life. Evidently the common practices of burial during his time had become less stringent. When the people of his town saw his devotion to the ancient ways, they began to follow his example. Confucius emerges as a man possessing a deep respect for the ties to the ancient traditions and to family worship, which in his teachings he was to promote. This incident also hints at the teacher of morality and the leader he was to become.

"It is Better to Study"

After mourning his mother for three years, he immersed himself in the study of the traditional Canons of Chinese life, particularly the way the ancient sages pursued moral virtue. For Confucius, study was the path to righteous living. The life of study remained a constant, and study was elevated to a virtue of itself. He observed that: "to study and, when the occasion arises to put what one has learned into practice, is this not deeply satisfying?" Confucius had a practical side, a strong wish to have an impact on the day-to-day life of the people. He did not want his teachings to die for lack of usefulness. Moreover, in a comment on a past experiment with abstinence and meditation, he said: "I once spent a whole day without food and a whole night without sleep, in order to meditate. It was no use. It is better to study."

Confucius emerges as the quintessential scholar and traditionalist who sought order and justice at a time when confusion reigned. For the rest of his life he wandered from place to place, hoping to put his ideas into practice and teaching his disciples the proper way to live and govern. But he found himself welcome in few of the princely courts, and only then because one of his students was employed there. For the most part he and his ideas were rejected. Perhaps Confucius was too much the idealist to negotiate the compromises that political power demands. Often great thinkers create the framework and others of a more practical nature must make it a reality. This was the fate of Confucius. He probably thought of himself as a failure, not realizing that in fact he was a visionary. It would be left to his students, numbering in the thousands, to carry on with his work and to institutionalize his ideas. They would be successful beyond his wildest dreams because Confucianism became the official state religion and moral standard of the Chinese people during the Han Dynasty and into the twentieth century.

Two Central Concepts: Chun Tzu and Jen

Confucius was a revolutionary thinker for his times. He instilled Chinese philosophy with a humanistic foundation and it is no wonder that European philosophers like Leibnitz, Wolff and Voltaire, as well as the American Thomas Jefferson, quoted his ideas to support their own. His humanism can be seen in two ways: firstly, in his notion of "Chun Tzu" or "The superior man," and, secondly, in his idea of "Jen" or "love."

Traumatized by the violence of the Warring States Period, Confucius wanted to remedy the "breakdown" of society with a government led by "virtuous" men. Philosophically, Confucius focused on the Tao of man rather than the Tao of Heaven, that is to say, he was far more concerned about people and their relation to society than the goings-on in Heaven or the spirit world. For example:

"The subjects on which the Master did not talk were—
extraordinary things, feats of strength,
disorder, and spiritual beings"[2]

or

"Chi Lu asked about serving the spirits of the dead.
The Master said, 'If you are not able to serve men,
how can you serve their spirits?'"[3]

It was not that Confucius denied the existence of the spirit
world, but rather he chose to emphasize the world of man.
Later, some would claim that his silence suggested that he understood the spirit world better than those who spoke about it.

Although the reality of competition and conflict during the
Warring States Period negated his idea of a moral world order,
Confucius thought it more normal for people to cooperate and
promote their common good. The means of achieving this ideal
society would be through the "superior man." These individuals
would be prominent members of society and government, who
would create the just and harmonious community. This "superior
man" contained none of the racial connotations of the superior
man as it developed in 19th-century Europe. Confucius taught
that ideally man should attain his position through character,
hard work, and perseverance and not through ties of blood or
heredity. He believed that education should be the prerogative of
the talented, meaning that any member of any stratum of society
could aspire to a position of leadership. Confucius' vision was of
a society based on merit, and was far ahead of his contemporaries, not only in China, but in Europe as well.

The word Jen (love, or benevolence) is central to Confucian
thought and, like his notion of the "superior man," was novel
and revolutionary in Chinese philosophy. Before Confucius, Jen

referred to the benevolent and just way a ruler governed his people. For Confucius, Jen was a concept based on man's rational mind. In order for the rational mind to perform its central task of revealing Jen, human beings were first obligated to do their moral duty — something that he defined as beyond self-interest and which he called righteousness (yi).

The question arises: how is one to determine his or her moral duty in a world where there are usually many possibilities? The right choice involves the invocation of wisdom (chih) for which one must use the rational mind of discrimination. How much love, for example, does one share with the family, the stranger, or even animals? To illustrate this idea of how Jen works in relation to the discriminating mind, the great Confucian, Mencius, explained:

> "As to animals, the gentleman is kind but not loving.
> As to persons generally he is loving but not affectionate.
> He is affectionate to his parents...." [4]

But can love be divvied up by the rational mind like so many pieces of candy or so easily compartmentalized? Can love be compelled or is it something spontaneous or, in some cases, earned?

The Confucian idea of love gives us a glimpse into the man himself, a scholar of the rational, who lived in an ivory tower of the mind, a teacher who suppressed passion as he strove to establish balance and order. What he achieved for himself, becoming the sage and scholar of equilibrium, so he wished to build into the institutions of Chinese society. Perhaps during the Warring States Period he had witnessed too much "passion."

Nevertheless, one can easily imagine this arid discrimination evolving into a philosophical system totally devoid of Jen, or love, and thus lacking any emotional impact. With so much emphasis on the discriminating mind, the spirit of love could become lost and lack any depth of genuine feeling. This is precisely the point that later Taoists were to criticize.

In the wrong hands the overly rational Confucius mind could go astray. It was adopted by the Legalists, for example, who set up a totalitarian government. They advocated an extreme interpretation of the Confucian notion of rational discrimination. The Legalists viewed society in black and white terms; if you were not with them, then you were against them. Yet Confucius himself was not a totalitarian thinker. As one modern scholar has noted: "He carefully avoided laying down rules...he believed that no creed formulated by another person can excuse any man from the duty of thinking for himself." [5] Moreover, we must be careful not to equate Confucius with all that Confucianism came to imply. In many ways Confucius emerges as a modern-day humanist and intellectual, who taught the freedom of ideas, promoted the rights of the downtrodden, sought to open learning to all who were qualified, and argued for a just and moral society.

The Nature of the Universe: Morality, Fate and Determinism

Implicit in Confucius' remedy for the problems of Chinese society is a strong dose of morality. He was a moral idealist who sought to merge the world of thought with the world of action. A good example is the concept of the "rectification of names," through which the name of a thing would correspond to its actuality. The philosophical implication of the word "father," for example, should correspond to the ideal role of a father in the world. Similarly the word "ruler" should denote a monarch ruling with benevolence and justice. In other words, reality should reflect the ideal.

In the "doctrine of the mean," which comprises some of the central ideas of T'ai Chi (and to which we will return in a later chapter), Confucius proposes the ideal life where morality is fostered by moderation and is complemented by a sense of balance and rootedness. He felt ill-at-ease with extremism of any kind.

Confucius was among those philosophers who reinterpreted the traditional concept of the Divine Creator: instead of Shan Ti, the Supreme Ruler, He was a god stripped of his omnipotence and now functioned like a constitutional monarch who obeyed the laws of Heaven and earth. Heaven's moral law operated like a machine whose mechanism, once set in motion, continued onward, subjecting everyone — including the Deity and mankind — to its laws. Confucius himself observed:

"Death and life have their determined appointment;
riches and honors depend upon Heaven." [6]

Given this high degree of determinism, how is the individual to shape his life? How can a person best mediate his or her fate? For Confucius, life is something like a game of chess. Although the rules are clearly laid down, the individual player can determine the way in which he or she proceeds. Some moves are obviously better than others. People are not as helpless as a bottle drifting at sea. They can decipher their fate and, to some degree, control it. The most felicitous method of acquiring control is through divination which, for the Chinese, meant turning to the "Book of Changes," the *I Ching*. According to Chinese tradition, Confucius read and re-read the *I Ching* so many times that he often broke its binding. Legend has it that he authored the "Ten Wings," the major commentary on this ancient text.

Conclusion

As Confucius looked out on the violence and deceit of the world around him, he must have seen a society bereft of love, and a ruling class steeped in avarice and greed with the blood of the people on their hands. He hoped that by using the rational mind, mankind could salvage the world from the wreckage wrought by the forces of the irrational. He was an educator who combined high intelligence with common sense. Within a few hundred years of his death, the aristocracy of the old order had faded away and a new nobility, nurtured on Confucian learning, emerged to take its place in the intellectual and governmental life of China. The scholar C. K. Yang summarizes the far-reaching contribution of Confucius as follows:

> "It (Confucianism) laid down the structural principles and sup-
> plied the key operational values for the basic Chinese
> institutions from the family to the state. The Confucianists —
> the scholars trained in Confucian doctrine — staffed the official-
> dom of the government, were members of the gentry in the
> local communities, and constituted the elite of traditional society
> in general. The influence of Confucianism permeated every
> fiber of Chinese society through some two thousand years of
> steady development, with only partial interruptions for brief
> periods. Traditional society cannot be properly understood
> without giving due consideration to the Confucian doctrine and
> the institutional attitudes of the Confucianists." [7]

Lao Tzu

Differences with Confucius

While Confucius established the basic principles and values of Chinese society, the philosophy of Lao Tzu profoundly influenced Chinese religion, government, art, medicine, and every other aspect of life, including Confucianism itself. The essence of Lao Tzu's thinking is found in a small book of approximately 5,250 words called the *Tao Te Ching*.

The *Tao Te Ching* has struck a chord in the West and East

alike. There are over forty translations in English alone and the Chinese have written hundreds of commentaries on its mysteries, including one by the T'ai Chi master, Cheng Man Ch'ing. The book itself is an alluring combination of poetry and philosophy, revealed truth and mystery, prose and aphorism. It discloses an impression of something intuitively half-seen, that will, with a little more effort, be revealed completely. *The Tao Te Ching* is wisdom literature at its best; it can be read many times without becoming dull, constantly enriching the reader with new insights and ideas.

Throughout the ages Lao Tzu and Confucius have shared the affection of the Chinese people. Though often in conflict, each school of thought attracted people simultaneously. Individuals were typically drawn to the politics and social awareness of Confucius and to the powerful, enigmatic poetry of Lao Tzu's philosophical insights. Cheng Man Ch'ing was one of those drawn to both teachers. He explained in his commentary on the *Tao Te Ching* how, by following Lao Tzu's method of cultivating the internal energy (Ch'i), he recovered from a life-threatening illness. Yet, in the same breath, he sings the praise of Confucius:

" Nevertheless I am a human being and as such must speak of the Tao of Mankind. My real desire, therefore, is to follow Confucius to the end. If it were otherwise...of what use would my life be to mankind? Although to seek a long life has its purposes, they (the methods of achieving longevity) are at a far remove from the study of the Tao of Mankind." [8]

Cheng Man Ch'ing, the public figure, is thus attracted to the method of achieving a just and healthy society as envisioned by Confucius, while the poet and physician in him acknowledges the efficacy of the Taoist way. Confucius and Lao Tzu represent two sides of a human dilemma; the longing to play an active role in creating a just society and the equally strong desire for quiet thought and personal growth.*

While affirming the validity of the Taoist healing techniques, Cheng Man Ch'ing is critical of Lao Tzu and the later Taoists who sought the elixir of eternal life by retiring to the mountains to unite with Tao. This spiritual path later became associated with the esoteric practices of religious Taoism. There are others, like the German scholar Richard Wilhelm, who argued that Lao Tzu advocated a totally different doctrine from that which became religious Taoism. [9] Yet it cannot be denied that Lao Tzu, and his Taoist followers, provided the major inspiration for religious Taoism, which would revere him as a saint in their religious pantheon. For some, the *Tao Te Ching* was elevated to something like holy scripture. Unfortunately for Lao Tzu, it was a guilt by posthumous association! The dead have no recourse among the living. One senses that Lao Tzu would have felt very uncomfortable as the patron saint of any formal institution, especially one like religious Taoism that would be officially recognized by the state, possessing a hereditary lineage, and practicing many elements of magic and folk superstitions. He was too much of an individualist and a non-conformist to be wrapped up in a tidy package for display as an icon of a formal institution.

Nevertheless, the criticism voiced by Cheng Man Ch'ing has a long history in Chinese thought. Lao Tzu and the Taoists were criticized by the Confucianists for being selfish because of their tendency to focus on the long life or health of the individual as

---

Cheng Man Ch'ing, one of the great modern masters of T'ai Chi, who also spent some of the last years of his life teaching in the West, is quoted frequently throughout this book. He was known as the master of five excellencies --- medicine, painting, poetry, calligraphy, and T'ai Chi. His books, many of which have been translated into English, remain an enduring legacy of his life's work.

opposed to the health of society as a whole. One important reason for this criticism centered on the difference between the Confucian concept of love (Jen) and that of Lao Tzu's. [10] The Confucian ideal of Jen tended to lead to a remote and artificial theory of love based on logic. Lao Tzu and his later disciple Chuang Tzu wanted to replace Jen with the notion of Tz'u which, for them, meant the "primordial, immediate source of love." By cultivating this wellspring of infinite love, the lover and the loved could attain a oneness in which the self is transformed into selflessness. This kind of love was at once both mystical and spontaneous and, precisely because of this, created a conflict with the Confucians in that it required a withdrawal from the world accompanied by an intense introspection. For the Confucians, this inevitably led to selfishness, which contrasted to the selflessness that Lao Tzu had envisioned as love's ideal.

Lao Tzu — Life or Legend?

Little is known about Lao Tzu's life, so little in fact, and the evidence being so unreliable, that there is a serious question whether Lao Tzu actually lived. Given the enigmatic nature of his writings, this would probably suit him.

The most famous story about him tells how he came to write the *Tao Te Ching.* According to legend, Lao Tzu held the office of archivist at the Imperial Court located at Luo-Yang in what is now the province of Henan. Frustrated by the chaotic state of the government, he resigned his post and set out on the back of a black ox to retire as a hermit in the mountains and to follow Tao. At the border an official asked him to leave something in writing which he had learned in his years of study. Some accounts record that the gatekeeper would not let him pass until he wrote his legacy. Lao Tzu complied and wrote the *Tao Te Ching* on the spot!

This story, similar to the one we cited earlier concerning Chuang Tzu's preference to be like a live turtle rather than a

Lao Tzu.
Courtesy of The National Palace Museum, Taipei, Taiwan

dead minister of state, is probably apocryphal but expresses the Taoist's dislike of government and his inclination to withdraw from the distasteful realities of society. From the Confucian perspective, it was proof of Lao Tzu's irresponsibility toward his fellow man.

Most of the details we have about Lao Tzu's life (and many historians, Chinese and Western, question their authenticity) come from the Chinese historian Ssu-Ma Ch'ien (163-85 BCE) who concludes that Lao Tzu, which means "the old one," was not his real name. His real family name was Li. He places Lao Tzu's birth about fifty years before Confucius, in about 590 BCE. The fact that Lao Tzu was a slightly older contemporary of Confucius tallies with the legend of their meeting at the Imperial Court when Lao Tzu was still an archivist. Lao Tzu, the elder of the two, and thus the one to be respected in the Chinese hierarchy of things, strongly criticized the ideas of Confucius, which the latter listened to in quiet dignity. Afterwards Confucius honored Lao Tzu with respect and awe, and described him as a "great dragon." By the time of the Han dynasty, this story had gained so much popular credence that there is an illustration of it on one of the tombs in Western Chaodong, where Confucius offers a pheasant to Lao Tzu as a sign of respect. [11]

Many Modern scholars suggest that Lao Tzu was a legendary figure and that the *Tao Te Ching* was written after the time of Confucius, in the 4th or 3rd century BCE.[12] This question is unlikely to be solved in the near future. For our purposes we shall leave it open and treat Lao Tzu as the probable author of the *Tao Te Ching*.

Tao

For Confucius, the word Tao, often translated as 'way' or 'path', or not translated at all, had a very clear and limited meaning. He used Tao to refer to the *way* of truth in an ethical or

religious sense of man's behavior or conduct in normative society. In the *Tao Te Ching* of Lao Tzu, the idea of Tao conveyed a
different and more grand meaning. Tao is the source of the universe; to glimpse Tao is to have an inkling of the way the universe works. Tao expresses what is natural, spontaneous and
beyond words. With Lao Tzu's Tao we enter the realm of the
holy because of its awesomeness. Although Tao is never understood as a god or a deity, it represents something so immense
and wonderful that the Tao cannot be named or even spoken
about except in riddles and enigmatic allusions:

"The Tao that can be told is not the eternal Tao.
The name that can be named is not the eternal name.
The nameless is the beginning of heaven and earth.
The named is the mother of ten thousand things." [13]

It is as though Lao Tzu, from the outset, wants to undermine
the Confucian notion of the rectification of names. The Tao is so
deep and so high that any attempt to name it would be an exercise in futility, because a name is a definition and a limitation
which is imposed on something by the human mind. The Tao of
Lao Tzu cannot be bought by the coins of logic. It can only be
intuited through its manifestations in nature which are the "ten
thousand things" of the phenomenal world, but the Tao itself can
only be glimpsed as through a glass darkly. Dark and dim, elusive
and intangible, these are the images that Lao Tzu employs to
describe the Tao, yet he insists that its essence is as real as its
multifolded images. He knows this by his observation of nature
and by his faith. [14]

And what was his faith? Like most Chinese, Lao Tzu believed
that there were patterns and order in the universe that manifested themselves in nature — like the seasons of the year, or the
cycle of night and day. So, too, must there be a dynamic essence

beneath the surface of things that is the source of creativity.

It might appear that Tao resembles the Western concept of God, but on closer inspection this is not so. The God of Judaism and Christianity is both the creator of the universe and the lawgiver, who requires human beings to follow his commandments or example. Significantly, this God plays an active role in human history for the well-being of his followers. For the Jews, God appears both as a redeemer from the bondage of Egyptian slavery and also as the author of eternally binding commandments. For Christians, Jesus appears as a divine being with a message of love and redemption for all mankind.

The monotheistic God of Western civilization rewards good and punishes evil, much like Shang Ti of ancient Chinese religion. He is masculine and can be aggressive but also compassionate like a father to his children.

The Tao of Lao Tzu relates to human beings in a very different way:

"Heaven and earth are not humane,
'treating the myriad things as straw dogs.
The Sage is not humane,
treating the people as straw dogs." [15]

In his lecture on this passage, Cheng Man Ch'ing explained that in ancient times the people made straw dogs as a substitute for the real animal in ritual sacrifices. Once the straw dogs had fulfilled their purpose, they were cast aside, thus leading to the idea that "the Tao of heaven and earth cannot be called humane." According to Lao Tzu, neither Tao nor the sage, whose goal it was to model himself or herself after the natural laws of Tao, existed for the benefit of mankind, yet mankind could benefit from the existence of a wise sage. Lao Tzu did not turn his back on his fellow man. However, true help sprang from being truly wise in the ways of Tao and not in the social contrivances of society's norms. Tao was not a lawgiver but rather a 'given,' a natural law unto itself.

The implications for Chinese and Western societies of the differences between the Tao and the Judaic-Christian God are absolutely crucial in understanding how each culture developed. In the classical Western religions man and god are in constant dialogue concerning right and wrong, reward and punishment. Tao, in contrast, is impervious to the call of man, and it is up to man to uncover the workings of the Tao and then, through spiritual cultivation, to live in harmony with its laws. A devotee of Tao uses meditation, which leads to inner harmony, to achieve intuitive knowledge of ultimate reality. The individual disciplined in Western religion would turn to prayer in order to unite with or beseech the God of creation. To mix together these cultural outlooks without a clear understanding of their differences, and their similarities, is to do both a disservice. Many people in the West, and even some in the East, confuse Tao and the Western God by identifying them as one and the same. This may be true on an esoteric or mystical level, in that all mystics strive to achieve union with God/Tao. But in terms of the historical and social context, this position is hard to sustain.

The difficulty of understanding Tao appears to stem from the way that many Westerners define it today; they use it as a popular synonym for "way" or "path" and they understand its function purely in the phenomenal world — the world of tangible existence. For Lao Tzu, there is another world which lies behind and is the source of the world of existence: this is the world of essence or non-existence, the Tao itself.

"Look, it cannot be seen—it is beyond form.
Listen, it cannot be heard—it is beyond sound.
Grasp, it cannot be held—it is intangible." [16]

Tao is not a thing in itself and yet it exists in all things of crea-tion. Tao is always changing, like masks of a talented actor, so that one never knows what it really is. If one wants to know Tao, Lao Tzu advises that only by "knowing the ancient beginning" can one find "the essence of Tao." [17] The great scholar and translator of the I Ching, Richard Wilhelm, explains it thus:

"...a primal view from one's inner depths will produce these images (of Tao) for oneself...These 'images of things' are the seeds of reality. Just as the acorn contains the oak, invisible and yet completely distinct..., so the 'things' of reality are contained in these seed-images." [18]

If we look at the process of an oak becoming a tree, we can gain an insight in the process of its growth and know something of its essence. However, Lao Tzu seems to be saying ("knowing the ancient beginning") that we can reverse the process — in-stead of becoming, there is also de-becoming — and thereby, know the idea that contained the oak before the seed, which is the oak without form. By analogy, Tao, while existing in the everchanging, phenomenal world, is ultimately the world beyond form. The famous Zen koan of "what did your face look like be-fore you were born?" is a re-statement of this process of "de-be-coming" back to Tao. In other words, it works both ways, forwards and backwards. If we can "de-become" to return to Tao, then we can also grasp the process of "becoming" in order to understand Lao Tzu's version of creation:

"The Tao begot one.
One begot two.
Two begot three.
And three begot
the ten thousand things

The ten thousand things carry yin and embrace yang.
They achieve harmony by combining these forces." [19]

Perhaps the most salient feature of Chinese philosophy —
and Lao Tzu is certainly no exception — is the belief in the dynamic and harmonic flow of all things in creation. From the
classical Western scientific viewpoint, a thing could not simultaneously exist and not exist. If it existed, it could be identified and
categorized, which suggests, at that point of identification, that
the thing is static and no longer changing. If there were change,
then the thing would be something new and require a new name.
For the Chinese, on the other hand, everything is always on "its
way to being something else." [20] There was no separating it out
of its natural setting. In other words, Tao-seed-sapling-tree-com-
post-soil represents a process of dynamic change. What was important for Lao Tzu was the process, and not necessarily the
particular manifestations along the way.

Lao Tzu's description of the process of creation reflects a dynamic flow in which "the ten thousand things" (quite a jump from
three) symbolizes the entire phenomenal world at a particular
moment in time.

What is the driving force behind the creative process?
Clearly, Lao Tzu is a child of the *I Ching* ('Book of Changes!')
which posits that the world is propelled by the polar opposition
of Yin and Yang ("The ten thousand things carry yin and embrace yang"). In nature, Yin and Yang are represented by the
integrated interplay of the receptive and the creative, dark and
light, negative and positive, female and male, spirit and material.
Hsiung Shih-li explains Yin and Yang in this way:

"That which is yin indicates form; that which is yang indicates
spirit. Ten thousand things, all carrying a form and hiding a
spirit, are in motion with the multitude. *When yin and yang*

harmonize the ten thousand things are transformed. This is called the union of ch'i." [21]

The uniting of Yin and Yang produce the generations of change and movement. If the ten thousand things carry Yin and Yang within them, then, according the process of de-becoming, so does Tao — which is both empty and yet contains the potential spark of Yin and Yang. This spark gives birth to one which divides, and gives birth to two which unite, like male and female. Once this process is initiated then the two give birth to a third, and so on to infinity, or in the words of Lao Tzu "to ten thousand things." This great polarity of Yin and Yang is called T'ai Chi which comes from the unity of one called Wu Chi ("the Tao begot one. One begot two."). Wu Chi is that aspect of Tao that represents pure emptiness or the Void, where only potential exists as an unformed reality. These distinctions are often blurred by the fact that some Chinese philosophers equated Wu Chi and Tao.

Lao Tzu's process of dynamic flow is stated a little differently in the Tai Chi Classics:

"T'ai Chi
comes from
Wu Chi
and is the mother of Yin and Yang.

In motion it separates;
in stillness they fuse." [22]

Thus, when speaking of T'ai Chi as a martial art as well as a process of dynamic flow and, in the same breath, as a state of meditative stillness, we are saying that T'ai Chi is a physical and spiritual replica of Lao Tzu's idea of creation. These ideas will be expanded later, especially in the chapter on Neo-Confucianism.

The Influence of the I Ching

Lao Tzu, Confucius, and practically every other Chinese philosopher were indelibly influenced by the *I Ching* and, as such, it is undoubtedly one of the most important books in world literature. In recent years the *I Ching* has also gained enormous popularity in the West.

The ideas contained in the *I Ching* are so ancient that they probably predate historical memory. According to legend, the original eight triagrams were created by Fu Shi (around 5000 BCE). King Wen and his son, the Duke of Chou (around 1150 BCE), wrote a commentary called 'The Decision.' We have already mentioned that Confucius reportedly added another commentary called 'The Ten Wings.'

One reason the *I Ching* is thought to be so old is that the names for the triagrams do not appear in other places in the Chinese language and thus may have been of foreign origin. [23] The *I Ching* is often mistakenly thought of as merely a book of divination, an oracle of the future. However, while the hexagrams can suggest a way of proper action, the quality of the questions themselves were crucial in understanding which path to take. Wilhelm points out that Lao Tzu's "whole thought is permeated with its *(I Ching's)* teachings" as was the thought of Confucius. [24] But what was different about Lao Tzu in the Tao Te Ching was that he "advocates that extremes be synthesized so as to form a new blend or harmony, whereas the Appendices (of the *I Ching*) simply advocate the taking of the mean or middle way between these two extremes," the latter being a Confucian idea. [25] In other words, Lao Tzu seeks to achieve the *intuitive* blending or harmonizing of opposites, while Confucius' approach is a way of *logically* choosing the middle path (the mean) between two opposites. These varying outlooks reflect not only differences in their philosophies but probably in their personalities as well.

The *I Ching* was a kind of cosmic treasure-map for men like

Lao Tzu and Confucius which enabled them to decipher the secrets of the universe and thereby gain some degree of control
over their lives in a world ruled by an impassive Tao. With *I
Ching*, the important point was to ask the right questions and
then be able to decode enigmatic answers. This required a man
or woman of deep sensitivity and profound knowledge, a sage of
the highest order, who understood the workings of the Tao and
could place human beings within its appropriate context.

Confucius and Lao Tzu understood this process in a very different way. Confucius approached the idea of knowledge with
the mind of a scholar: knowledge was to be accumulated and acquired like a businessman acquires assets, and then put to good
use. Lao Tzu, on the other hand, believed in a more intuitive way
which might be characterized as seeking "wisdom" in contrast to
"knowledge." He emphasized an internal, meditative search for
truth in which the seeker empties his heart and mind and allows
a "primal union" to occur between self and Tao.

Intuitive Wisdom

Lao Tzu rejected knowledge culled from the senses, like hearing or seeing, that mediate between the self and what is other or
separate from us. He greatly mistrusted these 'mediators:'

"The five colors blind the eye.
The five tones deafen the ear.
The five flavors dull the taste.
Racing and hunting madden the mind
Precious things lead one astray.

Therefore the sage is guided by what he feels
and not by what he sees.
He lets go of that and chooses this." [26]

Lao Tzu, the great nonconformist, shunned what much of the world honors. We can imagine that he was not the kind of man who easily made polite conversation at a gathering of his colleagues. From his writings, at least, he comes across as a misfit in normal society, a shy, retiring genius who is preoccupied with the world of his inner thoughts, which he expressed so powerfully in the *Tao Te Ching*. The picture he paints of the sage is that of a holy fool, clumsy and ignorant of society's ways, yet clinging steadfastly to the 'primal mother.'

Most men and women live by and are often dominated by the senses, though many seek some kind of objectivity and moderation in their lives, a function often facilitated by religion or societal norms. According to Lao Tzu, while learning may bring one closer to knowledge, it will distance him or her from Tao:

"In the pursuit of learning, every day something is acquired.
In the pursuit of Tao, every day something is dropped." [27]

What a shock those words must have been to his fellow librarians! But why did Lao Tzu reject knowledge acquired through the rational mind? Surely, as a civil servant and a librarian, his educational background would have focused on an orderly and scholarly sweep of the Classics. The answer is that he mistrusted this kind of knowledge for the same reasons that he mistrusted the senses. Both fanned the fires of desire which, being an extension of the ego, separated human beings from the "primal union" with Tao. Knowledge itself could become an object of desire. The more human beings know about what is possible, the more they want. This desire can become insatiable, like the proverbial child in the candy store. The wisdom of the sage is a process of conscious cultivation leading to innocence, or perhaps, better yet, a pure and undefiled state that is childlike without being childish!

The metaphor of the child is twofold. There is the child so

17 th-century illustration by Kano Yasunobu of the Chinese poet-sage Li Po.
Courtesy of The Jacob Pins Collection

bursting with desire that he cannot contain himself. This is not the idea Lao Tzu has in mind; rather it is the newborn babe who has just emerged from its mother's womb and is still in touch with a unity that is other-worldly. The sage is not a newborn, of course, but "like" a newborn who has traveled the road of knowledge and, at some point, found a parallel road called 'forgetfulness' out of which emerges a new reality. His knowledge and his past life are not lost but take a back seat to a new-found sense of innocence. Together, merging like two streams that become one, knowledge and innocence coalesce into wisdom. This new man is a sage who "has no mind of his own (and) he is aware of the needs of others." [28] Desireless, he is in perfect union with Tao and, as such, acts only in a natural way which the Chinese call Wu Wei.

Wu Wei is often translated as "no action." But it does not mean 'no action' in the sense of not doing anything. This is impossible because, as long as we are alive, we are doing something, even if it is something as simple as chopping wood or eating. Most scholars, like Joseph Needham, agree that it does NOT mean no action, but rather no *unnatural* action or no action that opposes Tao. In other words, the sage acts in the world in a natural way, according to Tao. The best analogy for Wu Wei is probably found in nature; the way water flows toward the path of least resistance, turning and changing course according to the lay of the land, filling and penetrating each rock and crevice, yielding to the hard stone, yet surrounding and having its way in the end.

This idea of Wu Wei is one of the central themes of Chinese thought and T'ai Chi. When comprehended and internalized, Wu Wei is a way of giving up in order to gain. In T'ai Chi terms Cheng Man Ch'ing called it 'investment in loss.'* Wu Wei is cru-

---

'Investment in loss' will be discussed in later chapters.

cial in apprehending Lao Tzu's vision of "primal union" with Tao.

Summary

According to tradition Confucius and Lao Tzu were near contemporaries. Whatever the historical truth, it is clear that each viewed Tao in different ways. It is as though they embodied the essence of the two principles of Yang (active) and Yin (passive). Confucius expounded a philosophy which demanded an active participation in the society of human affairs, Lao Tzu favored a passive withdrawal to the life of contemplation. Confucius emphasized the rational mind, with its ability to sort out information and reach conclusions; the way of Lao Tzu was to observe the workings of the Tao and to forget useless learned knowledge.

For Confucius, knowledge was masculine and actively pursued; for Lao Tzu, it was feminine and receptive, and revealed herself only through the passive observation of the wonders of nature. Confucius loved the ancient traditions and wanted to use them in order to revitalize traditional morality, Lao Tzu sought truth through non-conformism and individuality. Confucius sought to teach the Tao of man, Lao Tzu sought union with Tao itself.

The abstract nature of Lao Tzu's thought demanded an interpreter who could articulate his central concepts in a way that would make them as clear and as accessible as the ideas of Confucius. One such individual was Chuang Tzu, who flourished in the 3rd century BCE, and is generally considered to be Lao Tzu's greatest disciple. Indeed, by the 5th century CE, it was customary in China to speak their names in the same breath.

CHUANG TZU

Butterfly or Man: the Pervasive Unity of the Cosmos

Chuang Tzu was already mentioned in connection with the story of the tortoise, and his wish to drag his tail through the mud rather than be a minister of state. This parable, like hundreds of others, is characterized by a biting irony, robust humor, and, above all, penetrating lessons on morality that fly in the face of Confucian morality. Armed with these literary barbs, and a knack for incisive parables, Chuang Tzu took direct aim at what had become Confucian orthodoxy. Lao Tzu's criticism of Confucian thought is, more or less, implied; whereas Chuang Tzu's is explicit and unmistakable.

Chuang Tzu's intellect was very wide and impressive. He could outwit the logicians, and easily demonstrate the absurdity of their conclusions. Yet his stories also reflect the hand of a poet and the mind of a mystic.

One of his most famous stories has him awakening from a dream in which he appears as a butterfly. On waking, he wonders whether he is Chuang Tzu who dreamt he was a butterfly, or a butterfly who is dreaming that he is Chuang Tzu. In this story Chuang Tzu draws on a venerable Chinese tradition in which all creatures have a consciousness of their own as well as the ability to dream. This tradition allows him to posit a continuum between all aspects of the created world — inanimate as well as animate, abstract as well as tangible, the dreamer and the dreamed. Like mystics in other cultures, the idea of unity pervades his thought. For Chuang Tzu, Tao is the unifying principle as well as the source of all creativity in the world. Tao simultaneously transcends the phenomenal world and is the force that drives it onward.

Aside from his literary and philosophical accomplishments, Chuang Tzu is particularly significant in the development of spiritual cultivation and its varied techniques, which include T'ai Chi. He had a clear idea of what "self-cultivation" meant, both intellectual and physical. The nature of a sage and the way to get there often cropped up in his writings. His exposition of sagehood would dramatically influence Ch'an (Zen) Buddhism which would eventually be a factor in transforming Confucianism into Neo-Confucianism.

Critique of Confucius

Although Chuang Tzu employed a literary style that was different from that of Lao Tzu, his criticism of Confucian morality and virtue was essentially the same. Confucius, as we have already observed, believed that the "will of Heaven" represented the supreme power of the universe and that it reigned (rather than ruled) over a moral order independent and indifferent to human beings and their destiny. According to Confucius, man's fate was a result of the decrees of "Heaven" and did not depend on the virtuous actions of men and women. Nevertheless, in the social sphere, it was the moral obligation of people to act in a virtuous manner, even though such actions would not be rewarded. Confucius viewed his idea of love and benevolence (Jen) as being crucial in the development of the individual personality and that of society. The concept of Jen offered here is one based on a logical premise. It is rooted in the intellect rather than the emotions.[29]

Chuang Tzu believed that the logical mind could provide no more than logic itself and never fathom the depths of the mysterious Tao from which the primal source of love originates. The more one seeks the "virtuous way" outside oneself, as something that can be learned and acquired through the principles of logic, the less real that way becomes. This is often the case where one devotes his or her efforts in mastering the techniques of logic, and the end itself — in this case, the spirit of love — is lost and forgotten. Chuang Tzu's argument is reminiscent of the musician who practices scales all day but never enters into the heart of his music. In the end his music is sterile or stillborn.

"Te" — the source of individuality

Following the lead of Lao Tzu, Chuang Tzu explained why individuals are different in talent and inclination. The stakes were high because the implications of this idea countered the Confucian norms of moral and social conformism. Since Tao is the source of all things and "Te", Chuang Tzu argued, is what each individual thing obtains from Tao, it follows that "all things have their own spontaneous natures." [30] Form is created by the power of Tao, and receives its individual character through the endowment of "Te." So each individual form contains the combination, of Tao and "Te." Because of this combination Chuang Tzu believed that each individual or thing has the possibility and the inner ability to realize its own unique destiny. In contrast to Confucianism, which demanded obedience to traditional structures, despite individual differences, Chuang Tzu advocated a way which emphasized individuality and freedom, in which happiness is found through the realization of one's individual destiny.

He illustrated this point in his story, "Symphony For A Sea Bird." [31] A sea bird was blown ashore and landed outside the capital of Lu. The Prince ordered a reception, offering the bird wine. Musicians played music, while cattle were slaughtered and fed to the bird. "Dazed with symphonies, the unhappy sea bird died of despair." Chuang Tzu asks, "How should you treat a bird? As yourself, or as a bird?" He ends his parable leaving no doubt as to where he stands: "Hence the wise men of old did not lay down one measure (one way) for all."

Critique of the Logicians

Chuang Tzu's critique of the masters of logic was relentless: in this battle he gave no quarter. The problem with a morality based on logic is that the discriminating mind must choose one way and discard the others. While this method may make for a temporary kind of social harmony, it does not represent the truth based on Tao — because Tao contains all truth. Truth that is incomplete, in the long run, is bound to fail. Tao, based on tradition in order to promote social harmony — as taught by Confucius — was viewed by Chuang Tzu as merely a political and social expediency. It was not what he would call "ultimate truth." As touched on earlier, Lao Tzu posited that opposites play an important role in the world and that, without the one, the other could not exist:

"Under heaven all can see beauty as beauty only because there is ugliness.
All can know good as good only because there is evil." [32]

and later on:

"Yield and overcome;
Bend and be straight;
Empty and be full;
Wear out and be new;
Have little and gain;
Have much and be confused.

Therefore wise men embrace the one." [33]

The wise sage understands the relative nature of things and that the one extreme, or opposite, is dependent on the other. Thus the guiding principle of the true sage is to "embrace" all sides of the question. This is the state of "pure experience" which the modern philosopher and historian, Fung Yu-lan, defines as "...a state in which the individual is one with the universe...in which we have no intellectual knowledge...in which we accept the immediate presentation (or experience of the thing)...." [34] Events or ideas are thus taken at face value, and the experience or feeling of the thing occurs without allowing the intellect to intervene between the subject and the experience. Chuang Tzu explains Lao Tzu's understanding of the relation of opposites in this way:

> "Everything has its "that," everything has its "this." ...So I say,
> "that" comes out of "this" and "this" depends on "that"—
> which is to say that "this" and "that" give birth to each other.
> But where there is birth there must be death; where there is
> death there must be birth. Where there is acceptability there
> must be unacceptability; where there is unacceptability there
> must be acceptabililty... Therefore the sage...illuminates all in
> the light of Heaven" (Heaven here meaning Tao). [35]

In the realm of "pure experience," the sage feels the oneness
of all things because he avoids making distinctions which he
knows are false and misleading. Instead he looks at the essence
of things and not their functions. For example, from the perspective of the ones who hold a particular point of view, their viewpoint is the right one and the most logical. From the vantage
point of the sage, it is not the rightness or wrongness of the viewpoints but rather that they are all points of view resting on a
"viewpoint" continuum. Chuang Tzu would have us toss out the
individual viewpoints and hold fast to the entire continuum. The
mind of the sage is like a giant tent that encompasses all truths.

In one of his parables, he explained that "the purpose of a fish
trap is to catch fish, and when the fish are caught, the trap is
forgotten... once the words are grasped, the words are forgotten.... Where can I find a man who has forgotten words? He is
the one I would like to talk to." [36]

One is struck by his incisiveness as well as his wry sense of
humor. When the ideas are understood, and unity attained, there
is nothing more to say or actively to do. According to Chuang
Tzu's radical way of thinking, we could infer that once we have
grasped the essence of T'ai Chi — the principles and the movement — we no longer need the form.

The Mind of the Sage

It is the very essence of things, the great Tao, which the sage seeks, not the external trappings. The sage's place is at the center of the circle while, on the circumference, endless changes of rights and wrongs swirl around him. He is the calm eye within the storm who "abandoning all thought of imposing a limit or taking sides...rests in direct intuition." The mind of the sage completely binds itself to the pivot of the Tao and holds firm to its center.

In all likelihood, nothing describes the essence of T'ai Chi better than Chuang Tzu's idea of the pivot. In fact in Chinese the words T'ai Chi can be translated as "great pivot" or "axis," the center around which everything else revolves.*

Ideas similar to Chuang Tzu's are not unknown in the West. There is a famous Chassidic story of a Rabbi who is asked to arbitrate a dispute. The plaintiff stands up and ticks off all the wrongs he has suffered from the defendant. The Rabbi strokes his beard and says, "You're absolutely right." Then the defendant defends himself against the complaints of the plaintiff. The Rabbi nods his head and again says, "You're absolutely right." The Rabbi's wife, who was listening to the proceedings, exclaimed, "How can they both be right?" "You know," the Rabbi said softly, "you're right too." Perhaps Chuang Tzu and the Rabbi are trying to show us that it is a more profound truth that seeks peace and harmony rather the discord of individual viewpoints. There is something more to life than always needing to be right.

Nevertheless, there is a serious problem with Chuang Tzu's philosophy. In the wrong hands, it could sink into a morass of moral relativism in which everything is equal and thus everything is permitted (a powerful theme in the works of Dostoevsky). In-

---

*A definition of the words 'T'ai Chi' will be elaborated on in Chapter 6.

deed, on this basis, the ideas of Chuang Tzu were severely criticized by the Confucians and Neo-Confucians. The great Neo-Confucian scholar, Chu Hsi (1130-1200), portrayed Chuang Tzu in an uncomplimentary way: "Lao Tzu still wanted to do something, but Chuang Tzu did not want to do anything at all. He even said that he knew what to do but just did not want to do it." [37] Moreover, Wing-Tsit Chan points out that "...since the fifth century, his doctrines (Chuang Tzu's) have never been propagated by any outstanding scholar." [38]

Despite this, Chuang Tzu was highly regarded as to his ideas on how one approaches the path to sagehood. He was one of the first writers to amplify the concept of "self-cultivation" and its techniques. His powerful poetry and his deep insights — written with the authority of one who has been there — have attracted many fellow travelers throughout the ages. One could easily argue that T'ai Chi and all other forms of meditation, movement, and breathing exercises were influenced by his teachings.

In the Chinese way of things, for example, grace and even immortality, while sometimes conferred from above, could also be garnered by the learning and cultivating of certain esoteric techniques. This involved the alchemical manipulation of energy, on a spiritual and physical level. In some cases it involved the search for the elixir of eternal life. Chuang Tzu, like his mentor Lao Tzu, looked back to a time of ancient purity when the "true man" lived an idyllic kind of existence — a Chinese version of the Garden of Eden. The "true man" ate only plain food and "breathed deep. True men breathe from their heels (while) others breathe with their gullets." [39] The gullet runs from the throat to the stomach which suggests that, in Chuang Tzu's view, the true man breathes with his whole body. Cheng Man Ch'ing explains the process in this way:

"After the Ch'i (internal energy) sinks to the Tan T'ien (a

storage place for Ch'i about an inch or so below the belly-button), it is commanded by the mind and led to the hip joint, then to the heel. This process is referred to as "the true man breathing down to the heels." [40]

In another place Chuang Tzu pens a fanciful description of the true man:

"...There is a Holy Man living on faraway Ku-She Mountain, with skin like ice or snow, and gentle and shy like a young girl. He doesn't eat the five grains, but sucks the wind, drinks the dew, climbs up on the clouds and mist, rides a flying dragon, and wanders beyond the four seas. By concentrating his spirit, he can protect creatures from sickness and plague and make the harvest plentiful." [41]

Attaining Tao

The idea of "concentrating the spirit" is an essential part of Chinese meditation and yoga techniques, including T'ai Chi. It usually refers to the process of manipulating energy along the spine to the head. In one example Chuang Tzu seems to be using it in a purely intellectual sense when he has Confucius explaining to his disciples, "He keeps his will undivided and concentrates his spirit...," although here, too, he could be using the idea of manipulating the energy along the spine. [42] The later Taoists certainly understood Chuang Tzu in this broader sense.

In an ironic twist, a playful Chuang Tzu often uses Confucius to mouth the wisdom that he himself wants to tell his reader. We have already mentioned, for example, Confucius' observation that study is preferable to fasting. Chuang Tzu has Confucius explaining to his disciple Yen Hui the opposite — "You must fast!" Toying with his literary Confucius, Chuang Tzu suggests that Confucius had a deeper, spiritual meaning in mind, that is, "fasting of the heart," a phrase which is taken out of context because Confucius was merely referring to not eating. [43]

What Chuang Tzu means by fasting is achieving an inner unity that stills the senses through quiet meditation. Only then can "the whole being listen" to Tao and achieve unity and freedom. This is Chuang Tzu's way of answering his critics who argued that spiritual cultivation is a waste of time. Against this Chuang Tzu borrowed one of Lao Tzu's famous metaphors: that useless things can in fact be of great use.

> "Look at this window: it is nothing but a hole in
> the wall, but because of it the whole room is full
> of light. So when the faculties (the senses) are empty
> the heart is full of light." [44]

Chuang Tzu employs the above passage from the *Tao Te Ching,* which we quoted in the Preface, as a guide for meditation. It is part of his genius and originality that he often bounces off the ideas of others and rebounds with his own unique interpretation.

This theme of the importance of uselessness appears frequently in Chuang Tzu's parables. It was one way of defending himself and others against the Confucian criticism that Taoist sages and recluses did not contribute anything positive to the improvement of society. The sage referred to here is one who forsakes the Tao of man to follow the Tao of Heaven. In one conversation, Hui Tzu attacks Chuang Tzu by saying that his teachings are based on what is no use and, by inference, they are themselves useless. Chuang Tzu responded to Hui Tzu's criticism in this way:

> "If you have no appreciation for what has no use
> You cannot begin to talk about what can be used.

The earth, for example, is broad and vast
But of all this expanse a man uses only a few inches
Upon which he happens to be standing.
Now suppose you suddenly take away
All that he is not actually using
So that, all around his feet a gulf
Yawns, and he stands in the Void,
With nowhere solid except right under each foot:
How long will he be able to use what he is using?" [45]

Chuang Tzu is really saying that what is useful and what is useless depend on one another and, seen in that context, everything has a use. This is the enlightened viewpoint of the sage who stands at the center of things and thus he surveys the world from the widest possible perspective.

While Lao Tzu more cryptically alludes to the art of self-cultivation, Chuang Tzu is more explicit and elaborates with the idea of the 'fasting mind.' Like his mentor, he warns against relying on the senses themselves, but Chuang Tzu employs the metaphor of the senses to speak of the insight of intuition in the meditative process:

"Concentrate on the goal of meditation.
Do not listen with your ear but listen with your mind;
Not with your mind but with your breath.
Let hearing stop with your ear,
Let the mind stop with its images.
Breathing means to empty oneself and wait for Tao.
Tao abides only in the emptiness.
This emptiness is the fasting mind...
Look at the Void! In its chamber light is produced.
Lo! Joy is here to stay." [46]

These instructions are historically among the first to explicate the practice of meditation and of stilling the senses, which lead to the inner sanctum of Tao. There is no longer any separation between subject and object, which have merged into perfect unity. Chuang Tzu does not know if he is Chuang Tzu dreaming he is a butterfly, or a butterfly dreaming he is Chuang Tzu; they are one! This process allows us to glimpse into the lofty realm of pure experience where the enlightened one dwells: there is no beginning or end and, like Tao itself, the sage knows no boundaries and thus achieves the coveted goal of immortality (though not necessarily physically).

Unlike the theological tendencies of the West, in which immortality can be a reward for doing "good works," in China immortality was cultivated through the development of personal power, achieved by the sage through harmony with nature. This became increasingly true as belief in the power of the ancient god Shang Ti — and his ability to reward good and punish evil — declined. When the belief in Shang Ti's powers was strong, the Chinese turned to him rather than to nature for their spiritual and material sustenance. With the decline of this belief, the spiritual path of the sage focused on the harmony of Tao, man, and nature, rather than man and God.

In contrast, Western man's relation to nature tended to be either one of domination or subservience. It is probably not a coincidence that, as the belief in God's authority declined in the West, it was replaced by a growing faith in science and the ability of human beings to control and dominate nature. The relationship was not one of the harmony of equals, as was developed in China. This can be seen in Western art which often portrays nature not as it is, but rather projects onto it the power of human emotions; people take center-stage. In Eastern art the tendency is to portray the harmony of nature and man, which suggests a mood rather than human emotions. [47] If people are portrayed at

An example of "the grandeur of nature." Note the small figure in the snow on the right side. Streams and Hills under Fresh Snow by Kao K'o-ming (b. ca. 980, still living 1049).
Courtesy of The Metropolitan Museum of Art

all, they occupy a rather small place in the grandeur of nature.

These beliefs led to the development of fundamentally divergent outlooks between the East and West. It helps to explain how the search for harmony and communion with nature became the driving force behind the various methods and techniques in meditation and martial arts in the East. The sage that Chuang Tzu described was the scientist of his day in that he observed nature in order to understand the workings of the world and Tao. By the same token, the "true" scientist of today, like Albert Einstein and others, have become the modern sages and are often at the forefront of movements that view the interconnectedness of all things and events in our world. Interestingly, with the radical decline in the West of traditional beliefs in an omnipotent God, we are now witnessing the growth of an ecology movement — which seeks to redress the imbalance and disharmony between man and nature — as well as the growing popularity of Eastern meditation and martial arts.

Discipline and Spontaneity

The implications of Chuang Tzu's notion of self-cultivation are varied. Among the most important of these has to do with spontaneity. Because the sage dwells in unity with Tao, he or she is able to forget himself or herself and act in a way that is totally spontaneous, or in accordance with Wu Wei. Chuang Tzu gazes back nostalgically to a time when man lived in total concert with nature. He was so attuned with these natural rhythms that he was not aware of himself as something separate. His ego self was undeveloped and only potential. His rational mind did not design a plan to live by. Rather he acted spontaneously according to his deep connection to Tao. The true man was an artist whose canvas was life itself while the artist was a true man of Tao.

Chuang Tzu illustrates this idea with the story of a woodcarver who is asked to reveal his secret of carving a beautiful bell stand.

The craftsman recounts his process of setting "my heart at rest" and forgetting "praise or criticism," after which he focused on the single thought of the bell stand. The woodcarver continues:

"Then I went to the forest
  to see the trees in their own natural state.
  When the right tree appeared before my eyes,
  The bell stand also appeared in it, clearly,
  beyond doubt. All I had to do was to put
  forth my hand and begin."* [48]

Through the process of meditation, the woodcarver identifies himself so completely with his task at hand that he forgets himself and becomes one with the work of art to be created. This process is the key that unlocks the mystery of Tao and allows the bell stand to appear before his eyes.

For the martial artist and the T'ai Chi practitioner, these ideas of spontaneity are particularly significant. There is just one movement at a certain moment that is the right one. This is especially true in self-defense. Right preparation or self-cultivation can easily determine whether one is in concert with the Tao of one's opponent's movements or not. Just as important to Chuang Tzu was the attitude of the fighter, that is, his mental state.

He tells the story of a fighting cock who is not ready, according to his trainer, because "he is full of fire" and "ready to pick a fight." Later the problem is that he is "vain and confident of his own strength." Finally the trainer explains that he is ready:

"When another bird crows, his eye
  Does not even flicker.
  He stands immobile

Michaelangelo expressed similar sentiments.

like a cock of wood.
He is a mature fighter.
Other birds
Will take one look at him
And run." [49]

The training centers on preparing the bird's spirit. Like the woodcarver, the fighting cock, once purged of the demands of his instincts, becomes one with the task at hand. For students of T'ai Chi, this is an ideal to strive for; he or she is not "afraid of intimidation" because "he does not acknowledge death." Being at one with Tao bestows a kind of stoic imperturbability where "Mount T'ai could collapse in front of you," as Mencius explained, "and your complexion would not change." Like the water of Wu Wei, the student of T'ai Chi seeks the path of least resistance in order to accomplish his or her objectives. This is no small task and, given our instinctive natures to resist force with more force, requires enormous effort and discipline which, paradoxically, enables us to act freely and spontaneously.

Summary

Chuang Tzu was a master of parable. His goal was to teach men and women about the greatness of Tao, in order that they might realize their unique and ultimate potential for freedom and liberty. His was a way of living naturally and, at the same time, demanded hard work on the self in order to achieve selflessness and oneness with Tao. Chuang Tzu obviously had a great love for nature, which he perceived as a reflection of Tao. His influence on Taoism and Ch'an Buddhism was incalculable. Perhaps his greatest contribution is the sensitizing of each individual who studies his ideas to a profound awareness that through the effort of self-cultivation — be it T'ai Chi, yoga or prayer — one can be so much more than he or she ever dreamed possible.

PART 2

The Development of Chinese Religious and Philosophical Thought

CHAPTER 4

CHINESE BUDDHISM:
Its Growth and Its Influence

Chronologically our next stop ought to be Taoism, which developed in China during the third and second centuries BCE. However, it was the influence of Buddhism on Taoism that challenged the latter to become a more cohesive and dynamic force in the religious and political development of China. For that reason it may facilitate our understanding of Taoism by examining Buddhism first.

Historical Background

The rapid growth of Buddhism in China was primarily due to three factors which created an environment where a foreign religion could be accepted easily by the normally xenophonic Chinese: 1) the weakening of Confucianism as a religious force, 2) the disintegration of the Han dynasty, and 3) the devastation of the countryside by acts of nature in the form of floods and earthquakes.

During the Han dynasty, Confucianism became the official state religion, and Confucius himself was raised by the state to an almost godlike status, with sacrifices being offered to him in all schools. We can easily surmise that this turn of events would probably have been repugnant to Confucius, the humble philosopher of human rather than heavenly affairs. But the need of the state to imbue Confucianism with the majestic awe of religious authority prevailed.

Granted the vicissitudes of history, Confucianism proved to be remarkably resilient and remained the religious and moral measure for Chinese society until the twentieth century. The men of the bureaucracy, the cream of the intellectual elite, were solidly educated in the Confucian Classics, and they dominated the governmental and educational institutions of China. The triumph of Confucianism seemed so complete and unassailable that no religious force could challenge its hegemony.

But this was only one side of the coin. The fact that Confucianism had become so completely identified with the state meant that any failure on the part of the central government also reflected badly on Confucianism. In times of troubles, of which there were many, when the Chinese people needed compassion and miracles, Confucian ethics offered little in the way of solace or solutions to a beleaguered population. As a result many people began to search elsewhere and to tread the more mystical paths of Taoism and Buddhism. Moreover, periodically, oppressive rulers arose to plague the people and Confucianism suffered from the political backlash of "guilt by association." After all, it was the Confucian bureaucracy that obediently carried out the commands of the state. Thus, periods of chaos often witnessed the weakening of Confucian authority, and it is understandable why the triumph of Confucianism was less than complete.

Nevertheless, Confucianism demonstrated a remarkable talent to adopt new ideas from Taoism and Buddhism and adapt them to its ideological framework. This intellectual flexibility allowed Confucianism to survive, to reinvigorate its institutions with a new vitality, and to rebound stronger than before. The prime example of this was the Neo-Confucians of the tenth to thirteenth centuries.

Until the Han dynasty, debates in Chinese philosophy were an internal matter because China had little contact with the rest of the world, including the rich and fertile culture of India which sat on her doorstep. To the north, the Han extended the Great Wall in order to keep out the nomadic invaders who remained a constant military threat. Westward to India, it was a different matter. The Han Emperor Wu Ti (141-87 BCE) initiated several trade missions to India that radically transformed China's relationship with foreign peoples. By opening up a route that would become known as the Old Silk Road, Chinese goods flowed westward through India, Persia, Asia Minor, and finally Europe. In return, China received gold, precious stones, horses and a dynamic connection with the outside world which included the introduction of new ideas and a new religion from India called Buddhism.

The Beginnings of Chinese Buddhism

Buddhism came to China at a propitious moment. In the second century CE, the Han dynasty was clearly on the downside of its former glory and disintegrating rapidly. A number of power struggles had flared between certain noble families and various cliques of court eunuchs, which led to the weakening of the central government, bringing to mind the previous Warring States Period. In the provinces, free to impose their will because of a weak central government, wealthy landlords confiscated the lands of the peasant class and reduced them to abject poverty. On top of the economic and political chaos, nature wreaked havoc in the countryside with numerous droughts and floods, stripping the peasantry of what little they had left. Many became bandits, sold themselves into servitude or simply perished. The result of this kind of suffering was an upsurge in religious fervor among the general population who pinned their hopes for a better life on Buddhism and Taoism (Taoism also experienced an upsurge in devotees at this time and this is examined in the following chapter).

By virtue of its message of universal love and salvation, and a promise of an afterlife dependent on one's deeds (Karma), Buddhism appealed to all strata of Chinese society, who longed for even a hint of compassion and justice in a seemingly inhumane and unjust world. For the upper classes, who were basically Confucian in their outlook, Buddhism offered the concept of universal love which seemed very close to and later became identified with the Confucian idea of Jen. Moreover, after the Buddhist monasteries became established, men and women could retire behind their walls for a life of quiet contemplation, sheltered from the political chaos of the secular world. Concurrently, they were fulfilling a traditional Chinese ideal of retiring from society and cultivating wisdom and sagehood like Lao Tzu or Chuang Tzu before them. In short, Buddhism answered the longings of many people in Chinese society who had lost their faith and their traditional ties to the emperor and the Confucian establishment which upheld the moral basis for his authority and, by extension, the authority of the family.

The practice of retiring to a monastery and becoming a celibate monk or nun, and thus withdrawing from familial obligations, was viewed by the Confucians and the state as an affront to family life and to ancestor worship. This was one of the major reasons that led to later persecutions of the Buddhists.

By the time Buddhism arrived in China in the 1st century CE, it was already a mature religion with over five hundred years of development and tradition. Buddhism was born out of the searching for ultimate truth by Siddhartha Gautama, who lived in the sixth century BCE, about the same time as Confucius. After exploring the traditional Indian religions, the deprivations of asceticism, and the pleasures of a sensual life, while meditating one day, he suddenly realized that the answer to the sufferings of life lay within his own mind. He concluded that the cause of human suffering was the desire for the sensual things of this world and, if wrong-thinking about desires could be done away with, suffering could be eliminated and salvation achieved. From that moment on, he was known as the Buddha or the Enlightened One. Traditionally, Buddhists have called this process of Enlightenment, "The Four Noble Truths": 1) life is suffering; 2) suffering is caused by desires and lusting; 3) only by eliminating desire can suffering end; and 4) this is achieved by the "Eightfold path which includes right belief in the "Four Noble Truths," right aspiration, right speech, right conduct, right livelihood, right endeavors, right mindfulness, and right meditation. The implications of such a religious framework meant a life of rigid discipline in mind and body, a rejection of carnal pleasures, and an all-encompassing love for every living thing. In this way, the chains of cause and effect (Karma) could be broken and the Buddhist could enter into Nirvana, literally meaning "extinction," a state of illumination in which the ego has been extinguished.

In China, Buddhism was first thought of as a kind of Taoism, planted in India by Lao Tzu and now returning from there. According to one legend, Lao Tzu rode off on the back of an ox to India where he taught the concept of Tao. Another legend reported that the Buddha was actually a reincarnation of Lao Tzu. Adding to the confusion, the early translators of Buddhist texts often used Taoist terminology for Buddhist concepts. For example, the Buddhist idea of the "emptiness of all things" resembled the Taoist notion of "being and nonbeing," and thus buttressed the case of mistaken identity. In fact, in the beginning, many Taoists did not understand that there was any "fundamental difference between Lao Tzu and Chuang Tzu on the one hand and Buddhism on the other." [1]

This confusion actually helped Buddhism to grow in China. The Chinese, already familiar with what they thought were the concepts and terminology, more readily adopted Buddhism as

their own than they might have done with a totally foreign religion. By the 3rd century CE, most of the important Sanskrit texts
of Buddhism had been tranlated into Chinese. By the 4th century
the first Buddhist schools, known as the "Seven Schools," were
firmly established. According to one scholar, this now demonstrated that "the arena of Chinese philosophy was dominated by
Buddhists rather than by Confucian or Taoist thinkers." [2]

The phenomenal success of Buddhism in China can be attributed to its appeal to the various layers of society and the temporary waning of indigenous Chinese religious and political
institutions. This growth continued unabated in the 5th and 6th
centuries with the building of hundreds of monasteries, the acqui-
sition of large landholdings, and the conversion of many Chinese, including some monarchs, to Buddhism. The culmination
of Buddhism occurred with the establishment of Ch'an (in Japanese, Zen) Buddhism which represented the most "Chinese" of
the various branches that flourished in China.

Precisely because of its great success, Buddhism incurred the
wrath of the state and of those who upheld traditional Confucian
morality. As a result, there were a number of traumatic Buddhist
persecutions, the most severe occurring in 845 CE, when the
monasteries were dismantled, their clergy compelled to return to
secular life, and the Buddhist lands appropriated by the state.
Buddhism in China never fully recovered its previous glory after
this blow, although it remained influential until modern times.

Between the period of the early Chinese Buddhists of the lst
century and the Ch'an school of the 8th century, it is obvious
that a major transformation had occurred. Buddhism — in the
form known as Ch'an Buddhism — became thoroughly and un-
mistakably Chinese. This was very significant for Chinese society
as a whole, and Chinese philosophy in particular, because not
only would Buddhism influence the Chinese, but the Chinese
would return the favor by profoundly influencing Buddhism.

There are two kinds of Buddhism that came to China: Mahayana which develops the intellectual and philosophical side of the spirit, and Hinayana which emphasizes the ethical ideals in Buddhism.* Both Hinayana and Mahayana found a home in China. However, the latter became predominant because Ch'an Buddhism, which represented Buddhism at its height in China, was a part of the Mahayana school and seemed to mesh more easily with the Chinese character.

The Chinese developed their own way of categorizing Buddhism. [3] On the one hand, Buddhism is known as "Fo Hsueh" (the Buddhist learning) and, on the other, Fo Chiao (the Buddhist religion). For the Chinese people, "the Buddhist learning" exerted a profound influence from almost the beginning. The Buddhist ideas of the transmigration of the soul and the law of Karma were generally accepted by the populace as a whole and integrated into the Chinese worldview. One did not have to be a Buddhist in order to agree with and adopt certain Buddhist concepts or practices.

This inter-cultural flexibility stands in direct contrast to Western religious thinking, where one could easily be excommunicated for espousing ideas that resembled the ideology of another sect or religion. The Chinese, being both mystical and practical at the same time, sought the magical qualities of whichever religion seemed in possession of the power to bring them happiness and to ward off evil spirits. As C. K. Yang explains: "Magic was a tool for achieving results in a possibly threatening situation and was not a system of morality. Hence, a common man could worship a Buddhist god for general happiness of himself and his family, pray to a Taoist deity for the return of his health, and at the

---

This is an oversimplification of things, as there is an ethical side of Mahayana and a philosophical side of Hinayana. It is really a matter of emphasis.

same time practice Confucian morality." [4] Not only did the Chinese incorporate Buddhist magic, deities, and legends in their folklore, but it was not uncommon to see Buddhist and Taoist monks officiating side by side at a funeral service or some other communal event.

To draw a Western parallel — even with the recent advent of ecumenism — it is still rare to witness such cooperation between, say, a Catholic priest and a Rabbi, or even two priests of different Christian denominations, although this attitude seems to be changing.

Perhaps this suggests one answer as to why the Chinese were able to develop a unique mental and physical discipline like T'ai Chi. Openness and practicality in regard to the Chinese spiritual and religious outlook helped to prepare the cultural setting which allowed T'ai Chi to flourish — with its demands for both mental and physical flexibility and optimal movement. But more on this subject later.

Buddhist Influence on Self-Cultivation

In the domain of self-cultivation, it is difficult to distinguish between the techniques of the early Buddhists and the Taoists of the latter Han dynasty. Being influenced by the tradition of Lao Tzu and Chuang Tzu, the pioneer Buddhists did not understand meditation in the Indian sense of "concentration," but rather in Taoist terms of "conserving vital energy, breathing, reducing desire, preserving nature...." [5] The practice of Buddhist meditation that embodied breathing techniques can be traced to the arrival in 148 AD (?) of An Shih-kao, a Parthian monk, who taught meditative skills culled from Indian Buddhism and who pragmatically drew from Taoist terms in his translations in order to convey Buddhist ideas. [6] Later he translated an important Indian text on meditation and breathing which formed the basis of Ch'an (Zen) meditation.

Giant Buddha carved in stone in Central China.

Another Buddhist monk of the 4th century, Tao An, passed on a system of counting the breaths for the purpose of concentration, not unlike certain Zen practices of today. Tao An also taught various techniques of visualization which included the practice of picturing the Buddha in the mind's eye of the meditator. Visualization is the technique of utilizing the imagination to manipulate certain images or energy in order to attain a higher level of consciousness, personal power, or health. Historically, for practitioners of T'ai Chi and other Chinese health exercises, visualization of one kind or another represented a key component in one's daily practice. Its origins stem directly from these early Buddhist and Taoist traditions.

The fact that there exists a confluence of these two traditions is not surprising in that they shared a common purpose of transforming the self from its ego form to a nonego formlessness, thereby achieving unity with the universe.* The followers of Lao Tzu and Chuang Tzu, when characterizing the ultimate nature of the universe, spoke in terms of "being and non-being," while the Buddhists called it "emptiness." Both traditions shared an understanding that there exists a profound reality at the core of what people generally call the "real world" and that the mind is the vehicle to reach out, touch and even enter that deeper reality. What generally distinguished Taoism and Buddhism from each other was that the Buddhists perceived the world as being illusionary and empty, while the Taoists, despite the use of the suggestive term "non-being," understood the world as being real.

The Ideas of Seng-chao

As Buddhism matured in China, it became increasingly clear that Buddhism had its own philosophy that significantly differed

---

*This was less true for the later forms of religious Taoism which stressed the notion of immortality. More on this in the next chapter.

from Taoism. One of the most famous Chinese Buddhists was Seng-chao (384-414 CE) who would become the greatest teacher and translator of his time. When he was a young man, he discovered the works of Lao Tzu and Chuang Tzu and maintained a deep affection for them all his life. Once he began reading Buddhist texts, however, he donned the robes of a monk and later became the student of Kumarajiva, the most important Indian Buddhist of his day in China. Seng-chao represented a middle ground where genuine Buddhist thought mingled with indigenous Taoist ideas and, through his writings, a kind of homegrown synthesis was born that was both Chinese and Indian. As a native son, who was steeped in Chinese culture, Seng-chao planted the seeds of Buddhism firmly in Chinese tradition.

Seng-chao proposed a unique theory of the "immutability of things," unique for China of his time, but based in Buddhist thought of the Middle Doctrine from India. The position of the Middle Doctrine was that any statement concerning the existence or nonexistence of things could be refuted by means of a complex series of arguments. According to the Middle Doctrine, things in this world have no reality of their own, but only "exist by virtue of their relations (of one to another)." [7] Because something is not this or that, the followers of the Middle Doctrine did not choose between opposing positions and thus held to a middle way, which gave rise to their name. The followers of the Middle Doctrine held that only the Absolute has genuine or true reality.

One of Seng-chao's innovative ideas was to apply the Middle Doctrine to the concepts of *rest* and *movement* in order to demonstrate that, while seeming to be opposite, in reality, they are complementary and, with a proper understanding, they flow together and form a complete idea. This sounds something like a Buddhist reformulation of Yin and Yang. Seng-chao explained his idea in this way:

"As we investigate the meaning of not moving, does it mean to cast aside motion (activity) in order to seek rest (tranquility)? No, rest must be sought right in motion. As rest must be sought right in motion, therefore there is eternal rest in spite of motion, and as motion is not to be cast aside in order to seek rest, therefore although there is rest, it is never separated from motion. This being the case, motion and rest are from the beginning not different...." [8]

At first glance it may appear that Seng-chao is merely playing a mind-game with words. We all know that when we are riding in a car, we are moving and not at rest or when sitting at home, we are not moving. This is common sense. Yet on closer examination Seng-chao is telling us something profound. Indeed his ideas transverse hundreds of years and herald the ideas of modern physics. Albert Einstein's Theory of Relativity teaches that "mass (in this case, 'rest') has nothing to do with substance but is a form of energy (which is 'motion')." [9] In other words there is no such thing as absolute rest or absolute motion. They are *relative*. Einstein based his ideas on mathematics and the accumulated body of scientific evidence. It gives cause to wonder: on what did Seng-chao and the followers of the Middle Doctrine base their conclusions? How mighty their intuition proved to be!

But this is not to say that Albert Einstein and Seng-chao would see eye to eye in all things. For a Buddhist of the Middle Doctrine like Seng-chao, and unlike modern scientific thought, rest and motion are relative terms that represent two sides of the *same illusion*. In terms of traditional Chinese thought, *the dance of Yin and Yang is an illusion while only Tao — or in Buddhist terms, the Absolute — is real.*

We can see Seng-chao's ideas as they appear in the T'ai Chi Classics where movement and rest are viewed as relative terms, representing complementary dimensions of a larger unity.

"Be as still as a mountain,
move like a great river." [10]

"Being still, when attacked by the opponent,
be tranquil and move in stillness..." [11]

"Seek stillness in movement." [12]

From a perspective of T'ai Chi, Wang Tsung-yueh, one of the historical founders of T'ai Chi, wrote that being "still as a mountain, move like a great river" is a metaphor for developing a strong root and stance, while the "river expresses the infinite possiblities for transformation." [13] His interpretation merged a functional approach (root and stance) with an important philosophical point; the river can be understood as a metaphor for Tao which, like T'ai Chi, has "infinite possibilities for transformation."

Chen Wei-ming, a 20th-century teacher of T'ai Chi, interpreted "Seek stillness in movement" in terms of using "stillness to control movement" and the health benefits of sinking the ch'i (internal energy) to the tan t'ien (the center of the belly). [14] While both of these respected T'ai Chi masters approached stillness and movement from a martial arts or Taoist perspective, the roots of the idea that there is stillness in movement and movement in stillness can be traced to the Buddhism of the Middle Doctrine and to Seng-chao in particular, since it was he who clarified this paradox of stillness and movement, defined it in Buddhist terms of the Middle Doctrine, and brought it to prominence in Chinese thought.

Fa-tsang and the Golden Lion

Next to the Ch'an (Zen) school of Buddhism in China, the Hua-yen school or "Flower Garland School" was the most native

Chinese in its character, and also the most important due in part to its influence on the later Neo-Confucians. The followers of the Hua-yen school believed that an intimate relationship exists between all things, that everything is equal, and that, in the final analysis, all things are one. The teachings of this school are known as the "teaching of totality" because all things arise from oneness or unity and, taken together, form the unity itself.

The founder of the school was Fa-tsang (643-712) and it seems that, like Seng-chao, he was also influenced by the Taoism of Chuang Tzu. According to Fa-tsang, both the active and the passive (or, rest and motion) are empty and illusory and, because of this, can interpenetrate each other freely. Because of this freedom of flow between empty things, every phenomenon has the potential to be identical to every other and this accounts for the oneness and equality of all things in the universe.

But Fa-tsang dissented from Seng-chao's teaching regarding the reality of the world. He was of the belief that the world as well as the Absolute was real. According to Fa-tsang and the "Flower Garland School," by virtue of the unobstructed flow of all things, there was no essential difference between what he called an active event or form *(shih)* and Absolute Reality *(li)*. *As a consequence, the form and Absolute Reality are in constant flow between each other and, in contrast to Seng-chao, there is one complete world, not one of illusion and another of reality.*

In a famous story, the Emperess Wu asked Fa-tsang to lecture on Buddhism at the royal court. By way of an analogy to make his ideas more easily understood, he pointed to a statue of a golden lion and explained that the gold represented Absolute Reality or *li*, while the lion expressed form or *shih*. The gold assumes whatever form that is given to it by circumstances — in this case, the hands of the sculptor — and has no form of its own. On the other hand, the form of the lion has no reality of its own because it is entirely made of gold. Without gold there can be no form of the lion, and without form there can be no expression of the Absolute. They are mutually dependent. The lion and the gold exist at the same time each within one another and include one another. Moreover, both the gold and the lion are an expression of oneness, the highest principle of reality, which Fa-tsang believed to be Buddha-mind.

The ideas of Fa-tsang and the Hua-yen school reflect a sense of oneness and unity in the universe that philosophically conform to the Chinese view of things. Not only are they intellectually stimulating, but they also contain a practical side that can be applied to many areas, not the least of which is T'ai Chi.

Principle, Form and T'ai Chi

Here it is appropriate to interrupt our discussion of Buddhism and connect what we have just learned about Fa-tsang and his ideas to T'ai Chi, lest we try to do it later and lose our train of thought. T'ai Chi is a child of these and other ideas which we have or will examine.

The principles of T'ai Chi are elaborated in the written and oral traditions.* These principles are the ideas which, when taken as a whole, form the framework — the essence — of the movement or "form" called T'ai Chi. This framework functions somewhat like a trampoline. The student of T'ai Chi can use the spring of the principles to go much higher and further than if it was a solid floor with no life or give. These principles would, of course, remain a lifeless trampoline without someone to use and express them in the form. Just as the statue of the lion could not exist without the gold (principle), so the T'ai Chi form could not exist without its inner essence — the framework of the oral and written traditions.

*We will discuss these traditions in the appendix.

Thus, Principle and Form are mutually interdependent! The deeper one's understanding of the principles, and the ability to combine them with movement, fosters for the free flow from principle to form and back to principle. As Fa-tsang would put it, there is no obstruction between them, and thus no essential difference between principle and movement. They have become one. At that particular moment, we could imagine that someone is performing 'perfect' T'ai Chi, which would be a natural expression of Tao, or, in Buddhist terms, the Absolute.

Indeed this idea — that the T'ai Chi form is a reflection of Tao — can be found in the T'ai Chi Classics: "Although the changes are numerous, the principle that pervades them is only one."* [15] "Principle" of this quote can be —and often is — interpreted as Tao because, for the Chinese, Tao is the underlying principle that engenders and unites the entire universe and thus pervades every movement and change.

It might be argued that the raison d'etre for the T'ai Chi form and its principles, which together constitute a whole, is to increase the individual's awareness of Tao in daily life. Cheng Man Ch'ing recommended practicing the principles of T'ai Chi at any time and any place by seeking to "cultivate the Ch'i" or, while walking, by paying attention to the separation of the substantial and insubstantial foot.** "If you can do this," he wrote, "you can practice T'ai Chi Ch'uan at any moment, all day long." [16] It has been said among his senior students that they never saw him do the whole form because he said he was always doing T'ai Chi. For Cheng Man Ch'ing, there is no distinction between what he did in everyday living and what ultimately the Ta'i Chi form had

---

* See chapter six for a Neo-Confucian interpretation of these lines.
** This separation relates to an awareness of yin and yang and we will discuss it in Chapter 9 on the principles of T'ai Chi.

taught him when he was a student. This attitude is an excellent illustration of Chuang Tzu's story that, once the fish are caught (the principles), the trap (form) can be put aside. This is a level to which many aspire and few attain.

For the student of T'ai Chi, the goal is to embody principle and form so that they merge and reflect the essence of T'ai Chi. If this does not occur, the practitioner is doing something other than T'ai Chi. To draw an analogy with the golden lion: if the lion is made of brass, he may look something like a golden lion, but clearly he is not a golden lion. He is a brass lion. Without genuine principles, someone's T'ai Chi may look like T'ai Chi, but in fact it is something else.

In summary, when form and principle are in perfect harmony and the flow between them is natural and spontaneous, then form becomes principle and principle becomes form because, as Fa-tsang suggests, there is no barrier between them. The T'ai Chi player is no longer doing T'ai Chi: he or she is T'ai Chi! This is the threshold of the eternal present where one experiences total harmony with the universe and the loss of self that both Buddhism and Taoism aspired to. At this moment, if just for a moment, conscious thought is stilled and the struggle to overcome the physical limitations of the body is forgotten, and one can truly "flow like a great river."

Ch'an (Zen) Buddhism

Though probably few Westerners are aware of the Hua-yen or "Flower Garland School," most have heard of "Zen" Buddhism. Zen has fashioned a place for itself in modern Western culture through literature and film. Many people have sat Zen meditation or have tasted the simple pleasures of Zen cookery. In popular Western culture the name Zen often conjures up orientals in monk's robes sitting in meditation or the famous Zen Koans (riddles) such as "what is the sound of one hand clapping?" Zen, it seems, has arrived.

The word Zen is a Japanese translation of the Chinese word, Ch'an, which in turn is the Chinese for the Indian Sanskrit word, Dhyana. All these words contain essentially the same meaning: 'to be absorbed in meditation so that all dualistic distinctions of the mind are obliterated.'

Zen Buddhism came to Japan in the late 12th and early 13th centuries from Chinese Ch'an Buddhism which began its development in China around the 5th century. The famous Japanese Buddhist scholar, D. T. Suzuki, calls Ch'an Buddhism a "revolt" of the Chinese mind against Indian Buddhism. [17] By way of explanation, Dr. Suzuki contrasts Indian philosophy, which is "rich in imagination and wonderful in its capacity for speculation," with the Chinese mind which is imbued with Confucian morality, being ethically oriented, and less philosophical in its tendencies. This is not to say that the Chinese are not philosophical. In fact the contrary is true, but their philosophy tended to focus on the way to live one's life and shied away from the seductions of speculative philosophy. Moreover, the Chinese mind has a practical and down-to-earth bent that is clearly reflected in Ch'an Buddhism. For these reasons, Ch'an Buddhism represented the most thoroughly Chinese form of Buddhism as well as being the most influential of the Chinese Buddhist schools.

There is a famous story of a Zen master who was walking with his students in a forest. Reaching a river they found a young woman in distress, afraid to cross the water which she thought was too deep. Picking up the woman in his arms, the master carried her across and set her down safely on the other side. Then he continued walking as though nothing strange had happened. Since Buddhist monks are sworn to celibacy and not allowed to touch the opposite sex, his students were disturbed by his actions. Finally, one of them summoned up the courage to ask his teacher why he had broken the rules. The master answered, "I picked her up and set her down. Why are you still carrying her?" In a quintessential statement of Ch'an Buddhism, the master explains that he had acted not only morally and practically, but that he had done so in a spontaneous and natural manner. Simultaneously, he was warning his students about the pitfalls of clinging to the past. The master was clearly following the Zen way.

The Influence of Bodhidharma

The tradition of Ch'an Buddhism traces its lineage to Bodhidharma, the twenty-eighth patriarch of Indian Buddhism, who emigrated to China in about 475 CE. As Ta Mo, his Chinese name, he was the first patriarch of the Ch'an or Zen school of Buddhism. Although some Western scholars believe that Bodhidharma was more legendary than real, most Chinese and Japanese students of Buddhist history accept his existence as a historical fact.

After arriving from India, Bodhidharma spent most of his time in the north of China, first as the guest of Emperor Ta T'ung of the Liang dynasty and later in Loyang where, according to tradition, he passed the next nine years in deep meditation while facing a wall in the Shao Lin monastery. To this day, Ch'an Buddhism is often called "wall-gazing" or, in Chinese, "pi- kuan." Bodhidharma explained his method of "wall-gazing" in these words:

> "When abandoning the false and embracing the true, and in simpleness of thought abides in pi-kuan, one finds that there is neither selfhood nor otherness...He will not then be guided by any literary instruction, for he is in silent communication with the principle itself, free from conceptual discrimination, for he is serene and not-acting." [18]

Bodhidharma.
ourtesy of The Daitoka-ji Temple, Kyoto, Japan

Unlike the teachings of other Buddhist schools, Bodhidharma preached a message that focused mainly on attaining enlightenment through deep meditation. At the same time, he minimized the value of studying philosophical texts and the worshipping of images or idols. His was a way that went directly to the heart of the matter by focusing on each seeker's "Buddha-nature." There was no intermediary, just the wall of dualism that stood between the "gazer" and enlightenment. The net result of his philosophy was a moving away from an ideological or religious type of Buddhism, a deep awareness of the limits of reason or "conceptual discrimination," and an opening of the heart to a more spontaneous and natural way of attaining Nirvana. Bodhidharma possessed a penetrating intuition as to the nature of the Chinese mind and how to nurture it within Buddhist parameters. Indeed his words from the above passage bear a close resemblance to something Lao Tzu or Chuang Tzu might have said. In a pithy summary of his Buddhist beliefs, fearless as his likeness suggests, Bodhidharma chastises the Emperor Wu:

E. Wu: "I have built many temples and had many of the scriptures translated. Because I have brought many to Buddhism. What is my merit?"
B.: (testily) "None at all!"
E. Wu: "But tell me then, what is the essence of Buddhism?"
B.: "Vast emptiness."
E. Wu: "If all is vast emptiness, who are you?"
B.: "I do not know."

Notwithstanding Bodhidharma's fame as the father of Ch'an Buddhism and a Buddhist teacher of the first order, he is also credited by tradition as having invented the Shao Lin method of exercise and self defense. While teaching Dhyana concepts and meditation in the Shao Lin monastery, he discovered that his students were frequently ill and physically weak. As an antidote to this decrepitude, he installed a simple form of exercise in order to promote circulation, build up the Ch'i (internal energy), and loosen the joints.*

Later on, according to tradition, Bodhidharma and his disciples developed a system of martial arts and weapons-use known as Shao Lin Kung Fu. This style of fighting was based on the way certain animals — tiger, leopard, dragon, snake, and crane — attack or defend themselves. The combining of meditation and physical exercise was a revolutionary step for Buddhism which, in its Indian form, had stressed the ascetic side. Bodhidharma viewed the body and mind as a unity, and realized that the one could not be neglected at the expense of the other. Bodhidharma's path was one in which a balanced and healthy mind could not be separated from a balanced and healthy body; that the physical condition of the vehicle was as important as the mental state of the driver.

Whether or not Bodhidharma truly initiated the Shao Lin exercises is difficult to know with any historical accuracy. What does seem clear is that the Chinese wanted to see him in such a role, suggesting a cultural consensus that body and mind are one and are, more or less, of equal value.

If we compare these ideas with what was current in medieval Christian Europe, we would discover a completely contrary view regarding the body and mind. Christian theologians separated the mind and body, as they did with good and evil. The body was considered sinful, while the soul had the potential of attaining purity, but was contaminated and held back by the body's desires. The early Christian thinkers, most of whom held views as to the dualism of the body and mind, were influenced by Plato

---

*Some of these exercises can be found in Robert Smith's book, Secrets of Shaolin Temple Boxing.

Head of Bodhisattva, T'ang Dynasty (618-906).
Coutesy of Jacob Pins Collection

who believed that the soul was "infected with the evils of the body...." [19] According to Plato, the soul could be pure only after freeing itself from the body after death. Moreover, in Europe, sport and spirituality did not complement or reinforce one another. In Greece and Rome, sport was built on the cult of the body and the sensual idealization of the body as Beauty. The mind was considered as something separate from the body, except as a tool for victory in competitions.

In stark contrast to this approach, Bodhidharma integrated body and mind in order to achieve a spiritual goal — that of enlightenment. A dualistic understanding of the universe was completely foreign to Chinese culture. This kind of harmonious integration suggests one major reason for the attraction of T'ai Chi and other aspects of the Eastern culture in the West today. It reflects a changing attitude: that the body and mind must be sensibly integrated into a larger harmonious identity, that is to say, 'a balanced human being.'

Gradual versus Sudden Enlightment

Whether he himself or his accomplishments were historical fact or fiction, there can be no doubt that Bodhidharma influenced Chinese Buddhism in a major way. Similarly, the later doctrinal battle between the theory of "sudden enlightenment" versus "gradual enlightenment" would also profoundly affect the future of Ch'an Buddhism. This conflict became the yardstick by which the various schools of Buddhism measured themselves.

One of the first Buddhist teachers to criticize the gradual theory of enlightenment was Tao-sheng (360-434 CE), who believed that all beings possess Buddha-nature which, although hidden by ignorance, could burst forth with the insight of sudden enlightenment. The way that Tao-sheng explained his theory is most interesting because of its strong resemblance to the parable of Chuang Tzu: "...only those who can take the fish and forget the net are worthy to seek the tao." [20] For Tao-sheng, Tao represented enlightenment or true buddha-nature, and the net symbolized all techniques and teachings. He exhorted the seeker to leave behind the step-by-step approach of study and, through meditation, dive into the depths of oneself with abandon.

For Ch'an Buddhism, this doctrinal dispute culminated in the 7th century with Shen-hsiu and Hui-neng, the two greatest teachers of Ch'an Buddhism in their day. If Bodhidharma was the father of Ch'an Buddhism, Shen-hsiu and Hui-neng were his intellectual heirs that built it into two major ideological branches known as the Northern and the Southern schools.*

The Northern School of Shen-hsiu upheld the more traditional notion of gradual enlightenment; that Buddha-nature is revealed through levels of attainment. Shen-hsiu wrote a famous poem to illustrate his point:

"This body is the Bodhi-tree.
The mind is like a mirror bright;
Take heed to keep it always clean
and let not dust collect upon it." [21]

Sheng-hsiu is saying that the mind is pure and reflects pure emptiness. But if this is so, why is not everyone enlightened? The problem, according to Sheng-hsiu, is that the pure mind becomes soiled in its contact with the outside world and thus loses its pristine quality. The work of the Buddhist is to clean it through techniques of deep meditation and study, so that the mind can reflect its natural purity. The cleansing of the mind suggests a step-by-step process by which one eventually reaches the point where the Buddha-mind shines through in pristine radiance. This is the buddha-nature within every human being.

In response to Shen-hsiu, Hui-neng, who would establish the Southern School, wrote his own poem:

"There is not Bodhi-tree
Nor stand of mirror bright.
Since all is void, Where can the dust alight?" [22]

According to Hui-neng, the Buddhist need not busy him or herself with cleansing the mind. Since it is in Emptiness — beyond the pristine mind — where Absolute Reality is to be found, one needs only to go directly to that source of Buddha-nature. The experience of enlightenment is "sudden" because there is an abrupt leap of faith that transcends the boundaries of normal reason and consciousness, and one comes face to face and merges with Buddha-nature.

Where Shen-hsiu taught that the pure mind arises from the quietude of meditation during which wrong thoughts are eliminated, Hui-neng argued that the mind cannot be divided into a soiled part and a pure part, and that all its manifestations are reflections of Absolute Reality. In other words, there is not this mind or that mind: there is only the one mind, that of Buddha-mind. Moreover, Hui-neng believed that the very act of devoting time to cleaning the mind could prove to be a costly intellectual distraction that, in the end, could lead the devotee away from true enlightenment. This sounds very close to Lao Tzu's critique that 'acquiring knowledge' leads away from the eternal Truth of Tao.

While both Sheng-hsiu and Hui-neng conceded that the other had a point and neither held their position in total exclusion of the other, in essence the battle lines were drawn between these two theories as to the best approach for achieving enlightenment. At first Shen-hsiu's gradual enlightenment held sway and

---

For an excellent discussion of this dispute, see D. T. Suzuki, The Zen Doctrine of No Mind.

dominated the religious and intellectual climate of Buddhism. However, gradually, Hui-neng's Southern school superseded the Northern school and Ch'an Buddhism developed along the lines of sudden enlightenment.

More than one thousand years have passed since the time of Sheng-hsiu and Hui-neng. From the vantage point of the twentieth century, it is difficult to know with any certainty how much of their doctrinal disagreement was over the nature of enlightenment or how much politics entered into the picture. Probably, we will never know. But the important point to recognize is that both Sheng-hsiu and Hui-neng did not exclude entirely the other's point of view. This suggests that one cannot entirely abandon sound techniques for the lure of instant success — in this case, sudden enlightenment, or the ideal of freedom and oneness for a rigid methodology, which is gradual enlightenment at its worst. One senses that two great teachers like Sheng-hsiu and Hui-neng probably understood that each student of Ch'an Buddhism had his or her individual nature which required its own special kind of cultivation in order to achieve Buddha-mind. Gradual enlightenment and sudden enlightenment, it seems, represent two sides of the same coin.

The entire issue of sudden and gradual enlightenment naturally leads to the question: how does one progress on the path of spiritual, artistic, or scientifc enlightenment (here, meant in the larger sense)? Chuang Tzu's story of the woodcarver is apt. He saw the image of the bellstand in the tree and merely had to carve what was not needed. This might be classified as sudden enlightenment, but we must take into consideration that he was probably a master woodcarver, whose entire spiritual and artistic life had prepared him for that moment. Similarly, Albert Einstein worked for many years on his "Special Theory of Relativity." He said that it "began to germinate in me" long before the theory became clear and final. These are his words:

"Between the conception of the idea of this Special Theory of Relativity and the completion of the corresponding publication, there elapsed five or six weeks. But it would hardly be correct to consider this as a birthday, because earlier the arguments and building blocks were being prepared over a period of years, although without bringing about the fundamental decision." [23]

While it is difficult to describe the indescribable, many, who have been there, have tried to convey the experience of sudden enlightenment. One description is that it is like "the bottom of a tub falling out; when that happens, all its contents are suddenly gone." [24] In an instant fullness becomes emptiness. A Japanese Zen poem reminiscent of this is found in a number of versions. The poem tells of a nun carrying a bucket of water at night. She writes the following lines in response to the bucket suddenly breaking:

"The bottom fell out of the bucket carried by Chiyono;
Now it holds no water, nor does the moon lodge there."

The poem beautifully captures the sudden emptiness that the nun herself experiences. Her perception of the conventional world collapses to reveal another, profounder world behind it, an emptiness where the moon's reflection cannot be found. This incident was taken up and embroidered by others. A later version by another nun elaborates on the first:

"The bottom fell out of the bucket of that woman of humble birth; The pale moon of dawn is caught in rain puddles." [25]

Sudden Enlightenment and T'ai Chi

The scholar Chung-yuan Chang suggests that "the theory of sudden enlightenment...was a significant contribution of Taoism to Buddhist thought in China" and he cites Chuang Tzu's notion of breaking into laughter before finishing a story, as an example of sudden enlightenment. [26]

In this vein, there are stories of T'ai Chi masters — in particular Yang Pan-hou (1837-1892), the son of the founder of Yang style — who, as told by Chen Wei-ming, "would sometimes laugh happily or appear angry...At his level, these emotions spontaneously appeared without intention." [27] The fact that Chen — a famous teacher of the Yang style in China of the 20th century — would comment on a revered master's spontaneous display of emotions indicates that he believed there was something profound behind them, perhaps a state akin to enlightenment.

Indeed it is not unusual for practitioners of T'ai Chi to lose all sense of self, and of time and place, when practicing the form. The duality of subject and object merges and, for an instant, the doer becomes the dance itself. All that remains is laughter or tears or the calm emptiness of concentration, like whispers of an idea passing in the night. Or like the momentary residue of a snowflake that melts on touching the ground.

Another example of a kind of sudden enlightenment — as it relates to a breakthrough in T'ai Chi — is recounted by Cheng Man Ch'ing who tells of a dream he had in which his two arms were broken. He awoke anxiously and immediately moved his arms which, he realized, were in a state of "total relaxation." He explained the sensation thus:

> "The sinews of my arms were like a Raggedy Ann doll, and the joints seemed as if connected by an elastic band which allowed them to turn in any direction at will." [28]

Cheng Man Ch'ing made a monumental advance in his T'ai Chi because of his dream. Somehow, his subconscious was able to express itself in "reality." The duality of the dream world and

Cheng Man Ch'ing.
Photo by Ken Van Sickle

the waking world was obliterated and Cheng Man Ch'ing retained his dream experience intact on waking. This is reminiscent of Chuang Tzu's story of the butterfly in which he and the
butterfly — subject and object — become one. In the language of
R.D. Laing, reality can exist in many different "modes of experience." The loss of the ego-self, if even for a moment, like the
poems of the empty bucket, allows for a "sudden" transformation in the way one experiences the world. For Cheng Man
Ch'ing, the total relaxation he felt in his body suggests that his
conscious mind had finally let down its guard.*

In T'ai Chi, the problem of tension in the body is generally
understood as being rooted in the mind. If the mind is tense, then
so is the body. Complete relaxation can be achieved only where
the body and the mind and the various "modes of experience"
interact and interpenetrate freely, not in isolation, but as a
"teaching of totality."

One wonders if any kind of great leap forward, like the one
described by Cheng Man Ch'ing, can be accomplished without
the daily work of gradual enlightenment, which provides a foundation that prepares the diver for the great plunge. This is the
other side of the coin. Undoubtedly, Cheng Man Ch'ing had undergone countless hours of practice in which the idea of relaxtion
was firmly planted in his consciousness. To put it in sporting
terms, one is unlikely to hit a homerun if he or she is not playing
the game, which requires years of preparation and hardwork just

---

*In many primitive cultures, like the Punan Dyaks of Borneo,
there is the belief in two souls, a waking one and a dreaming one.
They do not recognize a clear distinction between these two states
of consciousness. The dreaming soul, for example, can take part
in the waking world. In Carlos Castenada's books, Don Juan, the
Yaqui Indian sorcerer, can also dream a 'double' who acts in what
we would call the 'world of reality' or the wakeful state.*

to be on the field. The same is true for the student of T'ai Chi. Without the gradual work of daily practice, it is unlikely that he or she will derive much benefit or insight at all from T'ai Chi.

What sudden enlightenment gave to Buddhism, and Buddhism gave to Chinese culture, was the freedom, we might even say, a permission, to transcend rigid concepts and regulations. It offered a way of seeing things fresh and anew; that each morning the sun rises as if it were the first dawn on the earth. It is not uncommon for T'ai Chi practitioners — students and teachers — to get stuck on rules and form. They often need the push or slap of "sudden enlightenment" to help them break out of their T'ai Chi ruts. Each time and moment that one does the T'ai Chi form, he or she should experience it as though for the first time, thus coming around full circle to where he or she began. To paraphrase a modern Zen teacher, Suzuki Roshi: ideally, T'ai Chi mind is Beginner's mind.*

Summary

By virtue of ideas, like sudden enlightenment and a well-organized monastic structure, that included a vast network of land-holdings with a taxfree status, Buddhism continued to prosper until the 9th century when the central government initiated a campaign of persecution against the Buddhists and their property. Yet, even into the 20th century, the influence of Buddhism on Chinese society was substantial and went far beyond their numbers.

Both Taoism and Confucianism borrowed heavily from Buddhist concepts. For example, the Buddhist idea of Karma became a part of the Chinese religious vocabulary. The Buddhist notion

---

Suzuki Roshi wrote an excellent introduction on Zen Buddhism called Zen Mind, Beginner's Mind.

of "emptiness" influenced Taoist ideas concerning the nature of "being" and "non-being." The Neo-Confucian doctrine of "seriousness" (Ching) found its roots in Ch'an Buddhism. Buddhist morality, like the prohibition of murder or theft, fit in well with, and indeed reinforced, traditional Chinese values. The Taoist religious hierarchy adopted many of the ways in which the Buddhists organized themselves, including the establishment of a monastic order and a new emphasis on studying Taoist texts. Buddhist breathing and visualization skills permeated the Chinese religious environment and became an integral part in the art of self-cultivation which both Taoism and Confucianism integrated into their respective philosophies.

With the arrival of Bodhidharma, the meditation techniques of Indian dhyana Buddhism (later to be known as Ch'an Buddhism) were introduced to China, along with an emphasis on integrating body and mind in order to spur on the advent of enlightenment. Later Ch'an Buddhists went a step further in using the sensations of the body to wake up the mind and employed shouting and beating techniques. This use of the body was entirely a Chinese innovation and was not known in Indian Buddhism.

Perhaps the most important contribution of Ch'an Buddhism to Chinese culture was its emphasis on freedom and spontaneity. Ch'an Buddhism taught that following a set of rigid rules of morality did not necessarily bring one closer to enlightenment. It taught a kind of simplicity and a natural way of being that resonated with Chinese culture and the teachings of folk heroes like Lao Tzu and Chuang Tzu. After attaining enlightenment, the enlightened one still carries water or chops wood. However, he or she does so naturally and spontaneously. As Po-chang put it when asked about the essence of Zen, "when hungry, eat; when tired, sleep." There is nothing special and, in a sense, something quite ordinary about being enlightened.

There are many in T'ai Chi who followed the path of Po-chang, just doing the form and following the principles. There are usually no fireworks, only the work itself. D. T. Suzuki relates a story of a monk who came to the master complaining that he was not learning enough Buddhist teachings. The master replied, "In the morning when you come and salute me with 'Good morning!' I salute you back, 'Good morning! How are you?' When you bring me a cup of tea, I gratefully drink it. When you do anything else for me, I acknowledge it. What other teachings do you want from me?" [29]

Every student of T'ai Chi yearns for the breakthroughs of sudden enlightenment. Usually, he or she experiences small breakthroughs of a little light. Occasionally there are giant steps forward. There are some students who "shoot through the stratosphere," aflame in their love for T'ai Chi. Often they burn themselves out before they reach the ground. Then there are those who persevere; they are usually the ones who become masters of their art and teachers of generations.

CHAPTER 5

VARIETIES OF TAOISM

Introduction

Taoism is a term that has come to suggest one unified movement when, in fact, depending on the tenor of the times, it could connote many different groups with often conflicting agendas. Taoism represents a colorful and important strand in the Chinese religious tapestry as well as being a significant philosophy and a radical political/social movement. In the realm of the arts — painting and poetry — one could say that Taoism signified the dominant force behind Chinese artistic expression. Poets and painters, who were not necessarily religious or philosophical Taoists, were sparked by the inspiration of Taoist ideas; for example, the love of and devotion to nature.

When people speak of Taoism, they are generally referring to certain basic ideas that most Taoists held in common. Specifically, most Taoists regarded the fathers of Taoism — Lao Tzu and Chuang Tzu — as the seminal philosophical inspiration of their movement. Yet, the Neo-Taoists of the late Han dynasty revered Confucius as a greater sage than Lao Tzu or Chuang Tzu. This may at first seem incompatible in light of the fact that Lao Tzu and Chuang Tzu saw themselves in opposition to the teachings of Confucius. On the other hand, the Neo-Confucians of the 10th to 13th century were greatly influenced by both Taoist and Buddhist teachings. It would be fair to say that of the three main philosophical and religious systems — Confucianism, Taoism and Buddhism — each, in its own way, contributed to the growth of the other. While there was great doctrinal and ideological infighting between the various competing religious groups, they were actively considering and assimilating each other's ideas that were deemed appropriate to their particular philosophical persuasion.

Religion in China

Historically most Chinese — unlike their Western counterparts — have believed that one need not adhere to the faith of one religion to the exclusion of all others. When placed in juxtaposition to Western religious culture, one can see just how different and almost shocking this idea is. As John Blofeld explains, "traditionally, most Chinese have been simultaneously Confucian, Taoist, Buddhist and followers of the ancient folk religion that never achieved a name of its own...Until the last century, *there was indeed no word for 'religion' in the (Chinese) language....*"[1]

In the West, each member of society belonged to a religious group which defined itself, at least partially, by its opposition to other religious groups. The Protestant Reform movement, for example, was a "protest" against many of the practices of Roman Catholicism. Religious orthodoxy was fervently upheld and one could lose his or her life by transgressing these articles of faith. By way of contrast, the Chinese did not necessarily belong to one religious group. Religion tended to be based on practical rather than ideological considerations — as we pointed out in the previous chapter.

The non-ideological character of the Chinese was confirmed by one of my Chinese teachers of T'ai Chi who pointed out that most Chinese Buddhists could accept Christ as a Buddha in their pantheon of saints whereas most Christians could not consider Buddha as a saint in theirs. In the same vein, he reminisced that as a student in China when he studied European history, he found it strange that Europeans fought a Hundred Year's War, at least in part, over religion. This is not to say that the Chinese were totally free from the convulsions of religious wars and persecutions, but when they occurred, they tended to be rare and not the norm. This good fortune was in part the result of the Chinese world view which held that the universe is a harmonious whole springing from one source, Tao. The concept of Tao lacks any of the human attributes of an imminent God, such as love, anger or jealousy, as in the West, and thus acrimonious religious divisions could be viewed as being patently false by definition.

Before the rise of religious Taoism during the late Han period, religion for the Chinese meant that the Emperor and his representatives throughout the realm offered sacrifices to Heaven and to various gods for the welfare of the entire communal order. As a member of society, each individual benefited from this communal religious experience. This kind of worship was not unknown in the West as it resembles the High Priest representing the entire Jewish people in the Holy of Holies on the Day of Atonement. For the Chinese people, this framework of representative religion was all they had known. It is doubtful how many had questioned or seriously considered another possibility. The fact of the matter is that there was little other than the state religion to choose from.

The rise of religious Taoism and Buddhism dramatically transformed the religious structure and, for the first time, religious beliefs did not depend on the communal order but rather on voluntary choice. Simultaneously, voluntary choice probably meant little or nothing to the vast majority of Chinese who were mostly illiterate peasants, living in tiny villages or in city slums, with little or no contact with the ideas of the educated elite. They lived their lives on the edge of subsistence where one miscalculation might destine a whole family to die of starvation. Even by the 1920s, one-half of all those born in China died before they reached twenty-eight years of age. [2]

As a consequence of their misery, the great masses of Chinese turned not to the Confucian Classics, which they could not read, or to the Confucian representatives of the Emperor, who were often unapproachable, but rather to the local priests of religious Taoism and/or Buddhism. In the mind of the common people they were wise in the formulas of magic and miracles which afforded relief from oppressive conditions. Being a resourceful people, the Chinese continued the practices of the state religion, Confucianism, and the worshipping of the ancient gods as well as incorporating Buddhism and Taoism into their lives. Essentially, after the Han dynasty, Chinese religion became an amalgam of many sources which created a colorful religious tapestry, to say the least. C. K. Yang describes what it would be like to step into a traditional Chinese home:

"The influence of religion on the traditional Chinese family life was everywhere visible. Upon entering any house, one saw paper door gods...painted on the doors for protection of the house and its family members against possible invasion by evil spirits. Near the door and on the floor was an altar to T'u-ti, the earth god, who protected the family against destructive influences...T'ien-kuan, the Heavenly Official, was in the courtyard, and wealth gods, who brought well-being and prosperity to the family, were in the hall in the main room of the house. There was the inevitable Tsao-shen, the kitchen god, on or near the cooking stove, who at the end of the year made an annual report to the Jade Emperor, the supreme god in Heaven, regarding the conduct and behavior of the family and its members, a report that would result in reward or punishment." [3]

The above description does not reflect the enormous influence of Confucianism, Taoism or Buddhism on daily and communal life. For example, if one wanted to build a new home, he would certainly consult the local astrologer for the most propitious time to begin the project. Equally important, in any project from building a home to digging a grave, was the expert in geomancy or "Feng-shui," literally meaning "wind and water," who determined the most favorable physical, climatic, and spiritual conditions.

Confucianism also permeated Chinese society and provided the moral glue that held society together. One of the best examples of Confucian influence that affected almost everyone in an immediate way was the cult of ancestors in which total respect and obedience was given to one's parents, not as individuals, but as abstract representatives of the family clan, which stretched back into the mists of time. This ingrained way of relating to one's parents was mystical and mysterious, and these all-powerful figures cast their shadows on the dynamics of all social relationships. Every individual felt the need to devote himself to someone more powerful, a parental figure, who could protect him against the vagaries of life. It is no exaggeration to say that religious feelings and morality penetrated every nook and cranny, from the highest to the lowest born, of each and every communal or personal rite of Chinese society.

Early Religious Taoism

In this environment, where religious expression was natural and abundant, Taoism of the Han dynasty flourished and attracted followers. Like Buddhism, its growth was prompted by the same conditions of political and social instability. In contrast to Buddhism, however, Taoism did not labor under the dismissive label of being something foreign or unnatural to the Chinese soul. Even before the Han dynasty, it was not uncommon for members of the royal family to patronize "fang shi" or Taoist sorcerers in order to cap their worldly power with the enticing brew of immortality. History records the untimely death of many a prince who died of the "elixir of immortality" that the fang shi concocted for him.

Nonetheless, the popularity of Taoism continued to grow when the pre-Han Emperor Ch'ih-shih Huang Ti (246-209 BCE) invited a large number of Taoist sorcerers to his court and commanded them to brew the elixir of life. He promised that the one who succeeded would reap a rich reward. How success would be determined is an interesting question in itself. In addition the Emperor demonstrated his own commitment by traveling to a Taoist holy mountain in order to offer sacrifices. Later he financed an expedition of young male and female subjects with the purpose of discovering the exact location of the "Islands of the Blessed" where the herb of immortality reportedly grew. It was said that he would wander up and down the beach, gazing eastward where he hoped to see the expedition returning.

During the Han dynasty, Taoism also had its adherents among the royal court such as the Emperor Wu who, like his predecessors, sought the elixir of eternal life and the "Islands of the Blessed." While the dream of immortality remained an important tenet of religious Taoism, some of its glitter was tarnished as it became less credible that real gold lay beneath its alchemical claims.

It was also during this period that Confucianism became the official state religion, due, in part, to its ability to support and ensure moral stability. This did not mean that Taoism or its writings were suppressed. The educated elite was certainly familiar with the writings of Lao Tzu, Chuang Tzu, and other sources of Taoist inspiration. Furthermore, the idea of immortality — that human beings could free themselves from the jaws of death — would hold a fascination for many Chinese, including some Confucians, until the modern era.

Taoism and Confucianism were not rival systems at loggerheads with one another. It is probably best to think of Confucianism as less of a religion and more of a system of morality that set the tone for the way society operated, whereas Taoism provided a mystical and spiritual home in which the soul could reside, take flight, and return. While Confucianism exerted a profound influence on politics and morality, Taoism was more influential in the realm of poetry and art. One could be a Confucian outside the home and a Taoist inside. Being a Taoist or a Confucian was sometimes simply a matter of what phase of life one was in. The scholar Burton Watson tells an interesting story that illustrates this point. [4]

There was a Confucian by the name of Yen Chun-p'ing who set up a booth for divining the *I Ching* in the marketplace. He explained that he used the *I Ching* as "an excuse to advise them (common people) on what is right," thus teaching Confucian ethics under the guise of divination. When he had earned enough money, however, he closed his stall and began teaching the ideas of Lao Tzu and Chuang Tzu. Often beneath the tough exterior of Confucian morality, one found the heart of a Taoist.

The Radicalization of Taoism

As religious Taoism penetrated and found a home in the beliefs and yearnings of the lower classes, it understandably became more radicalized, given the dire straits of the peasantry. These pent-up feelings of injustice burst out politically in the revolts of the Yellow Turbans and the Five Pecks of Rice sects. The Yellow Turbans were members of a Taoist sect known as T'ai-p'ing tao, "The Way of Supreme Peace," founded by Chang Chueh in the latter part of the 2nd century CE. They wore yellow turbans to symbolize their allegiance to the Yellow Emperor. Their leader, Chang Chueh, gained considerable fame as a healer who reportedly used magic to cure illness. However, in order for his magic to work, he required the sick person to confess his or her sins. The combining of the psychological and physical in order to affect healing was not unusual among Taoist healers like Chang Chueh. In 184 CE, the Yellow Turbans rose up in a violent rebellion against the Han dynasty. Although eventually defeated, and their leaders including Chang Chueh executed, the ideas of peace and equality that they fought for remained influential on both Taoism and the downtrodden masses of the Chinese people.

The Five Pecks of Rice sect (Wu-tou-mi tao) was founded by the Taoist Chang Tao-ling in the first half of the 2nd century CE and, unlike the Yellow Turbans which soon disappeared from history, lasted until the 15th century. The name, Five Pecks of Rice, was derived from the initiation fee to join the sect. The Five Pecks of Rice sect represented an authentic Taoist tradition in that Lao Tzu was venerated by its followers as a religious figure and the *Tao Te Ching* became its bible.

As with the Yellow Turbans, healing occupied a central role with the Five Pecks of Rice sect, along with the idea that physical illness could only be cured as the result of spiritual purification. The rebellion of the sect was put down by the central government in 215 CE, but not before they had controlled a large territory for about twenty years with Taoist priests in charge of the government, collecting taxes, and administrating justice. After the sect's defeat, a weakened central government allowed them to continue their educational activities and recognized the hereditary lineage of the sect's founders, the Chang family.

In the 5th century K'ou Chien-chih (363-448) became the sect's "Celestial Master," and this line of Taoism was elevated to the status of a state religion. K'ou established the first Taoist monastic institution, a priesthood, temples, and sacred texts, all of which were inspired by the example of Buddhism. With K'ou, Taoism established itself on a more or less equal footing with Buddhism and Confucianism as a religious and political force to be reckoned with. At the same time, many Taoists continued to cherish the ideals of Lao Tzu and Chuang Tzu that nonconformity and a rejection of all political structures were the only true way to uncover ultimate reality. As Chuang Tzu put it, they preferred to drag their tails in the mud than to become part of any political or religious establishment.

As a fuller picture of Taoism emerges, one can understand why Taoism can be so confusing for the Westerner. It can refer to the ideas of Lao Tzu and Chuang Tzu, the later philosophers known as the Neo-Taoists, the Taoist religion, and any number of combinations of the three including many sects that proposed their own unique interpretations of Lao Tzu and thus called themselves Taoists.

In a similar fashion to his understanding of Buddhism in Chinese society, the famous modern historian, Fung Yu-lan, divided Taoism into a philosophy, which he called Tao Chia (the Taoist school), and a religion, which is called Tao Chiao (the Taoist religion). [5] He observed that "their teachings are not only different: they are even contradictory." Lao Tzu and Chuang Tzu, for example, believed that in the natural course of things life is followed by death and that man should accept this arrangement calmly. On the other hand, one of the main tenets of religious Taoism was the doctrine of immortality and thus the avoidance of death. Interestingly, Fung argues that the Taoist religion, because of its ideas on immortality, was in the spirit of modern science in that it sought to "conquer" nature by escaping death through various alchemical techniques. Moreover the Taoists viewed the universe as being real, similar to modern scientists, and not an illusion as the Buddhists tended to believe.

Before we examine the religious Taoists whose ideas were seminal in the development of T'ai Chi, it would be beneficial to look briefly at "philosophical Taoism" both for purposes of definition and to understand the tenor of the times. In the same breath, a word of warning: one should not be too rigid in these definitions; the line between religious and philosophical Taoism can be sometimes vague and misleading.

Philosophical Taoism

With the collapse of the Han dynasty in 220 CE, China descended into a morass of intense political chaos and corruption. The Empire itself was divided into three competing states and, for about four hundred years, until the establishment of the Sui dynasty in 581 CE, Chinese society was ravaged and weakened by the onslaught of frequent wars and political intrigues. Because of the decline of the central government, nomadic invaders from the north managed to break through the Great Wall and conquer parts of northern China. Out of this period of decay, uncertainty, and devastation, a new philosophy know as "Hsüan Hsüan" emerged that reflected the disgust of certain intellectuals with the political climate. Modern scholars call this movement Neo-Taoism, because it represented a new interpretation of Lao Tzu's and Chuang Tzu's ideas. It was definitely not a strain of religious Taoism, yet Neo-Taoism contained mystical traits and a kind of spiritual romanticism in its love for nature.

The word "hsüan" means dark or abtruse and is found in the first chapter of the *Tao Te Ching* in which Lao Tzu explains that the Tao is so dark and mysterious that it cannot be named. By taking the name "hsüan hsüan," the Neo-Taoists were saying that they not only had uncovered some new and profound insight into the meaning of Lao Tzu, but they were also the true heirs of his tradition. While Lao Tzu was already popular with intellectuals during the Han dynasty, his fame coalesced around the movement of the Neo-Taoists along with a revival of interest in Chuang Tzu and others.

By opposing the arid, scholastic kind of Confucianism that had become institutionalized during the Han dynasty, the Neo-Taoists represented the ongoing philosophical tug-of-war between the followers of Lao Tzu and those of Confucius. The main bone of contention on the part of the Neo-Taoists was not, however, Confucius himself, whom they respected, but rather what the Confucians had turned him into. As Lao Tzu had done some five hundred years before, the Neo-Taoists challenged the orthodox beliefs of their day. They argued, for example, that Confucius should be seen as a great teacher and not as a god or semi-god that had inspired the state religion.

By virtue of their love of debate, the Neo-Taoists sharpened their oratorical skills on the Confucian establishment, thereby reviving a new interest in reason which became a pillar of future Chinese thought. Out of this electric, intellectual atmosphere, two schools of thought emerged: the Pure Conversation school and the Metaphysical school. In their fierce debates they rejected anything that smelled of politics and traditional morality while focusing their thoughts on flights of fancy, freedom, and plain fun. This daring serendipitous attitude was in sharp contrast to the seriousness of Confucianism and the stiffness of Chinese social conventions at large. In some ways Neo-Taoism is reminiscent of the hippie movement of the 1960s in that young people rejected the sexual and social mores of their parents and embarked on a new road which they hoped would lead to a deeper sense of truth and freedom. It was no accident that Lao Tzu and Chuang Tzu were "rediscovered" during the post-Han period in China and the hippie period in the West.

Undoubtedly the most flamboyant and perhaps the most famous of this unconventional trend were the Seven Sages of the Bamboo Grove (Chu-lin Ch'i-hsien), seven Taoist scholars and

The Seven Sages of the Bamboo Grove (pheasants and other birds were symbols of respect in Chinese culture).
Courtesy of The Princeton University Press

artists who would gather in a bamboo grove to practice the art of "pure conversation." With Lao Tzu and Chuang Tzu as their inspiration, they sought harmony with the universe and the Tao through the art of poetry, music, and the drinking of large quantities of wine. Their ideal was to act spontaneously on the spur of the moment — their notion of "wu wei" — as they cultivated their appreciation of the divine beauty of nature and delved into the secrets of the mysterious Tao.

The best-known of the Seven was Hsi K'ang who grew up in a wealthy family with strong Confucian ties, but found that his heart lay with the ideas of Taoism. He also practiced the Taoist techniques for longevity. While not a religious Taoist in the conventional sense, he was influenced by their ideas and methods for seeking immortality.

Another one of these sages was Liu Ling, about whom there is a famous story that illustrates just how unconventional he was.[6] It was said that Liu Ling always traveled with a servant who carried a bottle of wine and a spade for his master, the one to keep his master in good spirits and the other to bury him if he should die on the spot. The story conveys a sense of just how close Lui Ling lived to the precipice where his love and lust for life could easily plunge him into oblivion.

In another story Lui Ling would walk about naked in his home. To a Confucian visitor who found him in just such a state, Lui Ling explained that the whole universe was his home and his room was his pants. Because the visitor was in his room, Liu Ling asked him what business he had with his pants. The Confucian probably thought Lui Ling was simply out of his mind. But, for those like Lui Ling, there was method to their madness. The essence of their philosophy was a revolt against a conformist and strait-laced society bound hand and foot with Confucian morality. Their weapon was not necessarily the pen, but the sword of shock, which, at times, cut their opponents to the quick.

On the more conventional side of Neo-Taoism were philosophers like Wang Pi (226-249) who wielded his pen with great effectiveness. Wang Pi died at the young age of twenty-four, and yet he exerted a powerful influence on the Neo-Taoists of the time. There is no telling how much he could have accomplished had he lived a full life. In his short life he wrote an important commentary on the *Tao Te Ching* and the *I Ching* among other works. Wang Pi interpreted Lao Tzu in a novel way, giving rise to the name Neo-Taoism. However, there were many then and now, like Cheng Man Ch'ing, who believed that Wang Pi had diverged "from the meaning of the text." [7]

Nevertheless, Wang Pi represented the spirit of the age which was one of seeking, rediscovering and reinterpreting the past. He believed, for example, that Lao Tzu's idea of non-being (Tao) was actually pure or original being (Wu) and that there was but one unifying principle behind all things, and that was the principle of Tao. In order to return to one's pure being, it was necessary to return to non-being or Tao. The implication of Wang Pi's thinking seems to suggest that mankind can touch or comprehend Tao through self-cultivation techniques, which echoes or perhaps foreshadows Buddhist thought. This way of thinking apparently diverged from the direction of Lao Tzu and represented a new interpretation of the *Tao Te Ching* that was appropriate to the intellectual climate of the times. While Lao Tzu, like the Neo-Taoists after him, clearly believed that the Tao was pure or original being (Wu), the Tao also had no name and was not a thing. For Lao Tzu, the human mind could see how Tao worked in nature, but never fathom its essence.

An interesting point, which undoubtedly distinguished Wang Pi and his fellow travelers from other Taoists of their age, was that they honored Confucius as a greater sage than Lao Tzu or Chuang Tzu. Fung Yu-lan explains this anomaly in the following way: "When Confucianism triumphed over the other schools...in the thinking of such Neo-Taoists as Wang Pi and Kuo Hsiang, therefore Confucius was like a ruler, whereas Lao Tzu and Chuang Tzu were like his councilors." [8]

Here, one can see the overwhelming victory of Confucianism during the Han dynasty. The Neo-Taoists believed that Confucius had roamed in both worlds, the Tao of Heaven and the Tao of man, while Lao Tzu and Chuang Tzu had transcended the mundane world, traveling only the freeways of heaven. For the Neo-Taoists, roaming in one world was not enough and indeed was a one-sided approach to sagehood. In a surprising twist of logic, Wang Pi explains that because Confucius did not speak about non-being (Wu), he actually knew more about it than Lao Tzu and Chuang Tzu who often referred to it. [9] It was Confucius who said that if one hears the truth of Tao in the morning, he can then die at night. This suggested to the Neo-Taoists that Confucius was also knowledgeable about the Tao of Heaven.

Religious Taoism and Immortality

Religious Taoists charted a mystical course based on the early Taoist sorcerers, the Fang Shi. With regard to one issue in particular, religious Taoism parted company with Buddhism and practically all other religious and philosophical schools in China. The basic and unremitting goal of religious Taoism was the attainment of immortality through alchemical means, which included both external and internal techniques. This quest profoundly influenced Chinese thought, not only because it captured the popular imagination from prince to pauper, but it also encouraged the growth of Chinese medicine, pharmacology and martial arts.

We can well imagine what the Buddhists thought of this idea, given the fact that they denied any worth to the ego whatsoever. The attainment of Nirvana means the "extinction" of the ego-self; an idea in total opposition to the religious Taoist goal of maintaining the ego in a kind of purified transfigured form.

For their part, the Confucians were much too practical and rational to consider seriously the idea of immortality. Yet who can deny that escaping the jaws of ageing and death does not have its allure? Thus, there were those of all creeds who fell under its spell.

On a practical level, the religious Taoist ideal of immortality created a clear separation between the Chinese and Indian forms of Yoga. For Buddhists, yoga techniques were developed for the control of the body as a method of preparation for meditation and other spiritual endeavors. Most religious Taoists, on the other hand, believed that, if the mind, body, and cosmos could work in harmony and thereby manipulate the natural energy inherent in the universe, they could attain immortality through the techniques themselves.

In *The Secret of the Golden Flower*, a Taoist treatise on immortality reportedly from the 8th century, it is related that there are masters who "learn to circulate their energy independent of bodily existence and are still limited in that they are not immortal...." [10] This "circulation of energy" is the ability to manipulate one's inner energy (Ch'i) at will. At the very least, this suggests a high development of personal power, including the ability to be in complete control of one's health. But it was thought that one could take this idea a step further. According to Richard Wilhelm, a scholar of Taoism and translator of *The Secret of the Golden Flower*, by cultivating "an inner detachment from all entanglements with things" — which is the secret of the golden flower — it is possible "to preserve in a transfigured form the idea of the person..." [11]

For religious Taoists, the ability to manipulate one's internal energy was the path that led to personal power including self-defense, improved health, and ultimately immortality. These ideas were extremely significant for the development of T'ai Chi. The question of attaining immortality, though important, was not the only attraction for would-be devotees of Taoism. The manipulation of energy through meditation and visualization coupled with physical exercises — which would eventually include T'ai Chi — also provided the means of maintaining and improving one's health. By the twentieth century, this secondary benefit proved to be sufficiently enticing without the inducement of immortality, which came to be suspect in the modern world.

While immortality had affixed itself in the folk-imagination of the Chinese people for at least a millennium, a lesser goal of longevity and better health would be no less fundamental. In the T'ai Chi Classics, one author states the goal of T'ai Chi in just these terms:

"Think over carefully what the final purpose is;
to lengthen life and maintain youth." [12]

Nevertheless, for religious Taoists, the ideal of immortality and that of preserving one's health were conceptually and practically linked. They believed that there were two basic approaches in achieving immortality: the external (wei tan) and the internal (nei tan). The external method focused on manufacturing the "pill" of immortality. This pill or elixir was fashioned out of herbs, metals, and other natural ingredients in a laboratory setting (though perhaps primitive by modern standards) through the scientific methodology of trial and error. Chinese pharmacology is indebted to the results of these experiments. In the West, the connection between modern medicine and herbology was also apparent in, for example, the discovery of birch bark as the source for aspirin.

In contrast to external alchemy, the internal method centered on the development of the mind and body with the spiritual goal of transforming the consciousness of the seeker. The mind and body literally became an alchemical laboratory in which the pill of immortality was brewed out of the individual's inherent energies.

Chinese martial arts mirror these categories by their division into the external and internal schools. The external method (wei dan) stimulates one's energy (Ch'i) in a certain place by muscle exertion and concentration. The muscles are thus strengthened and are the source of the martial artist's power. The popular name for the external style is Kung Fu.

The internal method (nei dan) focuses on sending one's internal energy to the tan t'ien, a place where Ch'i is stored just below the navel, and then it is circulated throughout the body's pathways called 'meridians.' T'ai Chi is considered to be an internal martial art because it derives its power from the developing and circulating of this internal energy. The size or strength of the muscles is of secondary importance. In fact most teachers of T'ai Chi do not stress muscle development at all due to the notion that this could block the natural flow of Ch'i.*

The Historical Roots of Immortality

The religious Taoists were also known by the name "huang-lao" because they considered themselves devotees of both Huang-ti (The Yellow Emperor) and Lao Tzu. The earlier mentioned Yellow Turbans sect also traced its religious lineage back to Huang-ti. As the benevolent ruler of China's Golden Age, he received the homage of many diverse groups. He symbolized a mythical period of creativity and purity, not unlike that of the legendary King Arthur and Merlin. The Yellow Emperor not only established the basis of Chinese medicine, but was also credited with discovering the secret of immortality. Here again, healing and immortality share a common nexus and origin. From the

---

These ideas will be discussed at length later.

time of the Warring States Period, Taoists have revered the Yellow Emperor as a deity in the cult of immortals. A legend passed down from generation to generation has him ascending to Heaven on the back of a dragon with his entire household, a powerful image which became a popular subject for Chinese artists.

The underlying premise of Taoism was that human beings should live in harmony with the laws of nature. In the *Tao Te Ching*, Lao Tzu wrote:

"A man is born gentle and weak,
At his death he is hard and stiff
Green plants are tender and filled with sap.
At their death they are withered and dry.

Therefore the stiff and unbending is the disciple of death.
The gentle and yielding is the disciple of life." [13]

and

"Man follows the earth.
Earth follows heaven.
Heaven follows the Tao.
Tao follows what is natural." [14]

The thrust of Lao Tzu's observations is that men and women should look around them, determine how the universe works, and then live in harmony with Tao. Once they understand the way of the universe, it would be possible to choose a balanced and appropriate lifestyle which, at the very least, promotes good health and, taken to its logical conclusion, that is to say, complete moral, spiritual, and physical harmony with nature's laws, could lead to immortality.

This is a different tack from most Western religious thought. In Judaism, for example, the laws of nature are subservient to the laws of God. Jews seek harmony with God's laws and commandments rather than the laws of nature. Similarly, Moslems achieve immortality and the reward of Paradise by obedience to Allah's laws. In Christianity immortality is often a reward for the belief in Jesus as the Messiah. In all three Western or Middle Eastern religions, harmony with nature —even if such a state was thought possible — is not a prerequisite for attaining salvation from the cycles of birth and death.

For the disciples of Lao Tzu, each individual is an integral part of nature, a product of Yin and Yang, and a result of the creative process of Tao. Both Taoism and Confucianism, the two indigenous Chinese religions, share the view that the world is real. In contrast to Buddhism, the Taoist universe is not an illusion, but rather a dynamic extension of Tao, which is eternal, everlasting and continuously procreating. Therein lies the secret of immortality: if one can live in absolute accord with the Yin and Yang of the eternal Tao, the result will be that he or she can enjoy the pleasures of this world or, at will, dwell in the land of the immortals. If an individual wishes to remain in the world, health and longevity will follow them all the days of their life because they are the "disciples of life" and follow the "natural" way of Tao.

In the tradition of The Yellow Emperor and Lao Tzu, although of a much later period, lived the alchemist Ko Hung (284-364 CE) who wrote perhaps the most important book on Taoist alchemy called the *Pao-p'u-tzu*. This book explained the specific techniques and practices for attaining immortality and changing one's appearance, and included a vast array of other magical acts. Ko Hung's most important role was that of a compiler, for he gathered and published all of the most important Taoist teachings as to how one could achieve immortality.

Ko Hung believed that immortality could be reached only

through the alchemical interaction of the elixir of eternal life. While physical exercise, sexual yoga, breathing techniques, and meditation could prolong life, Ko Hung believed that only alchemy bestowed the gift of eternal life and supernatural powers like walking on water or communing with the spirit world. It was rumored that he may have gained his knowledge of alchemy not from traditional Chinese sources but rather from his visits to the aboriginal people in the tropical region near Canton. [15]

Surprisingly, Ko Hung was revered for his profound knowledge and understanding of the Confucian Classics. Like the Neo-Taoists, Ko Hung also held Confucius in high esteem and he represents another example of how the Chinese cultural tapestry was intertwined in a tight symbiotic weave. He upheld traditional Confucian ethics by arguing against the necessity of leaving one's family for the solitude of the mountains, although it was reported that he had done so himself. Ko Hung believed that, since the elixir could be manufactured at home, one could forgo the various yoga techniques requiring solitude. After all, by staying at home, the whole family could become immortal. Moreover, Ko Hung preached that immortality could not be achieved without practicing the Confucian virtues of good deeds, loyalty, friendliness, and trustworthiness. With Ko Hung, one understands just how deeply Confucian ethics had become ingrained in Chinese thinking. In this context, Fung Yu-lan's explanation, that Confucius had become a "constitutional ruler" who received homage from practically everyone, is right on the mark. In fact, it would be fair to say that the spirit of Confucius looms large in Chinese thought from the Han dynasty on, and any account that does not recognize his dominating presence would be less than complete.

The Western observer might think that in combining Confucian virtues and alchemy, Ko Hung is mixing apples and oranges. He appears to be using modern scientific methodology in the way he prepares the various herbs and metals for the elixir of immortality. At the same time, he claimed that the elixir will not work if it is not accompanied by Confucian ethics. From a modern perspective, we are quite certain that a drug, like an antibiotic, will be effective, whether or not the person taking it is virtuous or not. Virtuous behavior or thinking has nothing to do with the success or failure of the drug. For the Chinese, ethics could not be separated from any other aspect of life, and, as we have said before, it represented a worldview that everyone and everything was interconnected. Since the Chinese considered the mind and body as one entity, they could not conceive of the one working without directly influencing the other.

T'ai Chi represents a practical example in Chinese culture where body and mind are taught to act together as a single entity. If a person was doing the T'ai Chi form in just a physical way, without engaging the mind, his or her T'ai Chi would be considered "not very good" because it was merely external. An experienced practitioner of T'ai Chi can usually spot the "external" immediately. And, unlike many forms of Western exercise, T'ai Chi is understood by its followers as an "internal" martial art precisely because the mind is engaged as an active partner in the initiation and the nuance of every single movement. It is in fact meditation in movement. Thus, when performed well, T'ai Chi creates a mood like the flow of rain rather than the stunning crack of lightening. Yet within its rounded folds is hidden the blinding flash of potential that is often unknown even to the one doing the form. In the same way that Ko Hung could not conceive of physical immortality without an ethical mindset, so the founders of T'ai Chi required the active participation of the conscious mind to guide the body's energy and motion.*

---

*This is discussed more thoroughly in Chapter 9 on the principles of T'ai Chi.

The question arises: if Taoists like Ko Hung and others seemed to be on the track of a scientific method, why did a Chinese scientific tradition not develop similar to the one in the West? The answer lies in the deep mistrust that the Taoists held for reason and logic. Religious Taoism focused its energy on the powers of magic that would enable them to control nature, which marks only the beginnings of science in a Western sense.

Another equally important aspect of science is the emphasis on exactness and verification, which did not interest the Taoists. They sought to transcend the day-to-day world by living in the realm of myth that was not subject to the normal laws of perception and verification. Yet, because the Taoists closely observed the workings of nature, which they combined with a deep mystical intuition, they were able to evolve profound insights, many of which have been confirmed by modern science.[16] Moreover, the twentieth century philosopher and historian Fung Yu-lan believes that Taoism was "the only system of mysticism which the world has ever seen which was not profoundly anti-scientific." [17] Thus, religious Taoism contained some of the elements which might have led to a rigorous scientific methodology. Had it combined with, say, another system like Confucianism, which emphasized the rigors of logic, or one that combined logic with the observation and verification of the universe, the Chinese might have developed a scientific method long before the West. But that was not to be.

According to the religious Taoists, a person who becomes immortal, "hsien" in Chinese, does not only live forever, but he or she can become a powerful magician, enabling him or her to perform all manner of supernatural acts. The modern pictogram for "hsien" is a picture of a man and a mountain which suggests that someone who retires to the mountains is on a quest for immortality. The earlier pictogram for the word "hsien" was represented by a man ascending toward heaven. Clearly, in the

Chinese mind, man, mountains, and heaven are intertwined with the notion of immortality. Metaphorically, the intersection of mountain and heaven symbolize the place where mankind seeks that which is most pure and holy in him or herself, heaven being the abode of the gods or, in this case, immortals. The mountain represents the closest point to heaven that human beings can reach. A similar use of the man/mountain metaphor can be found in many cultures. In the Bible, for example, Mount Sinai is the meeting place for God and Israel.

Ko Hung divided immortals into three categories: celestial, terrestrial, and those who had given up the body. Celestial immortals fly to heaven with their bodies intact, like The Yellow Emperor, whereas the terrestrial ones dwell in forests or mountains. Ko Hung's death was considered of the third and lowest variety in that when he died, he was placed in a coffin, but later his body disappeared and only his clothes remained. The best-known immortals in Chinese mythology were the Eight Immortals who are often found in Chinese art and represent the eight conditions of life: youth, old age, poverty, riches, nobility, the common people, woman, and man.

Another well-known immortal, especially significant in the lore of T'ai Chi, was the Taoist sage Chang San-feng who is traditionally credited as being the creator of T'ai Chi Ch'uan. Historians are not absolutely certain that Chang San-feng existed or, because there are contradictions in the dates of his life, if there was just one or many Chang San-fengs. What seems certain about Chang San-feng and the other Immortals is that they represented a deep longing and pathos in the soul of the Chinese people for a better life than the one on earth. By cultivating a virtuous character, patience, perseverance, and a bit of luck, one might be visited by the spirit of the immortals, and have his or her life changed in ways little imagined but amply enlarged upon in the Chinese literary and oral traditions.

The Three Treasures

The Taoist cult of immortality as represented by Ko Hung was basically oriented to the outer approach (wei tan) because it sought immortality through the medium of medicines and herbs. In contrast, the inner approach (nei tan), of which T'ai Chi is a part, was equally important in the search for immortality and/or a longer life with improved health. It focused on strengthening, purifying, and balancing the internal energies of the body-mind. These energies are called the "three treasures:" Ching (essence), Ch'i (vitality) and Shen (spirit).

Each of the "three treasures" has two parts: an abstract and a concrete dimension. Ching, or essence, was thought of in terms of sexuality, its concrete dimension, while creativity symbolized the abstract level. Ch'i, or vitality, was viewed in the tangible world as breath and air while it symbolized the life-force in an abstract sense. Shen, or spirit, was related to the workings of the logical mind, and to intuitive and creative reflection in an abstract sense.

	Concrete	**Abstract**	**Body**
Ching (essence)	male sperm and female sexual fluids	creativity as the seed of life	genitals
Ch'i (vitality)	air and breath	internal energy and life force	stomach (tan t'ien) lungs
Shen (spirit)	ordinary consciousness thoughts and feelings	spiritual consciousness including that before birth	head/heart

The condition of the three treasures — their quality, quantity, and interaction — determined the mental, physical and spiritual

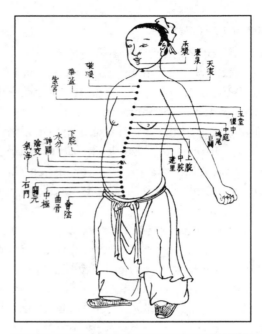

Front and back pathways to transmute internal energy.

health of the individual. Within this framework, through a multitude of healing arts and techniques that had developed over the ages from practical experience, it was thought that the seeker could transform his or her spiritual and physical condition for the better.

It is important to understand that man and woman do not stand alone in the universe as a bastion of the three treasures. Rather, the three treasures exist in the universe at large and human beings are a reflection of the universe's subtle nature, albeit in a coarser form. In other words, human beings are a microcosm of the universe and, as such, they represent all of existence, which includes, of course, the three treasures. *The essence of Chinese Yoga techniques is to reverse the process that led to a person's birth and thus return to the pre-birth, subtle state of his or her unity with the universe.* By reversing the birth process, one transforms his or her coarse body-form back into subtle consciousness. This process begins with transmuting Ching and Ch'i from their coarse to their abstract forms which leads to subtle Shen and the ultimate union of the human mind with cosmic consciousness. This occurs as a result of various intricate techniques of meditation and visualization.

In his commentary on the *Tao Te Ching*, the T'ai Chi master Cheng Man Ch'ing explains the process of transforming the three treasures in this way:

"To 'contain yang' means inhaling the Ch'i of heaven; to be 'wrapped by yin' means transforming sperm essence (ching) into bone marrow. The marrow flows inside the bones and the Ch'i circulates throughout — even to the feet — with the breath. When one arrives at this level, ones 'pulsing ch'is marry.' This is what Lao Tzu desires, this is what to study: the marriage of the ch'i is Tao or the province of men who are in communication with heaven." [18]

In other words, through the various yoga techniques of breathing ('inhaling the Ch'i of heaven'), the bedroom arts, meditation, and physical exercises that combine breathing and movement, one can strengthen and circulate the Ch'i and Ching. By focusing one's concentration, it was thought that the pulsing Ch'is would marry or merge, thus producing Shen (where men "are in communication with heaven"). Once subtle Ch'i was produced, the practitioner could achieve union with Tao. By virtue of producing and conserving the internal energy of the body-mind, that is to say, the marriage of the pulsing Ch'is, excellent health could be maintained and one's life prolonged.

To understand how the Ch'is marry and create shen, it might be helpful to analyze one of the breathing techniques used in T'ai Chi.* This type of breathing is called prenatal or reverse breathing and it is characterized by the contracting of the lower stomach on the in-breath and the expanding of the lower stomach on the out-breath. According to the Taoists, each person is born with prenatal Ch'i or, in other words, the life-force that each baby is endowed with before his or her birth. Some babies receive more than others, a fact which depends on the health of the mother and father, genetic inheritance, and other factors. Before the baby is born, he or she takes in its nourishment and oxygen through the umbilical cord and stores its energy in the

---

As a general rule, no breathing technique or, for that matter, T'ai Chi itself, should be tried without the guidance of a qualified and responsible teacher. These are powerful techniques and are dangerous if not done properly. Secondly, there are many different opinions about breathing in T'ai Chi. Some teachers prefer normal breathing, that is, on the in-breath, the stomach expands in contrast to that of prenatal breathing which is just the opposite. There are some teachers who do not want the student to pay attention to the breath at all. In short, this is a controversial issue and is beyond the scope of this particular discussion.

tan t'ien which is about two or three fingers below the belly button. The unborn child literally breathes, eats, and eliminates waste through the umbilical cord. Once the baby is born, breathing from the nose and mouth begins, which is known as postbirth breathing. This transition marks the end of prenatal breathing. However, if one closely observes the way a baby breathes, one will notice that the baby, while breathing through its nose and mouth, still uses its stomach with the in-breath and out-breath. The Taoists observed that, as one grows older, the tendency is to breathe higher up rather than into the stomach. The breath gradually moves higher and higher as one grows older until it flies out the mouth which culminates in death.

The Taoists hoped to accomplish two goals with prenatal breathing. They wanted to reverse the upward pattern of the breath, so that it would stay deep in the lower stomach. This was accomplished by harmonizing the movement of the stomach and the breath. They also wanted to strengthen and increase the prenatal Ch'i, which was stored in the tan t'ien, by mixing it with the Ch'i from the air that is inhaled into the body. The body thus becomes an alchemical test-tube in which the two Ch'is, prenatal and postnatal, are mixed and utilized to strengthen the body.

The Taoists understood the prenatal Ch'i as being Yang and the postnatal Ch'i of oxygen as being Yin. By contracting the stomach and tan t'ien as one inhales oxygen, the two Ch'is are joined together, married or merged, and, on the out-breath, the stomach is expanded and the "married Ch'i," newly bonded and instilled with vigor, is pushed down into the tan t'ien which multiplies and preserves the treasure of prenatal Ch'i.

In analyzing prenatal breathing, it is interesting to note how well this idea resonates with the larger philosophical framework of Taoism and Chinese philosophy. The Taoists clearly used their observations of nature in order to develop their ideas on self-cultivation. It is logical, though not necessarily true, that if the breath leaves the body through the mouth with death, one might be able to prolong life by preserving the breath as deep as possible in the body, in this case, the tan t'ien where life was first nourished.

For the Taoists, the infant represented the point at which the life-force was strongest and most Yang. Therefore, they observed the qualities of an infant, his or her way of breathing, and general suppleness of a child's body, and they sought to emulate these positive qualities. In the Taoist scheme of things, the baby was after all the closest to Tao, having recently come from there.* Moreover, in the *Tao Te Ching*, Lao Tzu extols the virtues of the "newborn babe" as the right example to follow.[19] In Christian tradition Jesus also points to the innocence of a child as a quality to be esteemed.

In addition, the concept of Yin and Yang is brought into the picture as an explanation of how the mixing of Ch'is are balanced. With the suggestion that the Ch'is "marry" and merge, the powerful imagery of sexuality, the honeymoon night of bride and groom, is intimated. The very act of a man and a woman that creates life is used as a metaphor for how one preserves life. Prenatal breathing springs from the experience of life itself. But even more, it is a kind of metaphysical poetry in which the life-force — Tao — rises up and expresses itself through the physical universe. And, while many aspects of the Chinese philosophical

---

* *My mother tells this story about her children. When I was about five years old, my sister three and my brother still an infant, we were sitting around the breakfast table. My sister and I were trying to imagine what god looked like. Suddenly I turned to my brother and said, "you should know, you were just there!" Throughout all cultures, the newborn represents that which has just arrived from another world, be it the world of God or, according to the Chinese, Tao.*

system that gave birth to techniques like prenatal breathing are not easily verified in a laboratory, they undoubtedly contain an intuitive wisdom and genius based on millennia of experience that, at the very least, can point the way to a qualitatively better and healthier life.

The Taoist way is a coherent system, in which the three treasures, as well as Yin and Yang, play an important role. Interestingly it knows no parallel in the West. In fact traditional Chinese medical charts, which are based on these ideas, portray an internal bodily terrain that is entirely different from those of the West. We have no medical tradition of energy pathways called meridians.

The example of prenatal breathing represents but one part of a many-tiered yogic structure. While words like Ch'i can be translated as something like "life-force," the ideas themselves and their framework have their own internal logic that reflects a mode of thinking which permeates all of Chinese culture. T'ai Chi mirrors this way of viewing the world. For this reason perhaps many Westerners are baffled by the T'ai Chi approach to keeping fit and healthy. To understand Chinese culture and, for our purposes, its relationship to T'ai Chi, the Westerner must begin to comprehend this unique way of viewing energy and the way it works in the universe. John Blofeld makes this point crystal-clear:

"People with a Christian or Jewish background are apt to suppose that absence of belief in an omnipotent creator-deity necessarily implies acceptance of the doctrine of materialism...A Taoist would be better pleased if you were to describe him as a follower of the doctrine that matter is essentially spirit; for...in fact his thought penetrates beyond such distinctions...He recognizes both spirit and matter to be indivisible manifestations of the formless, measureless, ever-existing, undifferentiated, and essentially unchanging Tao...." [20]

This is not to say that outsiders should accept the Taoist or any other system uncritically. However, in the same spirit that the Chinese learned and borrowed from others and thereby immeasurably enriched their culture, so we, in the West, are experimenting and enriching our own culture. With T'ai Chi and acupuncture, for example, flourishing in the West, and Western medicine being practiced side by side with traditional healing methods in China, there appears to be a genuine sharing of knowledge for the benefit of all. Hopefully, in the near future, solid evidence that measures up to Western scientific standards will accumulate on both sides of the Pacific and we will know more clearly what works and what does not.

Summary

Achieving immortality depended on the beliefs and inclinations of the seeker. Some masters of the three treasures like Ko Hung clearly believed that physical immortality was possible. Others, like Cheng Man Ch'ing, speak in vague terms of "communication with heaven," which suggests some kind of dialogue or I-Thou relationship, though not necessarily physical immortality in the sense that Ko Hung meant it. In the 20th century, the idea of physical immortality is less emphasized than that of a spiritual one. In 1935 John Blofeld met a Taoist monk at his monastery who clearly viewed immortality as a spiritual metaphor and not a physical reality:

"Immortals not only break wind or belch like other people, they die!...Becoming immortal has little to do with physical changes, like the graying of a once glossy black beard; it means coming to know something, realizing something — an experience that can happen in a flash! Ah, how precious is that knowledge!

When it first strikes you, you want to sing and dance, or you nearly die of laughing! For suddenly you recognize that nothing in the world can ever hurt you." [21]

One can almost reach out and touch the joy that resides in this modern monk's heart. His idea of immortality relates to a internal realization of the mind and captures the Buddhist flavor of "sudden enlightenment."

NEO-CONFUCIANISM: THE GRAND SYNTHESIS

General Background

common theme that runs throughout the history of Chinese philosophy and religion is the direct correlation between periods of political and social instability and the development of new religious and philosophical movements. Harsh conditions engender the best minds to ask questions and to seek solutions to the problems of their age. In China this occurred during the Warring States period when the ideas of Confucius and Lao Tzu emerged and formed the basis for two of China's most important traditions, Confucianism and Taoism. It was repeated with the dissolution of the Han dynasty which witnessed the rise of Taoism and Buddhism. And, again, against the backdrop of foreign invasions and the breakup of the T'ang dynasty (618-905), Chinese society once more was revitalized with the development of Neo-Confucianism which established itself from the tenth through the thirteenth centuries.

Neo-Confucianism is of paramount importance to any study of Chinese philosophy and religion because it introduced many of the ethical and metaphysical concepts that remain current up to and including this century.*

The Neo-Confucianism of the last eight hundred years is not the philosophy of Confucius per se, but rather represents the ideas primarily of Chu Hsi (1130-1200), the greatest of the Neo-Confucians. He and the other Neo-Confucians re-interpreted Confucius in light of the ongoing development of Chinese thought — a period of approximately 1,500 years since the death of Confucius. That Chu Hsi was spoken of in the same breath as Confucius and Mencius indicates the high esteem in which he was held by the Chinese people. Due to the efforts of Chu Hsi and his colleagues, Confucianism, in its Neo-Confucian garb, became the dominant philosophical force in China, Korea and Japan, overshadowing both Buddhism and Taoism.

Until the Sung dynasty (960-1279) Confucianism had not kept pace with the higher level of metaphysics that the Taoists and in particular the Buddhists had introduced. The Confucians had focused mainly on the ethical problems of society and the functioning of the governmental bureaucracy rather than the larger philosophical questions like the nature of the universe. This lofty ground was ceded to the Buddhists and Taoists almost by default. While the Confucian Classics contained a wealth of metaphysical material, they needed to be reinterpreted in order to stimulate new interest among the educated elite who had come to expect more profound patterns of thought. As a consequence Neo-Confucianism represented an amalgam of Confucian thought, influenced by Buddhist concepts and spiced by Taoist terminology. For Chu Hsi and others like him, ethics and education must coincide with a deep and profound inner cultivation of one's nature according to universal principles, as envisioned by Confucius.

It remains to be seen how much Western ideas and Communism will change the root culture and psychology of the Chinese people.

Influences on Neo-Confucianism

Challenged by the Buddhist and Taoist ideas of an ever-changing universe, the Neo-Confucians returned to the traditional Confucian source of inspiration, the *I Ching*. The Neo-Confucians completely rejected the Buddhist notion of characterizing the universe as essentially empty and illusory. They viewed the physical world as a harmonious whole that responded to the knowable laws (li) of a moral universe. At the center of the Neo-Confucian universe lay the laws of morality, not the "Void."

Borrowing from the Buddhist idea of sagehood that "you are the Buddha," Neo-Confucians strove to teach people how to be a sage in light of Confucian teachings. In contrast to the Buddhists, who sought to cultivate Buddhahood outside the boundaries of society, the Neo-Confucians remained inside the framework of the day-to-day activities of human beings. The Buddhist notion of pity and compassion for all creatures and all things was assimilated into the Confucian idea of universal benevolence (Jen) and a devotion to moral obligations.

Like Buddhism, Taoism also left its mark on Confucianism. The ideas of Yin and Yang and the Five Elements theories, while not the exclusive rights of the Taoists, had definitely become the pillars of their religious and philosophical system and, in the minds of many Chinese, carried Taoist connotations. The Neo-Confucians assimilated these ideas and elaborated on them, creating a metaphysical framework that was far more intellectually sophisticated than anything that had preceded them.

Chou Tun-i, Pioneer of Neo-Confucianism

In the ideas of Chou Tun-i (1017-1073), who is considered the "pioneer" of Neo-Confucianism, the concept of the "infinite" (Wu Chi) probably stems directly from Lao Tzu. [1] Moreover, some traditions claim that Chou received his famous "Diagram," which we will soon examine, from a Taoist priest. Be that as it may, it is clear from his "Diagram" that he faithfully adheres to the *I Ching* rather than to Taoist mystical cosmology — a direction that would influence all future Neo-Confucian philosophers.

It was important for any Neo-Confucian — who wished to remain under the umbrella of the Confucian movement — to steer clear of any hint that they harbored Taoist or Buddhist inclinations. Chou Tun-i followed the basic tenets of Confucianism: he identified his concept of Tranquility, for example, with the idea of Sincerity, which came from the "doctrine of the mean." For Chou, Tranquility had an active and a passive aspect and he emphasized both. Unlike the Taoists and Buddhists who tended to stress the passive side of Tranquility, which focused on meditation techniques and living a life separate from the mundane world, Chou Tun-i advocated the dynamic side of Tranquility. Chou envisioned the sage as an individual who cultivates and balances the Yin and Yang aspects of his or her personality. There was a time for the private meditative sage and an equal time for the dynamic worldly leader. This idea of a sage/king had been handed down from generation to generation of Confucians and Chou merged it with his notion of Tranquility.

Chou Tun-i's life was not unlike thousands of other middle-class young men and gave little indication of the greatness and fame he would achieve. He was born at Lien Hsi, a typical rural village, whose name came from a local stream. Chou's literary name, Lien Hsi, was borrowed from his origins. Apparently he spent many hours of his youth walking along this stream. His father was a magistrate in the bureacracy which suggests that Chou had access to a good education and govermental connections. After passing his exams, he became an official in the government and was known for his fair and judicious decisions. One of the most famous stories about Chou is that he refused to allow the grass to be cut in front of his window because he felt a deep empathy with nature. He died in 1073 at the age of fifty seven.

J. Percy Bruce, a Neo-Confucian scholar who visited the grave of Chou in the early 20th century, affectionately described the site in this way: [2]

"Behind the mound are three other tablets. On the centre one of these is inscribed a eulogy of the Sage by the general who restored the tomb. The tablet to the right...is to the memory of the Sage. The one to the left is the most ancient of all, and by far the most interesting feature of the shrine. On it is engraved the famous "Diagram of the Supreme Ultimate" (T'ai Chi T'u), with its accompanying monograph, which formed the basis of the Sage's philosophy and that of the Sung School (Neo-Confucianism)."

The "Diagram of the Supreme Ultimate" is important for these reasons. First, in one simple and concise stroke, Chou Tun-i summed up what had become the Chinese notion of the creation of the world and how that world functioned. True, there were and would be variations of his view, but his diagram and explanation became the standard; the starting point for others. Clear simplicity was Chou's genius: the fact that he could present such complex ideas in a distilled, easily understood fashion, leaving his reader with the impression that he had always known them. Second, Chou's conception of the Supreme Ultimate became the foundation of Chu Hsi's thought. Confucianism crystalized as a philosophy and as a movement under Chu Hsi's influence. However, not only did Confucians find the "Diagram" to their liking, but other schools in Chinese philosophy also adopted Chou's ideas as their own. Third, for our purposes of investigating the origins of T'ai Chi, the martial art, Chou's ideas were expressed in the T'ai Chi Classics, and thus influenced the way in which the founders of T'ai Chi understood their art.

It is significant that Chou based his "Diagram" on the appen-

Here is the Diagram as it appeared on Chou-Tuni's grave:

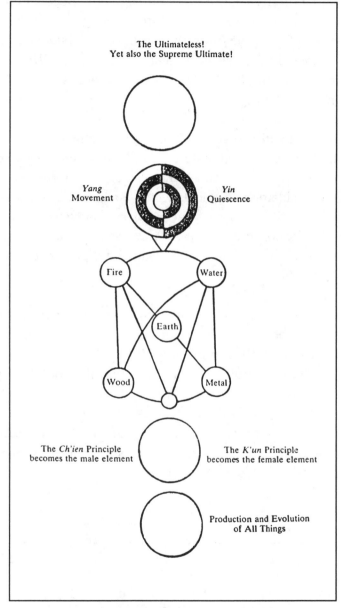

The Ultimateless!
Yet also the Supreme Ultimate!

Yang
Movement

Yin
Quiescence

Fire

Water

Earth

Wood

Metal

The *Ch'ien* Principle
becomes the male element

The *K'un* Principle
becomes the female element

Production and Evolution
of All Things

Diagram of the Supreme Ultimate (T'ai Chi T'u).

dices of the *I Ching* called the "Ten Wings," which were traditionally attributed to Confucius himself but, according to most
modern scholars, were written later during the early Han dynasty. While Chou was certainly influenced by specific Taoist
ideas, the fact that he relied heavily on the "Ten Wings" placed
him squarely in the Confucian tradition. Here is that crucial passage from the *I Ching*:

> "Therefore in [the system of] the Yi (I)* there is the Grand
> Terminus (Supreme Ultimate or T'ai Chi) which produced two
> elementary forms (Yin and Yang). Those two forms produced
> the Four emblematic Symbols which again produced the eight
> Trigrams (of the *I Ching*). The eight trigrams served to deter-
> mine the good and evil [issues of events], and from this
> determination was produced the [successful prosecution of the]
> great business [of life]." [3]**

Chou Tun-i's "Diagram" must be understood in a flow from
the top to the bottom. The empty circle at the top of the "Diagram" represents both the Infinite (Wu Chi) and the Supreme Ultimate (T'ai Chi). Chou's placing the Infinite and the Supreme
Ultimate together aroused a controversy as to whether they are
one or two separate entities. The problem was exacerbated because in his explanation Chou did not define the two terms.
Most Neo-Confucians accepted Chu Hsi's position that they are
one entity and we shall follow Chu Hsi here.***

---

* *Yi or I mean 'change(s),' which is the underlying concept of the*
I Ching *or the* Book of Changes.
** *The parenthesis [ ] are Legge's and ( ) are mine.*
*** *For more information see W. T. Chan, pp. 464-65.*

Wu Chi and T'ai Chi

The literal definition of the word "Chi" of T'ai Chi can mean "ultimate."* It can also express the idea of "pivot," "source," "root" or "axle." The word "T'ai" suggests the meaning of "supreme" or "great." Thus the concept of the "Supreme Ultimate" (T'ai Chi) can be understood as the source or root of the universe, on which all things pivot or turn.

From this understanding of T'ai Chi, it is not difficult to comprehend why the founders of T'ai Chi, the martial art, chose the "Supreme Ultimate" as its name. In the T'ai Chi Classics it is written:

"The motion should be *rooted* in the feet...
controlled by the waist." [4]

and

"The waist is like the axle...." [5]

All teachers of T'ai Chi emphasize that the body must move as one unit in coordination with the legs, waist, and spine. The analogy of Chou's Supreme Ultimate and the art of T'ai Chi is this: *just as the universe and all things contained in it revolve on its "pivot" in perfect harmony like a cosmic mobile, so does the motion of T'ai Chi grow out of the feet being rooted firmly in the ground and turning on the waist and spine in perfect harmony.*

The image of a mobile is particularly intriguing when considering how best to express T'ai Chi as a metaphysical concept as

---

* *The word Chi, meaning source, or ultimate, is not to be confused with Ch'i meaning breath or internal energy.*

well as physical movement. In its most physical form T'ai Chi contains the idea that one must allow the internal energy (Ch'i) to reach the top of the head. According to Cheng Man Ch'ing, this is accomplished through the notion of "suspending the headtop":

> "The process of "suspending the headtop" is similar to tying someone who has a queue to a beam so that his body hangs down in the air [above the ground]. He can rotate his whole body, but he can neither bend back nor drop his head, nor lean it to either side." [6]

Of course, he is not recommending that students of T'ai Chi actually do this, but rather he is using an image that transforms the body into a kind of an imaginary mobile. In this way the spine, neck, and head will be upright which will allow the transmuted Ch'i to become Shen and reach the top of the head.*

In its most ethereal form, T'ai Chi, the cosmic mobile, differs significantly from the human one suggested by Cheng Man Ch'ing in that it has no discernible or revealed source on which it hangs! This is because the Chinese understood the universe as a glorious harmony that revealed itself to human beings as pattern and order, turning and swirling in delicate balance. What could not be found — because it was beyond the capabilities of human beings — was the source or pivot on which the mobile rested. We could think of that pivot as existing in a dimension to which we, as finite beings, have no access, but can imagine it, theorize about it, only because we can see its manifestations in the physical world.

This helps us to understand the logic of Legge's translation of

---

This process in the context of T'ai Chi corresponds to the Taoist framework of the three treasures, which we referred to in Chapter 5.

the *I Ching* mentioned above where he designates T'ai Chi as the "Grand Terminus." Terminus means the station at the end of a railway or bus line. It is the "end of the line," the final place where human beings cannot go any futher because we are finite and the Supreme Ultimate is infinite. In this respect T'ai Chi (or the Supreme Ultimate) resembles the God of the West whom we cannot know when 'He' resides in the transcendent state of non-being.

The fact that the Supreme Ultimate is infinite suggests one important interpretation of why Chou included Wu Chi (infinite) in his uppermost circle with the idea of the Supreme Ultimate. [7] Because the word "T'ai" means "supreme," in that nothing can be added to it, T'ai Chi could be translated as the "Supreme Source" or "Supreme Root" of the universe. However, the word "source" or "root" contains the idea of place or location. In order to distance himself from the idea of something physical, Chou Tun-i, according to this theory, added the idea of Wu Chi as a kind of counterweight to thinking that T'ai Chi could be found on a map of the universe or be seen with the most powerful telescope.

Chu Hsi elaborated on the above idea from a different perspective. He, too, believed that T'ai Chi and Wu Chi were identical, but he held that Wu Chi is "the state of reality before the appearance of forms, whereas the Great Ultimate (T'ai Chi) is the state after the appearance of forms...."[8]

In other words Wu Chi and T'ai Chi reside together in the realm of the infinite. But T'ai Chi separates from Wu Chi when it becomes active and thus produces Yin and Yang which in turn are the creative agents of the material world. While T'ai Chi is both the creator and unifying force of the world of forms, it remains distinct from the material world. Chu Hsi explained it in this way:

"The Supreme Ultimate is inherent in, and cannot be separated from, the Two Modes (Yin and Yang); but the Supreme Ultimate is the Supreme Ultimate, and the Two Modes are the Two Modes." [9]

Following the above logic of Chu Hsi, one could also infer that even after they separate, Wu Chi remains within T'ai Chi. This is to say that everything we feel or see contains Wu Chi within it. The paradox is that Wu Chi and T'ai Chi are one and yet separate like a child inside its mother's womb. Thus, from this point of view, Chou put them together, not because he wished to guard against the idea that we might think the Supreme Ultimate has material form, but rather because they simply belong together, like Yin and Yang, which represent different qualities of a single unity.

It might be helpful in understanding the differing qualities of Wu Chi and T'ai Chi if we draw an analogy to Western religion. While the Supreme Ultimate and Wu Chi do not represent God as we know Him in the West or Middle East, there are certain elements which are similar. The God of Judeo-Christian-Islamic traditions has the characteristics of transcendence and immanence. God, in His transcendent state, is beyond any possible comprehension on the part of finite human beings.* It is only in His immanent state that He can communicate with human beings in a way that they can understand Him. An example of His immanent state, as it appears in the Bible or the Koran, is when God speaks directly to His prophets. Transcendence and imma-

---

* A word of warning to the reader: we are comparing the way that transcendence and immanence work within each system of thought. This is the similarity. We are not comparing the states of infinity or being of East and West which, in my opinion, would be like comparing apples and oranges.

nence represent two different ways of describing the one God. In the transcendent state God is neither he nor she, nor any other category, because we are speaking of something that is beyond human categories or comprehension. In the immanent state the fact that a masculine pronoun is used suggests limitation, or a kind of "contraction", of the infinite into the world of finiteness. Typically, mystics, in all traditions, seek to unite these two dimensions.

The same idea of transcendence and immanence is instructive in understanding Chu Hsi's idea of Wu Chi and T'ai Chi: they are one and the same entity, although Wu Chi represents the state of infinity similar to the idea of the transcendent God, who is beyond human comprehension, while T'ai Chi represents the transformation and appearance of infinity (transcendence) in the world of forms as the root principle of creativity.

Chu Hsi clarified the meaning of Wu Chi and T'ai Chi in response to the lack of definition bequeathed to him by Chou Tun-i. The reason why Chou Tun-i did not define Wu Chi and T'ai Chi is open to speculation. Perhaps we should not find this surprising. Lao Tzu also preferred to leave the "named" and the "nameless" shrouded in dark mystery. There is something awesome and overwhelming about contemplating the idea of infinity that engenders many different responses from finite human beings, not the least of which is the sense of fear and trembling. For others, contact with the concept of infinity fills them with an abiding sense of love and tranquility that opens their hearts and changes them forever.

Whatever their experience of infinity, most people find it difficult, or are unwilling, to speak of it at all — because words are often inadequate to express the powerful memory of the experience itself. In all likelihood this might be the reason that Lao Tzu and Chou Tun-i preferred not to define their experience. On the other hand, Chu Hsi, the man of reason, was able to reveal at least part of the mystery, or at the very least, create a coherent structure for understanding the relationship of the infinite to the finite. Not that he tried to define Wu Chi. Rather he endeavored to explain the relationship of T'ai Chi to the world of forms. His was an intellect that demanded clarity and reasoned response, unlike the master of paradox, Lao Tzu, who preferred mystery and poetic insights.

Neo-Confucianism and the T'ai Chi Classics

It is well worth noting here that in the T'ai Chi Classics, Wang Tsung-yueh (18th century) follows Chou's Diagram and Chu Hsi's line of thought. Wang begins his work in this way:

"T'ai Chi
comes from
Wu Chi
and is the mother of Yin and Yang."
In motion it separates;
In stillness they fuse." [10]

Stillness is the state in which Wu Chi and T'ai Chi are one entity and is the realm of the infinite before the world of forms. Once motion begins, Wu Chi and T'ai Chi separate and the latter enters the world by giving birth to Yin and Yang, which initiates the world of forms. The language that Wang employs harks back to the *Tao Te Ching* of Lao Tzu where it says: "the named is the mother of ten thousand things." [11] What cannot be named, according to Lao Tzu, is the "eternal Tao;" it remains "nameless" because its relationship to the "named" (T'ai Chi) is shrouded in darkness and mystery. It is possible that by understanding the "eternal Tao" (the nameless) as Wu Chi and the "named" as Tai Chi, Chu Hsi managed to throw some light on Lao Tzu's dark mystery and this expressed itself later in the T'ai Chi Classics by authors such as Wang Tsung-yueh.

Another significant observation of Wang seems to have been derived from Chu Hsi and the Neo-Confucianists. Wang states that "although the changes are numerous, the *principle* that pervades them is only one." [12] The fact that Wang uses the word "principle" is reminiscent of Chu Hsi who defined "principle" in a way that became the standard for Neo-Confucianism and thereby influenced Chinese philosophy as a whole. On the universal level, "principle" represented the highest standard of creativity and embraced all the multitude of things in the world of forms. Significantly Chu Hsi identified "principle" with the Supreme Ultimate. [13] If we substitute the Supreme Ultimate or T'ai Chi for the word "principle" in Wang's quote above, it would read this way:

> "Although the changes are numerous,
> *the Supreme Ultimate or T'ai Chi*
> that pervades them
> is only one."

We are thus reading Wang in the context of Chu Hsi. From this we see that he could be saying that there is but one "principle" (T'ai Chi) that resides in all movement and that "principle" comes from one source, despite the fact that "the changes (of Yin and Yang) are numerous" and thus appear to be inherently different. This, of course, is referring to the world of motion after T'ai Chi has separated from Wu Chi, produced Yin and Yang, and thus initiated the world of forms.

The question might be asked: why does Wang need two quotes that say essentially the same thing? The first quote ("T'ai Chi comes from Wu Chi...."), which opens his treatise, is a philosophical statement that informs the reader where he stands within the framework of Chinese thought. Wang wants the reader to know that T'ai Chi, as physical movement in the world of forms, mirrors the way the universe works and thus transcends any understanding or explanation in terms of moving the body this way or that. The source of all movement and creativity, whether it be a shooting star, the blooming of a flower, or a movement in self-defense, is the principle of T'ai Chi with all its multifaceted implications.

The second quote ("although the changes are numerous...") is placed within the context of T'ai Chi as a martial art. Wang is explaining how a defender must react to the movements of an "opponent." This is the practical, applied side of T'ai Chi. Wang is reminding T'ai Chi players that all efficacious movement in self-defense is natural and arises spontaneously out of a meditative state of tranquility or emptiness. This is the closest human beings can approach and stand before the awesome silence of Wu Chi. Here, in those quiet moments before beginning the T'ai Chi form, the individual stands tranquil and empty in the first circle of Chou Tun-i. We might even say that he or she becomes that circle.

It is not surprising that Chu Hsi influenced the T'ai Chi Classics. He was famous throughout China in his role as interpreter of Confucius, having written a commentary on almost all of the Confucian Classics. Moreover, Chu Hsi, like Wang Tsung-yueh after him, shared a common Chinese tradition that repeats itself, whether one is Confucian, Taoist or Buddhist. They believed that all things are born from one source and all things are intimately interconnected to each other. Most Chinese thinkers believed in the essential unity and harmony of all spiritual and earthly phenomena.

Earlier we mentioned the story of Chou Tun-i's refusal to allow his grass to be cut. In all likelihood his strong belief that all things grow out of the same source meant that he could empathize and feel the suffering of all living things, including the pain of grass being cut. Chu Hsi himself was known to speculate on whether or not plants possess a unique kind of intuitive wisdom. [14]

T'ai Chi and Yin/Yang

The opening paragraph of Chou Tun-i's explanation of the "Diagram," simply states the terms Wu Chi and T'ai Chi without any explanation. What follows is a description of how Yin and Yang developed. There is a disconcerting silence on the part of Chou regarding the transformation process from Wu Chi to T'ai Chi and then to Yin and Yang. Once he leaves the first circle (the top empty circle of the Diagram which symbolizes the world of the infinite) and enters the second circle (the world of Yin and Yang), Chou becomes far more explicit. Essentially Chou is following the *I Ching* which was quoted above: "...there is the Grand Terminus which produced the two elementary forms." Below are Chou's words, which we could understand as a a commentary to our passage of the *I Ching*. Their explicit intention is to guide the reader into the second circle of the "Diagram:"

> "The Ultimate of Non-being (Wu Chi) and also the Great Ultimate (T'ai Chi)! The Great Ultimate through movement generates yang. When its activity reaches its limit, it becomes tranquil. Through tranquility the Great Ultimate generates yin. When tranquility reaches its limit, activity begins again. So movement and tranquility alternate and become the root of each other, giving rise to the distinction of yin and yang, and the two modes are thus established." [15]

The above description of Yin and Yang is identical to that offered in chapter two. This understanding of Yin and Yang has probably not radically changed since the time of Confucius and the *I Ching* till the present day, although the Neo-Confucians developed an unprecendented philosophical structure in which Yin and Yang played a key role.*

Chou Tun-i's descriptions could be legitimately understood as a Chinese version of the creation of the world. It is a creation story that is unlike the one most Westerners are used to. Chou is saying that the world came into being through the spontaneous "movement" of Yang; something like the spontaneous combustion of fire. There seems to be an inherent potential for movement within the Wu Chi/T'ai Chi relationship. What jars the Western mind is that Chou's explanation lacks a First Cause or a God of creation that initiates the transformation process. Because of our culture and history, most Westerners think in linear terms which ultimately lead back to a First Cause. Our science, for example, is predicated on causality. The great benefit of linear thinking was that it propelled Western science to its high level of development.

In contrast, the image that emerges out of Chou's explanation is one of a perpetual pendulum of creativity swinging between the two poles of Yin and Yang. It is an image of circles and spirals rather than something linear. The potential for the pendulum always existed and did not require someone or something to set it in motion. *One must imagine that Yin and Yang always existed in Wu Chi. In stillness they existed only as potential; in motion they manifested as the creative process.* Yet potential and manifestation in the world are the same and, in Chinese philosophy, it was considered an illusion to think of them as different. They only "appear" to be different, but emptiness (Wu Chi) and form (Yin and Yang) are actually two aspects of the same reality. The waves on the surface of the ocean, for example,

---

The great 19th-century scholar and translator of the I Ching, *James Legge, argued with this position and believed that Yin and Yang originally were* symbols *for the quality of change and did not denote the* forces of change *in themselves, which came much later. (James Legge,* I Ching, *pp. 43-44).*

seem to be distinct from the ocean itself, but in fact they represent another form that the ocean has taken on and are in no way to be construed as separate realities.

Earlier, we used the image of the runner who expends his Yang energy which naturally flows into Yin because he now must rest (see chapter two). Although Chou's second circle predates the modern symbol for Yin and Yang of the two fishes, it represents the same ideas and is a description of the same universal laws.The concept of Yin and Yang is really a vivid portrayal of the universe as a dynamic system of "order" and "patterns" that are in constant motion, not from a First Cause like the striking of a billiard ball with a cue stick, but rather each billiard ball has its own inherent energy for flow and movement in relation to every other ball out of which emerges pattern, order, and harmony.

Unlike their counterparts in the West, historically Chinese philosophers were more interested in the practical side of "how" things worked, rather than where they came from.* Chou did not delve into why Yin and Yang exist. His was a "description" of the interaction between the two poles of motion and their effect on the world of forms. As a progeny of Chinese culture, Chou understood the workings of Yin and Yang, intellectually and intuitively, from his study of Classics like the *I Ching* and the *Tao Te Ching* and his own observations of nature and life.

One way of understanding the traditional Chinese view of "describing" the universe — which might be helpful to Westerners

---

European scientists, like Galileo, were treading dangerous waters if they denied existing theology, let alone the idea of a First Cause. In the 17th century Descartes divided knowledge into the domains of science and theology, which, however rigid, allowed scientists to focus on the practical side of their disciplines. The negative side of this division was that knowledge lost its sense of unity and wholeness ---something that did not occur in Chinese philosophy.

— is to examine the different approaches of East and West in the curing of illness. Western medicine concentrates its efforts on discovering the cause or causes of the illness and then tries to control or destroy that agent. This linear methodology of cause and effect has been very successful in many areas of health; for example, the using of antibiotics to destroy the bacteria of certain dangerous diseases. The Chinese physician, on the other hand, views disease as an imbalance of Yin and Yang in the patient's body. In analyzing the patient's condition the physician also examines his or her relationship with the external environment. Just as Chou Tun-i presented a description of "how" the universe functions in a balanced and harmonious way, so the Chinese physician strives to understand "how" the diseased person is no longer in harmony with his internal body and/or the external world. In Ted Kaptchuk's words, "Oriental diagnostic technique does not turn up a specific disease entity or a precise cause, but renders an almost poetic, yet workable, description of a whole person." [16]

Recent trends in the West, called the "systems approach," recognize the importance of examining the entire person, or society, including the social and biological environment, partly as a result of Westerners coming into contact with Eastern ideas and healing practices.

The Five Elements

The next step in Chou's Diagram is a representation of the Five Elements — Wood, Fire, Water, Metal and Earth — which are created from the activity of Yin and Yang.* While the principle of Yin and Yang is manifested as subtle energy in constant motion, the Five Elements imbue qualities and character to things

---

* See Chapter two for a more complete explanation of the Five Elements.

found in the material world. The Five Elements are something like the ingredients of a soup that coalesce to create a unique flavor.

The names of the Five Elements express certain inherent qualities which suggest how they function in the world. Fire, for example, has the quality of intense heat, moving upwards; earth implies stability, the foundation of life. Each entity in the universe has its own unique configuration composed of something of all the Five Elements, one being more dominant. A man or a woman, for example, is composed of the subtle principle of Yin and Yang which is physically and psychically manifested in the world through the confluence of the Five Elements. She might have a "fiery" personality, the quality of passion playing a domi-nant role, or he is very "earthy," the quality of stability being dominant. A Chinese physician might examine the pulses of a patient and discover an over-abundance of "fire" in the liver, an imbalance that results in a high fever or bouts of uncontrolled anger or passion.

The theory of the Five Elements plays a prominent role in T'ai Chi and corresponds to the five foot movements: advance (met-al), retreat (wood), look left (water), look right (fire), and central equilibrium (earth). Each posture in T'ai Chi can be understood in light of the Five Elements. The quality of fire, for example, is expressed by the "heel-kick" which is a strong straightforward kick to the groin area. "Repulse monkey" is a graceful, retreating movement symbolized by wood. By developing an understanding of the quality of each movement and then bringing that quality into the performance of each posture, the T'ai Chi student can deepen his or her understanding of the form, as we discussed in Chapter 2.

The founders of T'ai Chi not only adopted the name, the Su-preme Ultimate, they also understood that each time they en-gaged in the T'ai Chi form, they were recounting —we could even say dramatizing—the creation of the universe. This ultimate experience required both a profound knowledge of the Chinese creation story as epitomized by Chou's Diagram and an unwavering intention, a will of steel, in order to remain focused and thus to merge the physical with the spiritual. At the most fundamental level T'ai Chi is a microcosmic universe being created within and according to the laws of the dynamic macrocosmic universe, which is giving birth and sustaining life every moment. Perhaps most important, T'ai Chi can become a vehicle in which the principles of Chou's entire Diagram can be encountered at the very core of one's being because each individual contains the Five Elements in a unique code, the flow of Yin and Yang, and, at the deepest level, the stillness of Wu Chi and T'ai Chi.

Bearing this in mind, the words "T'ai Chi" can not only be defined as the Supreme Ultimate, but the doing of the T'ai Chi form can also be understood as the actual experience of the Supreme Ultimate!

Creativity and the Diagram

Moving down Chou's Diagram to the circle below the Five Elements, we reach the male and female principle, Ch'ien and K'un, which merge together to create all things. Ch'ien and K'un are represented by their respective trigrams in the *I Ching* and are more concrete and tangible than any of the ideas occurring higher in Chou's Diagram. The process is one of moving from the immaterial (Wu Chi) to the material world of things. Chou describes the "mysterious union" of the male and female principle in this way:

"When the reality of the Ultimate of Non-being and the essence of yin, yang, and the Five Agents come into mysterious union, integration ensues...The interaction of these two material forces engenders and transforms the myriad things. The myriad things produce and reproduce, resulting in an unending transformation." [17]

What Chou is saying, albeit in philosophical language, is that the interaction of the male and female principle produces the material world. His vision has the cloak of modesty but the image of "mysterious union" is really that of making love. No paradigm could be more concrete or appropiate for the way the universe creates than that of man and woman coming together and creating a child.

The result of a vibrant creative universe is represented by the last circle which is the culmination of all the principles that preceded it and reflects the concrete world of forms.

The Diagram and Confucian Morality

Chou Tun-i, a committed Confucian, could not complete his description of how the world was created without in some way linking this process to the Confucian ideals of morality. Chou believed that human beings are the highest form of life because they received the best and most subtle energy from the Five Elements which, in the Confucian worldview, corresponded to the Five Moral Principles of Benevolence (jen), Righteousness, Propriety, Wisdom, and Sincerity.

Chou interpreted the Confucian idea of Sincerity as being a deep and intuitive, even meditative, state of tranquility in which men and women could discover the true nature of good and of evil and thus correctly choose the "proper" course of action. In every aspect of life and creation Chou Tun-i and the Neo-Confucians viewed the universe as an integrated and interconnected whole where morality was conceived in, and flowed out of, the

---

*The corresponding Five Elements for the Five Moral Principles are Benevolence (love or jen) = wood; Righteousness = fire; Propriety = metal; Wisdom = water; Sincerity = earth.

Supreme Ultimate and its processes of transformation. The final destination of the Five Moral Principles was its flowering in the hearts of men and women.*

Ethical behavior always played a crucial role in Confucian thought and without such an attitude one could hardly be called a Confucian. The development of Benevolence (Jen) evolved over a long period of time, commencing with Confucius and being established, more or less, in its final form with the Neo-Confucians. What the Neo-Confucians contributed to the idea of Benevolence was to lift it out of the day-to-day world and extend it to the entire universe. This universal outlook can be traced to the influence of Taoism and Buddhism. Benevolence was not something that only man shared with his fellow man and the other creatures on earth, as Confucius understood it, but rather the entire universe was endowed with the moral quality of Benevolence, the seed of which could be traced back to the first circle of Chou's Diagram, Wu Chi and T'ai Chi.

This idea of Neo-Confucianism — that morality is rooted in the cosmos, and therefore constitutes a "natural" or " moral" law, as in the example of Benevolence, is not dissimilar to certain parallel concepts in the West.* However, due to the influence of Judaism, Islam and, to a lesser extent, Christianity, such a position was opposed by the idea of a transcendent God whose law was above that of nature and thus inviolable. This would help account for the contrast between East and West in their divergent views of nature. At least up to the 18th century, in the West, human beings were enjoined to follow God's laws, whether or not those laws contradicted a perceived harmony with nature. Endowed by God with His image, human beings generally viewed nature as a subject rather than as an equal, and as having "fixed laws" which only God, if He so desired, could contravene. Even

---

*See, for example, Dennis Lloyd, The Idea of Law, p 71 passim.

when, in more recent times, the concept of God faded from the equation, the idea that there are "fixed laws" in nature remained. The scientific method could and did thrive on such an attitude.

In contrast, Chinese philosophers believed that there existed an innate harmony and unity between the laws of Heaven, Nature and man that could be maintained only "if the appropriate ritual and customary observances were followed." Moral law was not only represented by a state of harmony in the universe but, according to the Neo-Confucians, it flowed out of the transcendent Tao. Thus human beings strove to be in harmony with the moral law as expressed in nature, and did not seek to control it. This outlook, combined with the lack of a concept of a lawgiver or First Cause, are two important reasons why the cultures of East and West are different, both in the realms of spiritual cultivation and of science.

Chang Tsai and the Concept of Ch'i

Another important Neo-Confucian was Chang Tsai (1020-1077), a contemporary of Chou Tun-i, who understood the evolutionary process of Yin and Yang and the Five Elements in a different light. He rejected Chou's thesis of Yin and Yang and the Five Elements as the basic causes or forces of change and instead replaced them with the concept of Ch'i. By doing so he elevated the idea of Ch'i to probably its most significant role in Chinese thought.

According to Chang Tsai, Yin and Yang were important, but only as actors being directed by Ch'i. He believed that Ch'i was a kind of miraculous energy in which the Supreme Ultimate and the Moral Principles reside. The grand implication of his thought was this: because Ch'i is the driving force of the universe and exists in all things, then everyone and everything is intimately connected by Ch'i; which we might imagine is like an electrical grid linking together an entire city or population. Thus Chang

Tsai, the Confucian, could argue that all things in the universe make up one large body, that all men are brothers, and that all things in the universe are deserving of love and respect. While differing from Chou, with respect to Ch'i, Chang Tsai exemplifies the attraction that the idea of natural or moral law held for all Chinese thinkers. Moreover, Chang Tsai's ideas recall the Buddhist "teaching of totality" of the Flower Garland School (Hua-Yen), yet another example of the influence various schools of thought had on each other.

Historically, the idea of Ch'i has been central to Chinese philosophy and culture. For Westerners, Ch'i is a problematic notion because it defies easy definitions or scientific classifications. Ch'i is often used in many different contexts and suggests diverse ideas of varying origins. Literally, Ch'i means "air," "vapor," "breath," "ether," or "energy." It can also refer to the emotional aspects of the personality or the external and/or internal strength of a person. Often among T'ai Chi devotees one will hear the phrase, "his or her Ch'i is strong (or weak)," which could mean that, in some way, perhaps occurring in the play of push-hands, someone has directly experienced the power of another person's "vitality." The implication is that the experience of this person's Ch'i was subtle, or possibly altogether shocking; that it caught the receiver of the Ch'i totally off-guard and rendered him or her momentarily helpless.

Traditionally the Chinese believe that a person will die when his or her Ch'i reaches a critically low level. The quality of one's health is not primarily dependent on the blood or the organs themselves, as is generally thought in Western medicine, but rather on the quality of the Ch'i which endows the functioning parts of the body with 'vitality' and keeps them in good working order.

By the time of the Neo-Confucians of the 11th and 12th centuries, Ch'i no longer merely meant "air" or "vapor." It had acquired an expanded definition which signified both energy and matter. The Chinese have another word, 'Chih,' which suggests only the world of matter. As one scholar explained, "...though chih is a form of ch'i, ch'i is not always chih." [18] In other words, while Ch'i makes up both energy and matter, that is to say, it exists in everything, it can also have the quality of being intangible and imperceptible to the human senses. An individual, for example, is composed of Ch'i which is both tangible to the senses (the body) and intangible to the senses (the internal energy or vitality). The Ch'i of the person's total being is the same Ch'i, although its manifestations can be different.

In contrast, we in the West are accustomed to a way of thinking, dating back at least to Plato, that energy and matter are two distinct entities. When we see a rock, we think of it as solid and inert matter. Ordinarily we do not perceive it as energy, although, from the viewpoint of modern physics, it is.

Another factor in the confusion regarding Ch'i is that Westerners are used to and expect a clear, systematic explanation of what a particular concept means. This does not occur with the idea of Ch'i. The Chinese have a different tradition which, as we have pointed out earlier, is less rigorously scientific and conceptual than ours in the West. They stressed the practical. As a concept, Ch'i corresponded to a "description" of the way things work in the world, and the Chinese felt no compunction or inclination to prove its existence. Ted Kaptchuk sums up the Chinese attitude toward Ch'i this way:

> "Neither the classical or modern Chinese texts speculate on the nature of Qi (Ch'i), nor do they attempt to conceptualize it. Rather, Qi is perceived functionally—by what it does." [19]

While the Taoists, especially the later ones, would probably not disagree with the Neo-Confucian view of Ch'i, they certainly stressed its immaterial and intangible aspect, as the vital "life-force" of the universe, the primordial energy, invisible and intangible, that bestows life on all living things. In the human body the center of Ch'i is called the tan t'ien which is just below the navel.* The tan t'ien functions like a bank account and the money stored inside is one's Ch'i. If a person continually withdraws from the account without depositing more money, he or she will go into overdraft. Depending on the banking system, at some point, the line of credit is cut off.** The same is true of Ch'i as the "life-force." If one does not continually replace and increase his or her Ch'i, the body will go into overdraft and become ill or even have its credit cut off, which means death. The Taoist alchemist, Ko Hung, lauds the value of Ch'i in the following passage:

> "Man is ch'i and ch'i is within each human being. Heaven and Earth and the ten thousand things all require ch'i to stay alive. A person that knows how to allow his ch'i to circulate...will preserve himself and banish illnesses that might cause him harm." [20]

Here Ch'i is the life-force of the universe, which works something like an electrical current that generates one's appliances. If there were no electrical current, the appliances would simply remain inert, empty shells.***

---

* See Chapter 5 on the workings of Ch'i and prenatal breathing.
** Banks in Israel allow large overdrafts with large interest payments while in the United States this is generally not the practice.
*** There is a growing body of scientific evidence in the West that Ch'i exists. In human beings it manifests as an electrical current that flows through the "preferential pathways" of the body. When stimulated, say, through acupuncture, this current can reduce pain and has the potential to heal certain illnesses. For the classic article, see Nordenstorm, Bjorn, American Journal of Acupuncture, *Vol. 17, no. 2, April-June 1989, p. 105-117.*

Chang Tsai, the Confucian, was clearly influenced by Taoists like Ko Hung. By advocating a position that the universe is composed of Ch'i, he was in effect claiming that the Supreme Ultimate is real and not illusion — a clear rejection of Buddhism. He also differed from the view of Chou Tun-i, whose idea of the Supreme Ultimate seemed closer to Buddhism in which the world of appearance grows out of non-being. For Chang Tsai, Wu Chi was not empty, but contained imperceptibly subtle Ch'i.

Chang Tsai held that the process of change occurs in the universe because the dispersion of Ch'i results in the dissolution of things, while the condensation of Ch'i results in the creation of things. By thinking of Ch'i in this way, Chang Tsai endeavored to explain how material and immaterial things are actually the same, despite their dissimilarity of appearance. When Ch'i disperses, it can ultimately return to pure spirit; when it condenses, it can evolve into material things. An example of this process, which we used earlier, is the transformation of water into different forms. When water condenses, it becomes ice, which is solid; when it dissolves, it becomes liquid. When water is boiled, it becomes steam, which is "vapor" — the least solid, almost intangible form of water. Despite the many differences in appearance, its essence remains the Ch'i of water.

While the Chinese experienced Ch'i as something real in their everyday lives, it could also be understood as a theoretical concept that forms the basis of Chinese philosophy, science, and medicine. According to Manfred Porkert, Ch'i, in theoretical terms, is best comprehended as a quality of direction, that is to say, of flow and movement oscillating between the two poles of Yin and Yang. [21] This continuous dynamic movement reflects a unified framework of relationships and patterns. Porkert explains Ch'i in this way: "Without relationship there would be no ch'i, because ch'i is not empty air. It is the structured pattern of relationships, which are defined in a directional way."

If we apply these ideas of Ch'i to Chinese medicine, we are not speaking of Ch'i as an actual substance that can be registered by scientific instruments, whose function is in some way to strengthen our immune system. Rather, Ch'i represents the relationships of flow and patterns of Yin and Yang within and without the body of each individual. The role of the physician then is to examine these relationships and to determine how best to bring them back into harmony.

While these ideas may seem unduly abstract, it might help to think of the relationships of Ch'i in terms of the physical or emotional attractions that certain people feel toward one another. Sometimes, we label these seemingly inexplicable attractions as "chemistry." We "know" that they are real, yet no scientific instrument can measure the attraction itself. Science can only measure the secondary results of the experience such as an increased heart rate or a blush.

Chang Tsai's ideas on Ch'i were extremely important in part because they had a major impact on Chu Hsi, the greatest of the Neo-Confucians. So pervasive and powerful was Ch'i in the physical universe that Chu Hsi believed it to contain the quality of buoyancy which created a force field and thus maintained order in the cosmos. If it were not for Ch'i, he argued, the earth would simply fall from her orbit. [22] Here, Ch'i seems to take on the quality of a kind of subtle and active substance, something more tangible than the "the structured pattern of relationships" described above. In the West a similar idea of a substance called ether, which existed in an invisible form, gained considerable currency in 19th-century physics as an explanation of how light waves moved through space.* This particular idea was conclusively disproved by Albert Einstein at the turn of the 20th century.

---

*It has been claimed that the 19th-century English painter William Turner depicted the tangible quality of ether in his many nature paintings.

Nonetheless, many Chinese believed in the buoyancy of Ch'i well into the twentieth century. As we shall see, it may well contain a significant insight into the concept of the quantum field in modern physics. The theory of the buoyancy of Ch'i worked something like the surface tension of water which is able to sustain heavy objects afloat like a ship in the ocean. Cheng Man Ch'ing — in a discussion of the soft overcoming the hard; a major notion in T'ai Chi which dates back to the *Tao Te Ching* — refers to Ch'i as something soft and immaterial and yet contains the strength to uphold the universe in its place:

> "Mass integration makes the difference. The entire weight of the galaxies of stars and universes do not rest on foundations more solid or weightier than they are themselves, but on the buoyancy of an immaterial "substance" referred to as ether (Ch'i)." [23]

At first glance these claims for Ch'i might appear somewhat fanciful and farfetched. However, in *The Tao of Physics*, Fritjof Capra explains the clear and compelling connection of the buoyancy of Ch'i and the quantum field in modern physics: "The Neo-Confucian developed a notion of ch'i which bears the most striking resemblance to the concept of the quantum field in modern physics. Like the quantum field, ch'i is conceived as a tenuous and non-perceptible form of matter which is present throughout space and can condense into solid material objects."*

In modern physics, both Einstein's theory of gravity and the quantum field theory propose that particles or objects cannot be separated from the space in which they exist. Similarly, Chinese thinkers, from Chang Tsai to Cheng Man Ch'ing, have consid-

---

*For a fuller discussion of Ch'i and modern physics, see Capra, The Tao of Physics, Ch. 14, especially pages 213-223.

ered Ch'i to be the common denominator of all things in the universe. The planets are made up of condensed Ch'i while the space surrounding them is composed of dispersed Ch'i, so subtle that it cannot be detected. Thus, every planet is interconnected with Ch'i, thereby forming an internal integrity of space and the planets, which Chu Hsi and Cheng Man Ch'ing described as "buoyancy."

There are many different ways to understand the concept of Ch'i, as we have seen. It is little wonder that the notion of Ch'i can be very confusing to Westerners. Simply put, Ch'i, which is as natural to a Chinese as his mother tongue, does not translate easily beyond the borders of the Far East. Ch'i can best be comprehended as a cultural concept, peculiar to the East, that defies an easy or a scientifically precise definition. Perhaps Porkert's way of viewing Ch'i as a pattern of structured relationships, rather than as substance, might be the best way for Westerners to begin to think about Ch'i. In this way Ch'i requires neither proving nor disproving. The individual can approach the merits of Ch'i with an open mind, and can explore its efficacy without having to force it into Western concepts; such as, if it exists, we must be able to measure it with scientific instruments.

In his television series, "Healing and the Mind," Bill Moyers, the distinguished American journalist, strove to keep an open mind about Ch'i as he experienced it from two masters, one of T'ai Chi and one of massage. He asked Dr. Lu, a chi gong expert: "...could you please explain how you use your mind and thoughts in order to emit chi?" Dr. Lu answered:

"The Chinese have a proverb which says, 'There are some things that can be sensed but not explained in words.' If you want to really understand the principles of chi gong, then you must practice it yourself. First 'come inside,' and then ask me questions. Don't ponder these principles when you are outside."

Dr. Lu's comments are reminiscent of the deaf man who peers through a window and sees people jumping around and performing all kinds of weird movements. He concludes that he has happened on an insane asylum. Actually what he sees is the joy of people dancing at a wedding party. He can't hear the music and thus remains on the "outside."

In the end we may discover that the reason for the power of Ch'i in Chinese healing and martial arts stems from a conditioned belief in it by a people whose cultural worldview is sustained and strengthened by such ideas. Moreover, many well-informed people of the East and West, including scientists, have come to the conclusion that merely the belief that something works may be the most powerful tool in assuring that it does. The Placebo Effect supports this point of view. For Westerners, cultivating the mysteries of Ch'i — the sense and perhaps the nonsense — may be the ticket for a fascinating and fruitful journey of self-discovery.

Chu Hsi and the Idea of Principle (li)

Chu Hsi initiated some important changes in Chang Tsai's concept of Ch'i. He grappled with Chang Tsai's ideas, modified them, and eventually presented his own ideas on Ch'i which would dominate the future of Chinese thought. The problem with Chang Tsai's explanation of Ch'i, as Chu Hsi saw it, was that the dispersion or condensation of Ch'i did not clarify why a flower became a flower or a human being became a human being. Chu Hsi reasoned that there must be some principle involved that determined what the pattern of Ch'i would be. He called that principle "li" and argued that the Supreme Ultimate must be composed of li, and not Ch'i as Chang Tsai thought.* Thus the

---

*Chu Hsi's 'li' brings to mind 'te' of Lao Tzu and Chuang Tzu, which was discussed in Chapter 3.

various multitude of things become what they are because there is the "li" of a flower or the "li" of a human being that exists within the Supreme Ultimate.* When Ch'i condenses, it does so within the context of a specific organizational pattern of li that determines the nature of the condensed Ch'i. The relationship of li and Ch'i is intimate, complementary, and interdependent.

Li is the guiding principle of Ch'i and Ch'i is the vehicle through which li is manifested in the world.** There cannot be li in the world without Ch'i, and by the same token, there cannot be Ch'i without li. W. T. Chan explains the interrelationship this way:

> "Principle (li) needs material force (Ch'i) in order to have something to adhere to, and material force needs principle as its own law of being...." [24]

Li is like the potter and Ch'i the clay. Without the potter there could be no pot; without the clay the potter has nothing with which to create.

While the Taoists approached Ch'i in a practical way, as energy that could be manipulated for their own purposes, Chu Hsi, more rigorous in his philosophical outlook, created a comprehensive system which sought to satisfy the unanswered questions in Chinese philosophy within the context of Confucianism.

Chu Hsi and the Notion of Sagehood

The interrelationship of li and Ch'i, as developed by Chu Hsi, would play an important role in the Neo-Confucian under-

---

*One wonders if Chu Hsi's 'li' was a philosophical heralding of DNA.
**This is reminiscent of Fa-tsang's metaphor of the golden lion, which is recounted in chapter 4.

standing of self-cultivation. Until the time of Chou Tun-i, meditation and self-cultivation techniques tended to occupy a secondary
role in the Confucian way of spiritual growth, while study of the
Confucian Classics represented the recognized path to the realization of sagehood. Due to the influence of Taoism and Buddhism, which had their own frameworks of spiritual
self-cultivation, the Neo-Confucians were spurred on to develop
a system of their own that corresponded to their way of perceiving the world.

By the 13th century, and probably much before, techniques of
self-cultivation had become an acceptable and appropriate chan-
nel for the attainment of sagehood based on the Confucian
model. A major goal of Neo-Confucianism became the teaching
of certain meditative techniques, so that human beings could ac-
quire wisdom and thereby realize their full potential as wise and
judicious human beings. Not that study, scholarship, and proper
moral behavior were no longer taught, but rather they were valued along with methods of self-cultivation. Even though the Neo-
Confucians were influenced by Taoism and Buddhism — a fact
they were loath to admit — they nevertheless maintained their
unique Confucian character. Unlike Buddhism, which sought to
promote buddhahood in the confines of the monastery, or Taoism whose devotees retired to the solitude of mountain and forest
retreats, Neo-Confucianism, in keeping with the tenets of Confucius, fostered the cultivation of wisdom and morality within the
boundaries of the mundane world.

Chou Tun-i's approach to attaining sagehood lay in a state of
tranquil meditation, which he defined as "having no desires." According to Chou, when a person has no desires, he or she can be
straightforward and impartial and thus act spontaneously and
naturally, which is ultimately the moral way. In this thought one
can hear a not-so-distant echo of Ch'an Buddhism.

Chu Hsi believed that, because human beings had received

the best and most subtle kind of Ch'i, this endowed them with the ability to reason and to be moral. This "quality" Ch'i was very important, according to Chu Hsi, for developing self-cultivation and thus attaining sagehood. Chu Hsi drew the metaphor of a pearl (li) lying in water (Ch'i). When the water is pure and clean, the beauty of the pearl is able to shine through and be seen in all its glory. If the water is muddy, the pearl may not be seen at all, or at least, its beauty seen in varying degrees of clarity. The point of his concept of self-cultivation was that human beings had the possibility of purifying their Ch'i and thus allowing the "pearl of wisdom" to shine through. While li came directly from the Supreme Ultimate and remained the same in regard to its purity, Ch'i as material or immaterial force could be transformed into a higher and purer vehicle of li.

For some Neo-Confucians like Chou Tun-i, the muddled morass of selfish desires could be cleared by a quiet kind of introspection which he called "tranquility." Others like Chang Tsai believed that human beings could change the nature of their Ch'i by "doing away with one's desires, controlling one's imagination, (and) suppressing the search for fame and money." [25] Chu Hsi suggested a third way in which the reasoning powers of human beings, intuitive introspection, and the sheer force of will played dominant roles. To uncover the universal truth of li, he recommended following a two-fold path:

1. Extending knowledge through the investigation of things. To know li (Supreme Ultimate), one must employ the mind to investigate the material world which will lead back to a deeper knowledge of li.This is not unlike a scientist on the trail of a great discovery. Chu Hsi likened the result of this quest to a kind of "sudden enlightenment," which is reminiscent of certain Buddhist ideas.

2. The above investigation required "attentiveness of mind" which meant that the purpose of the task must be kept foremost in one's mind at all times. This "attentiveness" contained a large element of will.

Summary

In the great tradition of Chinese self-cultivation the human mind is the source of all spiritual and physical transformation. It has the ability to adjust or ease the "decrees of Heaven," although not the power to veto or change them entirely. In this sense we could say that Chinese religion contained a very humanistic, anthropocentric philosophy. Men and women could expect very little in the way of compassion from Heaven, which tended to be impervious and "ruthless" toward mankind, treating them as "straw dogs." Unlike the general trend of Western religion, where the individual could cultivate a relationship with the Divine Being in the hopes of ameliorating his or her fate, the Chinese developed the powers of his or her mind in order to work with, to anticipate, and to harmonize the "will of Heaven" with the yearnings of mankind. For Neo-Confucians, self-cultivation implied not only the changing of one's temperament by controlling selfish desires, it also meant the uncovering of the universal truth of li in the Supreme Ultimate on which the laws of human ethical behavior were based.

By the time Chu Hsi died in 1200, the practice of self-cultivation was very much part and parcel of the Confucian tradition and thereby ensconced in the mores of the governmental and social elite. While the traditions of Taoism, Buddhism, and Confucianism had their own values and beliefs which led them in different directions, certain ideas were held in common which they borrowed from one another. The idea of the sage who practiced the art of self-cultivation symbolized a shared tradition that united all of them.

Against this background of cultural confluence the stage was set for Chang San-feng, a Taoist monk and traditionally acknowledged as the creator of T'ai Chi Ch'uan, who lived just after Chu Hsi's death and was purported to be "knowledgeable about all ancient forms of wisdom, including the I Ching, Confucianism, Buddhism, and Taoism...." [26]

PART 3

The Creation of T'ai Chi Ch'uan

THE ORIGINS OF T'AI CHI CH'UAN FOUNDATION AND FOUNDERS

We have completed our exploration of the religious, philosophical and cultural background of T'ai Chi. We can now turn our attention to the founders of T'ai Chi and the specific ideas which inspired them to create their unique discipline. Though little can be authenticated about the historical tradition itself, the legends and stories that arose around the founders of T'ai Chi tell us much about the nature of their art.

The Foundation of Self-Cultivation

Before the first millennium CE, it is unclear exactly what the Chinese were doing in terms of physical/spiritual self-cultivation. From various literary sources we can conjecture that certain practices were beginning to develop. Early hints at self-cultivation can be found in "The Yellow Emperor's Classic" when Ch'i Po, the Emperor's adviser, reminds him that the "ancients kept their bodies united with their souls." About the same time Lao Tzu recommends some kind of spiritual/physical self-cultivation:*

---

* If one accepts the dates that modern scholars place Lao Tzu and "The Yellow Emperor's Classic," in about the 3rd Century BCE.

That is why the Sage governs himself by
relaxing the mind,
reinforcing the abdomen,
gentling the will,
strengthening the bones."* [1]

It is well worth noting that both Ch'i Po and Lao Tzu speak of
cultivating the mind and body in the same breath. Chuang Tzu,
Lao Tzu's great disciple, was one of the first to clearly suggest
that there existed some form of special exercises based on the
movements of animals to cultivate the mind and body. He spoke
of the ancient sages who "breathed through their heels" or
"swayed like a bear...and stretched their necks like a bird."

The common thread that unites the ideas of Lao Tzu and
Chuang Tzu – and nearly all Chinese systems of self-cultivation –
is:

1) relaxing the mind,
2) breathing in a conscious manner,
3) the imitation of animal movements (this being prevalent
where movement composed a major part of the activity, in
contrast to the various forms of sitting or standing
meditation).

---

*Cheng Man Ch'ing interpreted Lao Tzu from a perspective of
Taoist techniques of spiritual cultivation, more so than any
commentary or translation that I have read, and thus, Tam Gibbs,
who was his student, follows this line of thought in this
translation. Moreover, Cheng Man Ch'ing has a very interesting
interpretation of Lao Tzu's words in his commentary on pages
28-29. These ideas constitute the basis of the many different kinds
of self-cultivation techniques, including T'ai Chi.*

The Meditative Mind

The notion of "relaxing the mind" was a code word for achieving an inner harmony and tranquility through meditation. All three major religious movements in China developed some form, method or technique of quieting the mind. It is clear that one of the major characteristics of Chinese religious practice was the art of meditation, in the same way that prayer was central to religious practice in the West. By virtue of the fact that, in the Chinese mind, the universe was harmonious and orderly, and thus reflected the nature of Tao, men and women could unite with Tao only by first creating within themselves order and harmony.

All of the religious movements in China viewed desires and the senses with mistrust, and as potential harbingers of chaos in the process of meditation. The objective of self-cultivation was to elevate the spirit and mind not by adding new facts of knowledge (though Confucianism leaned more toward this approach) but rather to reveal the place of human beings in a harmonious and orderly universe. Chinese culture, as we mentioned earlier, did not separate the mind and body as was done in the West: they believed that matter and spirit were made up of the same essential "material" called Ch'i. In striving for spiritual enlightenment through self-cultivation the Chinese sought to empty out the mind and not to add more facts to one's body of knowledge, or to pile more muscles on one's intellectual physique, but rather to refine the mind and body — in a balanced accord — in order to unify with Tao. Even later Confucianists could agree, at least to some degree, with this goal.

The most extreme statement regarding the way to self-cultivation, and the conflict between intellectual and intuitive knowledge, as we pointed out earlier, was made by Lao Tzu, who wrote:

"In the pursuit of learning, every day something is acquired.
In the pursuit of Tao, every day something is dropped." [2]

For Lao Tzu there was an inherent conflict in adding more things on top of the Tao that one once had naturally as a child, and subsequently lost in the process of maturing. According to Lao Tzu, becoming a scholar in order to achieve enlightenment was like searching for the proverbial needle in a haystack by piling on more hay.

The logical mind could also be a trap because it could ensnare the meditator in a morass of linear thought which diverted him or her from being sensitive to the infinite Tao. At its best, logical thinking functioned effectively in the finite world of definitions and limitations, but could not enter into the room of intuition and insight.

Ch'an Buddhism created the ideal tool, the Koan, to show the limits of the logical mind. The correct answer to "what is the sound of one hand clapping?" for example, did not hinge on logic but rather on the insight of the individual student. There was not one answer but many, and the correctness of the answer depended on how the Zen teacher, presumably enlightened himself, perceived the level of his student's spiritual consciousness.

The nature of the logical mind is to think in terms of dualities; the meditative mind dwells in unity, free from the entanglements of the mundane world. The poet Wang Wei (701-761), deeply influenced by Buddhism, beautifully summarized the qualities of the quiet mind:

"In late years, I love only the stillness,
The world's affairs no longer trouble my heart.
Looking at myself: no far-reaching plans;
All I know: to return to familiar woods—

The pine winds blow and loosen my sash;
The mountain moon shines upon me playing the lute.
You ask for reasons for failure or success—
Fisherman's song enters the river banks deep." [3]

As in poetry, the image of the fisherman is often portrayed in Chinese painting. He symbolized that the frantic pace of the world has been forsaken for a quiet patience and tranquility, his line sinking deep into the river's silence.

Breath

In the East there is a long tradition of meditation accompanied by various breathing techniques. When Chuang Tzu speaks of "breathing through the heels," he was perhaps referring to the way the Chinese in his day sat in meditation. Moreover, the balancing of one's Yin and Yang Ch'is could be interpreted as combining meditation and breathing techniques.* In its early historical meaning Ch'i was defined simply as "breath," and only later did it develop a more complex interpretation in Taoism and especially in Neo-Confucianism.

The importance of breath soon becomes self-evident to anyone who embarks on meditative practices. Most of the time our breathing is uneven and shallow. We rarely savor a full portion of fresh air or become conscious of our breathing. The breath is often taken as an involuntary mechanism of the body, like the blinking of an eyelid or the digestion of the stomach, and not something which can be consciously regulated in order to relax the mind or improve one's health. The crucial importance of the breath is not an idea exclusively held by the East. In Genesis God "breathed" life into man. It could legitimately be argued that the

---

* See chapter 5 on Taoism.

Silent Angler in an Autumn Wood by Shen Chou, 15th-Century.
Courtesy of The Metropolitan Museum of Art

less we breathe, the less we are alive.

The Taoists wholly adopted the life-giving qualities of breathing and it was always included in their spiritual practices, whether they were seeking union with Tao or physical immortality and eternal youth. In the Chapter on Taoism we spoke of prenatal breathing in which the devotee seeks to bring his or her breathing deep into the tan t'ien. The deeper one breathes, using the mind to direct the Ch'i, the closer one approaches the ideal of the child and its natural youth. The symbol of death is shallow breathing where the breath gradually rises until it flies out of the mouth.

Ko Hung, the taoist alchemist of the 4th century CE, advised people who wished to maintain their youth and health to practice the vigorous discipline of breath control:

"In the beginning to learn the proper use of breath, one should inhale through the nose. Stop up the nose and mentally count one's heart beats. The breath should be exhaled through the mouth. In this method of breathing, everyone should make it his aim that his own ears might not hear the sound of either inhalation or exhalation. The rule is to inhale generously and exhale sparingly. One should suspend the feather of a wild goose in front of the nose and mouth that the feather might not stir while the breath is being expelled...After a very long period of time one should be able to count a thousand heart beats. When a old man has arrived at that stage, then he will be transformed into a young man...." [4]

For the early Taoists like Lao Tzu and Chuang Tzu, breathing did not represent merely a method by which to drink from the fountain of youth. Rather it provided a way to achieve mystical union with Tao. The basic idea was that breathing allowed the meditator to "empty" him or herself because "Tao abides only in emptiness," and if one is full of him or herself, there will be no room for it to enter.

In contrast, the Buddhist way of breathing reflected their philosophic inclinations and focused primarily on bringing "mindfulness" to their meditation practices. Mindfulness was one of the steps of the Buddha's "Eightfold path" and came to mean not only choosing the "right " subjects for thought, but also the ability of the meditator to maintain his or her undivided attention on the task of meditation. In order to accomplish this, focusing on counting the breaths was an effective technique for grounding the flights and fantasies of an untamed mind. Unlike Taoist breathing, the Buddhists emphasized "normal" patterns of breathing; inhaling the breath and expanding the diaphragm and then exhaling, the diaphragm contracting naturally. The Buddhists stressed that the exhalation of breath was a kind of 'emptying out' process. In contrast to what Ko Hung recommends above, the Buddhists did not seek immortality or eternal youth, but rather union with the Void. The Buddhists believed that the Taoists were egoistic in seeking immortality and were merely filling themselves up with (hot) air.

Both Taoists and Buddhists practiced slow and long techniques of effortless breathing. It was hoped that this kind of focusing and breathing would bring about a clarity of the mind. Buddhist initiates often began their meditation practice with nothing more for instruction than to count their breath from one to ten, repeatedly, until the mind was trained to keep its focus. Anyone who has tried this technique can attest to the degree of difficulty involved, despite the apparent impression of ease.

Animal Forms

There is clearly a natural relationship between relaxing the mind and breathing in the process of meditation. What is somewhat surprising to the Western mind is the assimilation of meditation and breathing techniques with animal forms of exercise.

This historical watershed is marked by Hua T'o (141-203 CE), a famous physician and the father of Chinese anaesthesiology, who introduced a system of renewing one's vitality with a combination of mental, physical and breathing exercises called "Tao Yin." He is also credited with being the creator of Ch'i Kung exercises known as "The Sport of Five Animals."*

A graphic description of Hua T'o's art was given by his student, Wu P'u:

"The Immortals of ancient days, while performing the inhalation process, passed their time like dormant bears, looking about like owls, twitched and stretched their limbs and joints in order to hinder the advance of old age. I have an art, called "The Sport of Five Animals," namely a tiger, a stag, a bear, a monkey, and a bird, by which illness can be cured and which is good for the movements of the feet when they accompany the process of inhalation...Whenever you feel unwell, stand up and imitate the movement of one of these animals." [5]

According to Waysun Liao, Hua T'o also invented a fighting martial art based on the movements of animals called "The Five Animal Games" which was the first known system of martial arts in China. [6] Several hundred years later Bodhidharma, an Indian Buddhist monk, arrived in China and introduced a program of physical conditioning in the Shao Lin monastery which was based on the animal forms and probably yoga techniques of his

---

Today there are literally hundreds of Ch'i Kung exercises which roughly means "developing the internal energy." The term covers a wide range of mind, body and breathing practices. Many consider T'ai Chi a form of Ch'i Kung, albeit a more complex and arduous one with implications of self-defense.

Bear

Tiger

Crane

Deer

Monkey

The five animal forms of Hua T'o.

native India (See Chapter 4).*

We might ask: why did the Chinese choose animals on which to base their systems of exercise and martial arts? Nothing like it occurred in the West. We do have the connection between families and their coat of arms, for example, characterizing a positive or noble quality which they wished to portray. In the Bible we also hear of Jacob's last testament to his sons in which he likens Judah to the nobility of a lion or Dan to that of a snake. But in this context it is symbolic and poetic. In Western sport, which perhaps bears the closest resemblance we have to Chinese health and martial exercises, there is no example of imitating the movements of animals.

It is possible to speculate on some of the reasons for this unique development. The most obvious is that the Chinese recognized in the various animals, like the tiger, certain qualities of ferociousness combined with power and grace which they could imitate and utilize in their systems of health and self-defense. We have also discussed previously the emphasis that the Taoists and the Neo-Confucians placed on the observation of nature. No doubt the animals of China's varied climates came under close scrutiny, and the Chinese, being a practical people, put that information to good use. Chinese artists indeed were taught to become "like" their subject matter in order to depict them in their

---

* There are some who argue that Bodhidharma -- or, at the very least, his followers -- was a major influence on the creation of T'ai Chi. There are others, like Cheng Man Ch'ing, who believed that the art of Bodhidharma only develops "hard Ch'i" and thus is an external system which is totally separate from T'ai Chi (Wile, Cheng Man-Ch'ing's Advanced T'ai-Chi Form Instructions, p. 13). See, too, Chi Kung by Dr Yang Jwing-Ming chapters 2 and 3 for an excellent explanation of the difference between the internal (nei dan) and the external (wai dan) styles of martial arts and Chi Kung.

paintings "from within." When a calligrapher draws the Chinese symbol for water, for example, he might imagine the experience of floating or swimming in a lake. Similarly, the devotee of this kind of martial art strives to imitate the positive qualities of the particular animal that the form seeks to represent.

Another reason for the use of animal forms was that, from a Chinese medical point of view, animals were perceived as being naturally more healthy than human beings. Cheng Man Ch'ing, who was also a doctor of traditional Chinese medicine, explained that because the animals do not stand erect like man, they are healthier: "...their internal organs are mostly suspended from a horizontal spine. The least movement of the animal exercises the whole set of its organs." [7]

The Chinese notion of utilizing animal movements for exercise or self-defense did not encourage anyone to become an exact clone of a tiger or a deer. As Cheng Man Ch'ing pointed out, there is an essential physical difference between mankind and most animals in that, aside from man's larger brain capacity, human beings walk upright. In Chinese medical thought the spine of man, if held in the proper equilibrium in relation to the rest of the body, could provide human beings with more than a modicum of good health. This is one reason why T'ai Chi emphasizes holding a tensionless, "plumb-erect" spine as though it were a "string of pearls."

What the Chinese hoped to accomplish by imitating certain attributes or movements of animals was to combine them with man's innate intelligence and physical abilities. In contrast to primitive societies, there was no element of worship or of becoming the animal itself in a trance-like state. On the contrary, the mind of man retained a balance of clarity, rationality, and intuition.

With respect to man's unique physical abilities, mention should be made of the ideas of Moshe Feldenkrais, a Western master of movement and awareness, who was also a teacher of Judo. He agreed that the animals had certain advantages over man in locomotion but he also pointed out that the erect spine of man freed the hands for creative work. This fact led to the making and wielding of weapons which have made man more powerful than the animals. Feldenkrais also noted that man has the potential to move quickly on his axis, most notably in the rotation of a bullfighter as he evades the bull's charge at the last moment. [8] This idea is "pure" T'ai Chi because the rotation of the body and stepping aside leads the bull's strength into emptiness (we shall speak more of this later). In all likelihood Feldenkrais was influenced by his training in Judo which contains the idea of yielding to strength in order to gain the upper hand.

A further reason why the Chinese health and martial arts emulated the animals could be understood as growing out of the larger Chinese vision of the universe. Believing the cosmos to be a unified whole with everything being connected to everything else, they did not look down on the animal world as being inferior, but rather recognized that each part of the universe had its place and role to play in the cosmic drama. The vitality of a tiger might have a different quality from that of human beings but the basic element that united all living things, the Ch'i, evolved from the same origins of the Supreme Ultimate. This profound sensitivity to all things, organic and inorganic, opened up a broad intellectual horizon so that the Chinese might learn from all things, including the animal world.

It is possible to contrast this view of the Chinese with the prevailing notion in the West regarding our relationship to the creatures of the world. In Genesis, God made all the living creatures after their kind, but God said, "Let us make Mankind in our image, after our likeness: and let them have dominion over ...(all the earth's creatures)." [9] Man has received from God not only "dominion" over the creatures, but also something unique and

Godly, a soul, that reflects the nature of the Divine Being.* As a consequence, the role of animals in Western society was that of a servant — something to be 'served' on man's dinner table, a hunting trophy to be hung on the wall, or, at its worst, a pest to be eradicated. This kind of attitude did not create an intellectual climate where Western man was inclined to learn from his fellow creatures. However, it should be pointed out that the idea of "guarding" nature has become more fashionable because it is has become increasingly clear that, as the Chinese have known for centuries, we are all interconnected with everything else and the fate of human beings hangs on the way we view every living thing on the planet, including the Earth itself.

The final reason for the development of animal forms was the absolute need for an effective system of martial arts for both individuals and groups of people like the monks of the Shao Lin Monastery. Throughout most of Chinese history the peasantry was both oppressed and poverty-stricken, often to the point of starvation. As a result, bands of roving brigands filled the countryside and made traveling a most dangerous endeavor, even on the country's major roads [10] Entire villages developed their own systems of martial arts which they employed to protect themselves and which they kept secret, so that the element of surprise could be utilized to its best advantage. An excellent example of this was the Ch'en family village out of which, by most accounts, T'ai Chi originated.

In almost all the martial arts of China the strengths of animals and even insects were imitated. One famous insect form is called

---

* *This idea of dominion must be balanced against what God tells Adam later; that he must "guard" the Garden of Eden. [Genesis 2:15] The root of the Hebrew word is "shomar" which can mean to keep or to guard. In the West, the notion of dominion has often 'dominated' that of 'guarding.'*

the Praying Mantis style. While the imitating of animals may at first seem strange to people of the West, when put in the context of Chinese culture, the logic grows more natural and compelling.

The Historical Origins of T'ai Chi

Having discussed the philosophical and historical roots of T'ai Chi, we can now examine the founders of T'ai Chi themselves — from the perspectives of historical research, mythology and folklore.

Historically, T'ai Chi is composed of the many cultural streams that have been described in this book. Like the Yellow River stretching across the breadth of China, its waters fed by innumerable brooks, rivers, and tributaries, so T'ai Chi combined and grew with the various types of meditation and visualization techniques, Tao Yin and Ch'i kung exercises, the many kinds of breathing techniques and the martial arts which included the animal forms. T'ai Chi also absorbed traditional Chinese philosophical concepts which consisted of an amalgam of Confucianism, Taoism and Buddhism, Yin-Yang, the Five Elements theories, and medical principles which had combined with Taoist meditation techniques and were characterized by the circulation of the Ch'i through the body's meridians.

Out of this natural organic process, T'ai Chi began about 300 to 400 years ago as a martial art that was separate and distinct from the other forms of self-defense in that it emphasized relaxation, softness, and the circulation of Ch'i to achieve its goals, whether they be self-defense, improved health, or immortality.

When exactly T'ai Chi emerged with a distinct identity is difficult to pinpoint with any historical accuracy. We know that the T'ai Chi of today is very different, at least in appearance, although not in principle, from the T'ai Chi of yesteryear. Chen Wei-ming, an important teacher of the Yang style, who opened a T'ai Chi school in Shanghai in 1927, said that early T'ai Chi was probably practiced by holding single postures — apparently there were only thirteen, far fewer than we have today — and that only much later Wang Tsung-yueh (18th century) connected the postures in a flowing sequential order. [11] The flowing movements and set order of T'ai Chi are a few of the most common characteristics of modern T'ai Chi, although many teachers recommend the practicing of single postures as a form of standing meditation.

Probably the most accurate records as to the origins of T'ai Chi date back to the Ch'en family of the 17th and 18th centuries. The Yang style, named after the Yang family, was an outgrowth of the Ch'en style and became the most popular form of T'ai Chi in China and Taiwan in the 20th century.

If we retain the image of T'ai Chi as a river, it is perhaps impossible to sort out a precise point where we can say: "this is now The T'ai Chi River." While the safest historical point of reference for T'ai Chi is the Ch'en family in the 18th century, most of its devotees trace it back to the legendary founder Chang San-feng. No discussion of the origins of T'ai Chi would be complete if the life of this remarkable man were not included.

Chang San-feng

All cultures have their heroes and heroines who represent the highest aspirations of a people or nation. For Americans, Abraham Lincoln epitomized the qualities of honesty and courage. For the Chinese, Confucius symbolized the qualities of the wise and scholarly sage who sought to educate all people in the "right" way to live. These real people, who take on mythic proportions, became symbols as to how a culture would like to view itself as well as giving their stamp of approval for something fantastic or daring that ordinary people might shy away from. The result is that myth and events interact to create a cultural history that is no less real or valid "even if it did not happen" because

Chang San-feng.

ordinary people believe in their myths, draw on them as acts of faith, and ultimately institutionalize them as icons of their common heritage. They also remind people that suffering is temporary and purposeful in the larger scheme of things. Historically, the Chinese people, especially the lower classes, have known more than their share of suffering. In such circumstances, mythic figures can help people to rise above and transcend the fetters that often bind them to the drabness of day-to-day life. Heroes and heroines trumpet a call to redemption.

One of these mythic characters was Chang San-feng who was undoubtedly the most significant figure in later Taoist history. Traditionally, he is credited with having mastered Taoist yoga techniques which enabled him to achieve immortality. His accomplishment as a spiritual master was on such a high level that, according to tradition, he reappeared in his physical form after his death.

By some accounts he was born at the end of the Sung dynasty (late 13th century), which would make him almost a contemporary of Chu Hsi. Others place him in the Yuan dynasty (1278-1368). He supposedly lived in his physical body for over two hundred years. Because of the many conflicting dates of his life, some scholars have wondered if there were more than one Chang San-feng.

It was said that Chang San-feng was a huge man, towering over seven feet tall with the build of a solid tree who moved with the delicacy of a graceful bird. His face bore the shape of the full moon and his large eyes peered out with kindness and compassion for all living things. His hair was wild and unkempt as would be expected of a man who lived alone in the mountains far away from society, yet he exuded a sense of warmth and gentleness to all he met. Having mastered the art of regulating his body temperature, he wore the same light clothing in summer or winter. Apparently he could sit in the freezing snow and his body remained warm and comfortable. When he traveled, it was said, he could traverse half of China in one day.

As a young man, in the typical fashion of middle to upper classes, Chang San-feng passed his examinations and became a government official. At this point in his life he was an ardent follower of Confucius and was well-versed in the Classics including the *I Ching*. After the death of his parents he resigned his position, gave away all his property, and became a wanderer and a seeker of truth. Eventually he found a home in the Pao-Gi mountains, which are known for their three pointed peaks. Here he chose a new name for himself, San-feng, meaning 'three peaks.' According to one tradition, it was in this period of his life that he began his studies of Bodhidharma's exercises at the Shao Lin Monastery. Later he met a Taoist monk who taught him the method of attaining immortality which he practiced diligently until, after moving to the Wu-Tang mountains, he experienced a "great realization" and became one with Tao. Each dawn he would rise early and sit alone in deep meditation, tasting the subtle elixir of heavenly and earthly Ch'i which he mixed and circulated with his knowledge of Taoist breathing techniques.

It was in the Wu-Tang mountains that Chang San-feng created T'ai Chi Ch'uan and that is why the internal system of martial arts is associated with the name of these mountains. *According to Cheng Man Ch'ing, Chang San-feng's outstanding innovation was to apply "the philosophy of Huang Ti (The Yellow Emperor) and Lao Tze to boxing, substituting pliability for hard-hitting muscular power."* [12] This idea is absolutely crucial if one is to grasp the innovative nature of T'ai Chi.

---

* *Cheng Man Ch'ing was a vigorous supporter of the view that Chang San- feng was the creator of T'ai Chi (see Wile, Cheng Man Ch'ing's Advanced T'ai-Chi..., p. 11).*

As an immortal and adept in Taoist magical arts, Chang San-feng possessed extraordinary powers which are demonstrated in the following story.*

One day he met members of the Mongolian royal family who were on a hunting expedition in the Wu-Tang mountains. Chang San-feng was on his own hunting expedition but his was for herbs rather than game. The Mongolians ordered him to move on but Chang answered that, while they hunted with bows and arrows, he only used his bare hands. Then, with the grace of a deer, he jumped high in the air and snatched a pair of hawks that were flying by. Needless to say, the Mongolians stood in awe of this extraordinary physical feat. Chang then set the two birds in each of his hands and no matter how hard the birds tried to fly away, they could not leave his palms. The reason for this is that a bird needs to push off from something solid with its feet in order to launch itself into the air. Chang's sensitivity was so well-attuned that he could slightly withdraw his hands as the hawks began to push off.** He explained that he loved all living creatures and had mercy on them. He held his hands steady and the birds lifted skyward.

The Mongolians were incensed by his impertinence. One drew his bow and shot an arrow at Chang San-feng who caught it with his teeth. He threw the arrow into a tree and then told the

---

*There is a strong element of Chinese patriotism here. The Mongolians conquered all of China by 1279 and ruled for about one hundred years. The ethnic Chinese considered them foreign oppressors.

**There are others like Lenzie Williams, a well-known American teacher of T'ai Chi, who suggest that the story is about "the sinking of the inside of the palm due to the internal qualities that he cultivated." This subtle difference demonstrates the inclination of T'ai Chi practitioners to delve deeper into their art — 'deeper' meaning more internal.

Mongolians that violent weapons were not his way, an echo of Lao Tzu's words (*Tao Te Ching,* Ch. 31).

Legendary stories like this one about the life of Chang San-feng are significant precisely because of what they reveal about the ideals of Chinese culture. In addition to his extraordinary physical powers and patriotism he demonstrated a deep compassion for all living things.

Moreover, the wedding of the Yellow Emperor's medical theory and the ideas of Lao Tzu (pliability and softness) as a substitute for "hard-hitting muscular power" in martial arts was a powerful and radical statement in Chinese culture. The early religious Taoists had fomented social revolutions with this volatile mixture. Yet, for this formula to take hold, at least in the imagination of martial artists, it required a mythical figure of Chang San-feng's stature to ensure its credibility. T'ai Chi rubs against the grain of the way most people think of martial arts or self-defense. The usual response to force is more force and not softness and sensitivity. With Chang San-feng as T'ai Chi's traditional founder, the art gained an aura of authenticity and respectability that enabled it to grow in status as a rival to the many other established forms of Chinese martial arts. Later, tales of T'ai Chi's legendary fighters would further enhance and secure its reputation.

Chang San-feng and the Origin of T'ai Chi

There are several stories as to how Chang San-feng came to his realization and thus created T'ai Chi. By far the most well-known is the battle between the snake and the crane — a further example of Chinese tradition drawing on animal behavior as a model.

In this version Chang San-feng was sitting in quiet meditation in his hut. Suddenly he heard a noisy racket outside his window and, looking outside to see what was going on, he saw a snake with raised head ready to defend itself against a crane in the tree above. Suddenly the swift crane dived at the snake and thrust its sharp beak at its head. The supple snake evaded the crane's attack and lunged at the crane's exposed neck. The crane quickly raised its right wing and brushed away the snake's dangerous strike. Repulsed by the bird's wing, the snake curled around and attacked the crane's left leg. Lightening quick, the crane swept away the snake's charge with its left wing. The bird struck again and again at the snake but was unable to gain the advantage or to inflict any damage due to the soft circular evasions of the snake. Finally the two opponents grew weary and the struggle ended with no clear winner, the bird flying away and the snake disappearing in the grass.

According to tradition, this primal struggle afforded Chang San-feng a profound insight which ultimately led to the creation of T'ai Chi Ch'uan. He learned that the soft could overcome the hard from the suppleness and pliability of the snake's circuitous movements. This was one of Lao Tzu's key principles and the battle of the snake and the crane confirmed its applicability to martial arts. Their struggle also highlighted the paramount importance of quickness and change in martial arts. The fact that both the snake and the crane quickly yielded or attacked, as the situation required, demonstrated the crucial aspect of an intuitive and instantaneous understanding of Yin and Yang in the context of fighting. Thus the T'ai Chi symbol of the two fishes — which embodies the concept of Yin and Yang — was well suited to become the name and the emblem of the emerging martial art, T'ai Chi. Moreover, several movements in T'ai Chi were named after this great battle, such as "Crane Spreads Her Wings," "Brush Knee Twist-Step" and "Snake Creeps Down."

A Critical look at the Origins of T'ai Chi

Even if we were inclined to accept Chang San-feng as the

creator of T'ai Chi Ch'uan on the basis of these stories — and there are many who do — several major obstacles stand directly in our path which are not easily brushed aside.

The historical evidence that supports Chang San-feng as the "father" of T'ai Chi is extremely scanty and inconclusive. Chang may be the "adopted" father, but he would probably lose any claim to paternity in a court of law. In the classic book, *Chinese Boxing*, its author, Robert Smith, presents the views of Chou Chi-Ch'un on the origins of T'ai Chi. Chou demonstrates convincingly that Chang San-feng could not have been the founder of T'ai Chi. [13] Even if we assume that Chang San-feng was the founder of T'ai Chi, there is a large gap of about three to four hundred years between his life and the man who is often credited as being the second link in the T'ai Chi chain, Wang Tsung-yueh.

To further complicate matters, there are those who argue that two Wang Tsungs lived in different periods and, due to the similarity of names, people naturally confused them. Chen Wei-ming, who we mentioned earlier, accepts this thesis and suggests that Chang San-feng transmitted his T'ai Chi to the earlier one, Wang Tsung. [14] It was later transmitted to Wang Tsung-yueh. This conveniently circumvents the problem of the three to four hundred year gap between the lives of Chang San-feng and Wang Tsung-yueh, assuming that both men lived extremely long lives and Chang San-feng was born in the late 14th century. However it proves nothing about the claim that Chang San-feng was the founder of T'ai Chi. On the other hand, Wang Tsung-yueh seems to have been a living person who actually influenced the history of T'ai Chi and we will speak of him shortly.

There is yet another opinion that suggests T'ai Chi came from neither Chang San-feng or Wang Tsung-yueh, but rather from the larger area around the Ch'en village in Honan province and "actually had its source in the masses...." [15] T'ang Hao, a historian of the martial arts and T'ai Chi, claims that Ch'en family T'ai

Chi bears a close resemblance to a book of the 16th century which was based on the popular styles of boxing in and around the Ch'en village. Thus the Ch'en family incorporated these boxing styles into what later became known as the Ch'en style of T'ai Chi.

While interesting as speculation, all these theories have their shortcomings, being based on few verifiable facts. We simply don't know with *reasonable historical accuracy* who founded T'ai Chi. This does not mean its founder will always remain a mystery. Some enterprising archaeologist may uncover a tombstone which contains diagrams, explanations and unimpeachable evidence as to who the creator of T'ai Chi was, or if such a person ever existed.

Having said that, Wang Tsung-yueh probably still represents the best lead in tracing the beginnings of T'ai Chi in that he is most often credited with having been the first "known" successor to Chang San-feng. Many historians of T'ai Chi agree with this premise, even though it has been argued by some that Wang might not have been a real person and that his work was authored by someone else.* Nonetheless Wang is usually credited with transmitting T'ai Chi to the Ch'en family in the 18th century, and authoring the "T'ai Chi Ch'uan Lun" of the T'ai Chi classics, although this, too, is open to debate. The scholar Douglas Wile was correct in warning his readers about the pitfalls in discovering the true origins of T'ai Chi: "...abandon all hope ye who search for certainty." [16]

Wang's "Tai Chi Ch'uan Lun" — assuming he wrote it — is the most philosophical of the Classics, and connects T'ai Chi, the art of movement, with the concept of the Supreme Ultimate (which was discussed in the chapter on Neo-Confucianism). The

*See T. Y. Pang, On Tai Chi Chuan, pp. 267-269

reader will recall Wang's statement: "T'ai Chi comes from Wu Chi and is the mother of Yin and Yang. In motion it separates; in stillness they fuse." For this reason alone, he would be very important in the history and development of T'ai Chi. Wang's treatise is clearly the most scholarly and philosophical of the Classics.

There is another equally important reason why Wang Tsung-yueh plays such an important role in T'ai Chi. According to one well-known tradition, he is a mystery man who suddenly appears and transmits his secret art, T'ai Chi, to the Ch'en family.* *The one fact that almost everyone agrees on is that the Ch'en family practiced something called T'ai Chi, although there is a wide range of opinion as to where they got it.* There is no less a range of varying opinions as to where Wang Tsung-yueh received his knowledge of T'ai Chi.

The tradition of Wang transmitting T'ai Chi to the Ch'en family has been told in the following way: One day, as Wang was passing through the Ch'en village, he happened to see the villagers practicing a style of boxing. He made a few disparaging remarks in public regarding their skill. Of course this angered some of the villagers who challenged him to a fight. Wang made quick work of his challengers. Recognizing that Wang had unusually high skills as a martial artist, they begged him to stay on and he agreed. According to the story, Wang taught them something he called T'ai Chi. Whether or not Wang's teaching was merely a modification of what the Ch'en family already practiced or was something entirely new, we do not know.

There is another tradition that claims the Ch'en Family taught T'ai Chi to Wang. This is disputed by others because in his writings Wang does not credit the Ch'en family as his teachers, which goes against the accepted custom.

The Ch'en and the Yang Family Traditions

The Ch'en family kept the art that Wang had taught them a tightly held secret and it was not taught to anyone outside of the village until the arrival of Yang Lu-shan (1799-1872), who was to become the founder of Yang style T'ai Chi and patriarch of the Yang family. *Another fact that nearly everyone agrees on is that Yang Lu-shan received T'ai Chi from the Ch'en family.*

Yang, reputedly of peasant origins, came from the north of China and was a devoted student of the martial arts. He had learned the hard style of Shao Lin boxing but was not satisfied with it. After hearing about a secret style of boxing in the Ch'en village, he immediately traveled there but was refused admittance as a student because he was not a member of the Ch'en family. Legend has it that he remained in the village, working as a servant and hoping to find a way to learn the Ch'en's secret martial art.

One night Yang heard a noise coming from the courtyard. He leaped out of bed and furtively crept up to the fence which surrounded the courtyard. There, through a hole in the wall, Yang saw the Ch'en family practicing their T'ai Chi. From that night on, he watched through the hole and diligently practiced what he had learned. Eventually he was caught and brought before the elder of the Ch'en clan, Ch'en Chang Hsiang (1771-1853), who wanted to see what Yang had learned before they threw him out. The Ch'en elder was so impressed with Yang's ability and perseverance under difficult conditions that, contrary to tradition, he permitted Yang to remain and learn the Ch'en style T'ai Chi. Within a relatively short time Yang became one of the top students in the Ch'en village, which still exists in modern China.*

It is possible today to study Ch'en style T'ai Chi in the Ch'en family village. For the experience of a Westerner, see Herb Rich, "A Bitter-sweet Journey to Learn Ch'en T'ai Chi in China." (T'AI CHI vol.15, no.3, June 1991, p. 12).

Yang Lu-shan and the Popularization of T'ai Chi

Yang Lu-shan sparked a revolution in the development of T'ai Chi. Through his efforts T'ai Chi left the narrow confines of the rural Ch'en village and moved center-stage to the capital of Peking, from where it spread throughout China. Yang became famous not only as a martial artist, but also as one of the first masters to teach openly.

The reason for the popularity of the Yang style is an interesting story in itself and is intimately connected to Chinese history of the nineteenth and early twentieth centuries. During this period China suffered the humiliation of European and Japanese colonialism. A new technological world was emerging in which firepower greatly decreased the importance and, in most cases, completely nullified the military effectiveness of the traditional Chinese martial arts. The Boxer Rebellion of the early 1900's proved this beyond any doubt to the martial arts community when many fighters, believing that they were immune to bullets, dashed headlong into the fire of foreign guns and were cut down.

In the light of the sobering reality that China was a weak sister in world affairs and being exploited by more powerful nations, Chinese nationalists adopted a new strategy which they hoped would make China strong and ensure her a prominent place among the nations of the world. One of the first results of their actions was the overthrow of the autocratic and inefficient Ch'ing government and the establishment of a Republic by Sun Yat-sen in 1912.

In this era of profound change in both traditional attitudes and societal structures — which witnessed the attempt of the nationalists to bring China kicking and screaming into the modern age — the Yang family modified their T'ai Chi and introduced a style that stressed elements of health, physical fitness, and techniques of personal self-defense. Their genius was an ability to keep the essence of their art while at the same time making it available to the population at large.

If one compares the Yang and Ch'en styles of today, one is struck by the fact that they appear to be almost completely different systems.* The Ch'en style is filled with daring and dynamic movements, with changes of pace, of incredible, explosive energy, powerful kicks and punches, jumps and even a fall to the floor, where the Ch'en stylist does the splits. This kind of T'ai Chi requires hours of prodigious practice, an athlete of unusual abilities, and a superb teacher.

The Yang style, in contrast, has been toned down and is much less demanding physically. It reflects a distinctly meditative quality in its smooth, sinuous movements that flow "like a great river." The watchwords of the Yang style are "relax" and "softness" and, among the many principles of T'ai Chi, Yang stylists consider these two qualities the first among equals. Almost anyone can work on these ideas, although to put them in practice on a deep mental and physical level can be as difficult as performing the powerful movements of the Ch'en style. But the very nature of the evolved Yang style — its softness — made it accessible to most people, young and old alike. The Yang style easily conformed to the practitioner's abilities, age and objectives, which thus enabled it to reach a wide audience.

Most early martial arts teachers tended to keep their art secretive and unavailable to the public. One reason for this attitude was that anyone who gained a reputation as being a good fighter faced a constant barrage of challenges from other martial artists seeking to establish a reputation. In that respect China was reminiscent of the gunfights in the "wild west."

Yang Lu-shan, the father of the Yang style, seems to have

---

*The Ch'en style has also undergone changes but it appears much less so than the Yang.

broken with the tradition of secrecy. The reason he gave was based on patriotism and must be viewed against the background of China's exploitation at the hands of the 19th-century Western imperialism. "We are poor," Yang explained,

> "because we are weak; truly weakness is the cause of poverty...The virility and vigor of the Europeans and Americans goes without saying... From my youth I have always considered helping the weak as my personal responsibility. I have seen popular martial arts performers whose spirit and physique are in no way inferior to the so-called muscle men of the West...I begged to learn their art, but they kept it secret and would not tell me." 17

It was later, Yang relates, that he learned the art of the Ch'en family. After teaching in Peking, he witnessed the improvement of his students' health and he realized that T'ai Chi could play a role in saving the nation by strengthening the weak. The result of his ideas was revolutionary and, in the twentieth century, T'ai Chi grew from a little known art to a popular exercise which can be found today in almost any Chinese park.*

It is clear that T'ai Chi has been and still is undergoing a natural process of change. What most people are doing today is probably quite different from the T'ai Chi done in the 19th century and even more so the further back we go, say, to the time of Chang San-feng in approximately the 14th century, assuming there was then such a thing as T'ai Chi.

---

* *Chen Wei-Ming, whom we mentioned earlier, said that in the 1920s, when he opened his school in Shanghai, few even knew the name of T'ai Chi but "within four years Taichi had become very popular." (*Tai Chi Ch'uan Ta Wen, p 11).

The Skill of Yang Lu-shan

After Yang left the Ch'en village for Peking, he soon became famous. He was known as "Yang, the unbeatable" because of his martial arts prowess. Once he was challenged by another boxer who struck Yang's stomach with tremendous power. At the same moment Yang gave a deep belly-laugh which threw the boxer to the ground. Legends like this one established Yang Lu-shan's fame as a martial artist par excellence.

Another story tells of a Shao Lin monk who approached Yang while he was meditating. [18] The monk offered his salutations and then suddenly, like a tiger, flew at Yang with his fists. Yang depressed his chest and patted the monk's fist with his palm: "As if struck by a bolt of lightning, the monk was thrown behind a screen, his body still in the attitude of attacking with clenched fists." With a bit of comic understatement thrown in, the monk apologized and said, "I have been extremely rude." After asking Yang what had happened to him, the monk said that he had never met someone with Yang's martial arts' abilities and begged to be accepted as his student. The master did not answer in words but instead reached up and caught a bird in his hand. Then he opened his hand — reminiscent of Chang San-feng and the hawks — but the bird could not fly away because of Yang's sensitivity to its trying to push off. From this story it is clear that Yang had assimilated the T'ai Chi prowess of Chang San-feng. "This hardly deserves to be called miraculous," Yang explained,

> "If one practices T'ai-chi for some time, the entire body becomes so light and sensitive that a feather weight cannot be added without setting it into motion and a fly cannot alight without the same effect."

This quote of Yang comes directly from the "T'ai Chi Ch'uan Lun" of Wang Tsung-yueh in the T'ai Chi Classics. [19]

In the stories about Yang Lu-shan (and there are many more),* one finds a strong emphasis on the power and efficacy of T'ai Chi as a martial art rather than as a method for developing better health or other Taoist spiritual pursuits. One reason for this is that Yang lived in the 19th century when martial arts still radiated an aura of invincibility prior to the Boxer Rebellion. T'ai Chi also faced stiff competition from many other martial arts systems such as Shao Lin Kung Fu. The fact that Yang easily defeats a Shao Lin monk was intended to show the superiority of T'ai Chi in the realm of the fighting arts.

The way in which Yang describes the results of practicing T'ai Chi— "the entire body becomes so light and sensitive"— is the kind of talk that would catch the attention of a martial artist seeking to utilize the full potential of his abilities. This is not the language of the street-fighter or the brawler but rather suggests that intelligence, sensitivity, and perseverance are the keys to becoming a successful boxer.

Yet, from a T'ai Chi perspective, these qualities are understood differently than the way of other martial arts. They are qualitative rather than merely those of degree or nuance. Most traditional T'ai Chi teachers, including those of the present time, reject the notion that T'ai Chi is simply a "soft" form of Kung Fu. In Yang Cheng-fu's Ten Important Points with a commentary by Chen Wei-ming, for example, it was put this way:**

"USE MIND AND NOT FORCE...In practicing T'ai Chi Ch'uan the whole body relaxes. Don't let one ounce of force remain in

---

* See Jou, The Tao of Tai-chi, pp. 43-44
**Yang Cheng-fu (d. 1936) was the famous grandson of Yang Lu-shan. Chen Wei-ming was Cheng-fu's student as was Cheng Man Ch'ing.

THE YANG FAMILY
Yang Lu-shan (1799-1872).

Yang Chian (1839-1917).

Yang Chao-hsiung (1862-1930).   *Yang Cheng-fu (1833-1936).*

the blood vessels, bones, and ligaments to tie yourself up. Then you can be agile and able to change." [20]

When Yang Cheng-fu and others speak about not using force, they mean exactly what they say. Not using force or staying soft are not poetic metaphors. The problem of using words to explain this idea is that they are symbols which, for most people including many students of T'ai Chi, have little relation to reality. It is easy to "think" that one is relaxed until attacked. That is why just doing the T'ai Chi form with the feeling of relaxation and softness can be a supreme act of illusion. Only by experiencing a threat, and working on staying soft and relaxed, can one progress in this area. This is the underlying concept of push-hands where one faces the threat of being pushed by his or her partner, and hopefully begins to learn the true meaning of Yang Cheng-fu's words.

The question often arises: do the principles of T'ai Chi actually work in a fighting context? It is not easy to find the truth of the matter if one only relies on the legendary stories of T'ai Chi masters, which often assume mythic proportions. One believable story is told by Robert Smith, a man well-versed in the "harder styles" of the fighting arts. Smith, who became Cheng Man Ch'ing's student in the late 1950's, was invited to attack Cheng, and this is his description of what happened:

"Informal and friendly it should have been, but frightening is what it actually was. Against that there was no defense. I am certain that no one has ever been struck more quickly and often in such a short span of time. Fortunately, he put little energy into the strikes." [21]

Summary

Under the influence of the Yang family, T'ai Chi became well-known in China. After Yang Lu-shan left the Ch'en family for

Peking, the center of Chinese culture and politics, he became the martial arts instructor for members of the royal family and other well-connected aristocrats. Later, he also began to teach openly to all who wished to learn. This was a revolution for not only T'ai Chi but for Chinese martial arts in general, where secrecy had provided a sense of security in a lawless society.

In the twentieth century, the Chinese were undergoing a period of reappraising their traditions in light of Western ideas, which many feared would overwhelm Chinese culture. One consequence was that Chinese martial arts began to be practiced openly. They were viewed as something positive and tangible, and a source of pride for the Chinese people. From the 1920s onward, T'ai Chi benefited from this positive sentiment and grew in leaps and bounds, and it continues to do so today, being influenced by numerous teachers from various traditions. Although relatively young by Chinese standards, T'ai Chi has established itself as one of the most important contemporary techniques of self-cultivation. Today the original Ch'en style is being "rediscovered" and a number of offshoots from the popular Yang and Wu styles are flourishing in both the East and the West.

The marriage of Chinese philosophy and martial arts that gave birth to T'ai Chi Ch'uan was a stroke of genius on the part of the Chinese people. It was somewhat surprising that such diverse elements could find one another and create a multi-faceted system of movement that is unique, iconoclastic, and ultimately practical, not only in terms of martial arts but also regarding a wide range of human development. In surveying the origins of T'ai Chi one is left with the distinct impression that it could have only been created in China. Most martial arts systems employ the notion of Yin and Yang, techniques of meditation, and methods of training the Ch'i. What separated T'ai Chi from the other schools is that its founders took Lao Tzu literally:

"Under heaven nothing is more soft and yielding than water.
Yet for attacking the solid and strong, nothing is better.
It has no equal.
The weak can overcome the strong;
The supple can overcome the stiff.
Under heaven everyone knows this,
Yet no one puts it into practice." [22]

Lao Tzu had to wait something less than two thousand years for someone to put his ideas into practice. Today his words echo through every T'ai Chi school, in every session of push-hands, in the quiet thoughts of every serious student of T'ai Chi.

T'AI CHI CH'UAN AND PUSH-HANDS: THE FORM AND THE FORMLESS

One of the most intriguing aspects of T'ai Chi is that it can represent something quite different to different people, and even something different to the same person from one moment to the next. For some, it might be the supreme system of self-defense. Another's fancy, especially lovers of movement, might be drawn by T'ai Chi's dancelike qualities. Yet another may seek better health or peace of mind. Today, T'ai Chi is an art for all seasons and, as such, the sum of its parts are seemingly greater than the whole.

Until now, we have focused on the content and development of Chinese culture and philosophy and how T'ai Chi grew out of it. With that as a basis, we can now change our approach. Let us turn our attention to the nature of T'ai Chi and to how Chinese culture is reflected in its ideas and practices. In this chapter the T'ai Chi "form" and the exercise called "push-hands" will share the spotlight and move to center-stage.

The Form

Imagine that one day, early in the morning, you go for a walk and find yourself in a lovely park with open spaces embroidered with many groves of large trees, bursting with the green leaves of spring. To your left, a man is throwing a ball for his dog. The dog, little and wiry, ferociously chases down the ball and retrieves it for his master. You watch for a moment and then you notice that there are paths that zig this way and that. You follow one and come to a hollow surrounded by bushes which opens onto a small pond. Birds are singing. Occasionally fish breech the waters of the pond. Near the water's edge, you see a weathered, wooden bench. You sit down. Directly in front of you, a willow tree catches your eye, its branches and leaves painting impressionist shadows on the brownish, still pond. For some reason, the willow's thick, twisted trunk grows almost parallel to the ground and then, suddenly and gracefully, the tree soars skyward, its sinewy branches softly swaying in the morning breeze.

In a small, flat grassy area, slightly in front of you and to your right, a man of average size appears and stands facing the pond. There is nothing unusual about him; except that his bearing is plumb erect, his gaze straight ahead, and his feet form a 'V,' heels touching. You sense a purposefulness in the way he is standing. No one naturally stands that way. He does not seem carefree or unintentioned in contrast to the way you feel. He does not acknowledge you, and it is clear that this is his special place. He must come here regularly. As he holds his unusual pose, he radiates a relaxed, meditative stillness, practiced, but not for effect. Whatever he is doing, it is not for you anymore than it is for the fish or the birds. Today you happen to be sitting near his "place." Watching him, and trying not to be too indiscreet, you wonder, what will be?

He stands in his quiet pose for several minutes. What is so unusual about this moment? You feel as though your world has suddenly quieted down. The predictability of your everyday rhythms has collapsed. Little changes catch your attention. The occasional song of a bird seems clearer than before. The dew drips from the willow's leaves onto the pond. Little ripples form and sail away. You feel slightly uncomfortable, like an unwanted intruder, and you wonder if you should leave. Perhaps you feel some indignant resentment that he has changed the mood, your mood. After all, you were here first. Perhaps it bothers you that he can affect you without even lifting a finger. Yet his stillness has somehow enabled you to hear the song of the birds and the softness of the breeze in a way that is more pronounced and clear. You reconsider your resentment. Your mind, which an instant before was cluttered with thoughts, is slowing down and focusing. You like that; along with his uncanny ability to do absolutely nothing but stand and profoundly influence the world around him.

So there he remains, relaxed and unperturbed, like a statue that lives. For, despite his stillness, you can see the gentle heaving of his chest and back, expanding and contracting with the even rhythm of his breath. Occasionally you notice his eyes blinking and his body gently rolling back and forth on the bottoms of his feet. Then, purposefully, he sinks into his right foot while his body remains erect. He moves slowly and deliberately — he appears to glide in slow motion. He steps to the side with his left foot, shifts his weight, and turns to the right. Then he turns back to the center, his weight now evenly distributed. As he straightens his knees, his arms, with relaxed wrists, begin to float upwards like clouds across the sky or like a bubble drifting to the water's surface. You are fascinated by the fluency of his movements. You have the sense that his body is bereft of bones and flesh and is composed of water, flowing and floating in the air. He moves in perfect, exquisite harmony.

He sinks his weight into his left foot and simultaneously turns to the right, his hands now parallel as if they were holding a ball. When he steps out with his right foot, you notice how gently it touches the ground; so soft and delicate that the dewy turf might be thin ice that he is testing as he gradually bears his weight down upon it.

It occurs to you that he has done these movements many times before, hundreds, perhaps thousands. He is too deliberate, too intentional, to be spontaneous. Yet there is a quality of suppleness and pliability that leaves the impression, if not the certainty, that he is totally free. He is willowy like the branches of the willow tree in front of you, yet solid and rooted like its trunk. He is graceful like a dancer but this is no dance that you have seen before. You are struck by the clarity of each movement as his body cuts through the air like a knife. Throughout, his face remains calm, yet intent like a cat stalking its prey.

Watching him, you wonder if you could do what he is doing.

Snake creeps down.

He begins to form postures that seem more difficult. As he shifts his weight back, his backside drops down, almost touching the ground. Then moving forward, he presses his weight onto his front foot, while lifting the knee of the back foot to the height of his solar plexus. He is standing on one leg, perfectly balanced.

Later, he stands on one leg and kicks with the other, his arms rounded and opening like a flower in full bloom. You see the self-defense application, an obvious kick or strike with the hand, but you wonder, 'why so slow?' What is the purpose of his dance?

As questions crowd your thoughts, he finishes the same way he began, his feet forming a 'V' and his body standing plumb erect. You want to talk to him, but you feel intimidated. After a moment or two, lingering in quiet solitude, he turns and walks away, disappearing along the meandering path that makes its way through thick bushes and stately stands of towering trees. You feel enriched yet incomplete. And you wonder, what was that all about? What a strange and wonderful way to start the day!

The Meaning is in the Mind of the Beholder

T'ai Chi can be understood in a myriad of ways. Two people performing the T'ai Chi sequence may look similar, yet may experience very different things. T'ai Chi is an "internal" art and each person internalizes something different from it. While the vast majority of people practicing T'ai Chi today are interested in its health benefits, there are many who are concerned with becoming one with Tao, learning T'ai Chi as self-defense, or developing the ability to concentrate while moving. It is possible to attain all of these objectives through T'ai Chi.

Someone might practice Taoist yoga techniques to achieve union with the Tao and better health. Another person might seek to become an expert in self-defense while also improving his health. An actor might study T'ai Chi to improve his powers of concentration and to be more graceful in his movement. T'ai Chi is eminently practical and can be used as an effective tool in almost every aspect of one's life. Precisely because it is an internal art with an emphasis on understanding who we are as human beings, it can have a profound influence on anyone whose inclination is to go beyond the surface meaning of things.

Keeping this in mind, our mythical T'ai Chi man might have been practicing certain breathing techniques to circulate the Ch'i throughout his body's meridians for better health. He might have been developing a deeper root and strengthening his legs. He might have been working on self-defense techniques by visualizing attacking and yielding to an imaginary opponent with each movement of the form. Then, too, he might be on a high level of meditation where he can actually feel one with Tao. Of course, he might have been thinking about the fight he just had with his wife or what he planned to eat for breakfast.

In T'ai Chi the mind is the message. The most important benefits of T'ai Chi will be determined by one's intention as well as the effort one is willing to devote to its fulfillment.

The Idea of Tao and T'ai Chi

The great philosophers of China believed that ultimate truth resided in Tao which is nameless, unknowable, indefinable, undifferentiated and eternal. Tao was often symbolized by Wu Chi and T'ai Chi, and characterized as emptiness and the void. From within this apparent emptiness, Tao contained the potential for creating form through the movement of Yin and Yang. Although these ideas are perhaps best demonstrated in Chou Tun-i's Diagram, they are much older than Chou's explanation, being traceable to the furthest recesses of Chinese antiquity.

In Chinese thought, human beings stand at the center of the universe and are the meeting-place of Heaven and earth. Each person, while being a separate part of the cosmic whole, contains Tao within him or her. Through the personal cultivation of one's deepest intuition, the seeker could glimpse and even unite with the nameless source of all things — Tao. At the highest levels of T'ai Chi, and with the help of various methods of spiritual cultivation, this union of man and Tao could be consummated. It is possible that, while doing the form, our T'ai Chi man was in pursuit of the elusive Tao. The Yang family described these aspirations thusly:

"When one can magnify the tao by means of man, and know that the tao is not apart from man, then we can begin to discuss the unity of Heaven and earth. Heaven is above and earth below; man occupies the center. If one can explore the Heavens and examine the earth, unite with the brightness of the sun and the moon, be one with the five sacred mountains, the four great rivers, prime and decline, and the alternation of the four seasons, participate in the flowering and withering of the trees and grasses, fathom the fortunes of ghosts and gods, and understand the rise and fall of human events, then we can speak of Ch'ien and K'un (triagrams of the I Ching) as the macrocosmic Heaven and earth and man as the microcosmic Heaven and earth." [1]

Human beings are here viewed not only as the creators of harmony between heaven and earth, but also as mirrors in which Tao is revealed in the cosmos. These ideas are common and pervasive to Eastern philosophies and traditional societies. They are less acceptable to the scientific, positivist modes of modern Western thinking. "Traditional man knew that the world is one," explains Edward Goldsmith, "that it is alive, orderly and hierarchically organized, and that all living things that inhabit it are closely interrelated and cooperate in maintaining its integrity and stability." [2]

In Western religions a similar chord was struck; man is made in the image of God, suggesting that man is a microcosm in which it is possible to glimpse, and for mystics, to unite with the macrocosmic God.

Clearly, the Yang family considered its art of T'ai Chi in a larger context than merely as a self-defense technique, as physical exercise or as an elixir to better health. The Yang family viewed T'ai Chi as a spiritual quest of the highest order. This was not to denigrate the other benefits of T'ai Chi, of which the Yang family were well aware. Rather they understood the larger potential of T'ai Chi and wished to secure its rightful place under the umbrella of Chinese culture and wisdom.

T'ai Chi provides the opportunity for people to broaden horizons far beyond what they probably thought possible. In the loftiest of realms we are speaking of T'ai Chi as an "art" that approaches the intensity of a religious experience. In this context T'ai Chi is a discipline whose purpose is to aid the modern seeker in rediscovering the inherent harmony of the universe and his or her place in it.

From what we have learned about Chinese philosophy, it is not surprising that the Yang family would integrate the idea of bodily movement and the concept of Tao. This represented the highest level of spirituality where body, mind, family, community, country, world, and universe become one.

T'ai Chi Artist, T'ai Chi Warrior

T'ai Chi was born in the context of self-defense and was called a 'martial art.' This suggests that the practitioner viewed him or herself as a warrior as well as an artist. In China the artist sought to express the nature of the world, which was understood as the harmonious interplay of the dynamic forces of Yin and Yang. The world was not an expression of the artist's ego (at least not flagrantly), but rather the artist strove to be a tool with which the natural harmony of Tao could be evoked. This naturalness occurred because a profound awareness of Tao had been awakened in the consciousness of the artist. As a result, the "true" reality of things emerged out of his or her art.

Like the painter or poet, the martial artist knew that to reach the highest levels of his martial abilities, he must become profoundly sensitive to the primal source of the universe — the eternal Tao. Ultimately he sought to unite his mind with Tao in mystical union. The logic of being a martial artist was that, if the warrior becomes one with the universe, he knows the opponent inside and out. The founder of Aikido, Morihei Ueshiba, explained it as follows:

> "Regardless of how quickly an opponent attacks or how slowly I respond, I cannot be defeated... As soon as the thought of attack crosses my opponent's mind, he shatters the harmony of the universe and is instantly defeated regardless of how quickly he attacks. Victory or defeat is not a matter of time or space." [3]

Ueshiba's words are a radical statement of the power of harmony and would probably find favor in the minds of many martial artists, although only the most accomplished would be able to translate them into action. For the artist of T'ai Chi, the body and mind are the paintbrush or pen with which, in the act of creation, to unite with ultimate reality. Again, in the words of the Yang family:

> "The whole universe is one great T'ai-chi; the human body is a small T'ai-chi. The human body being the essence of T'ai-chi, one cannot but practice the Great Ultimate Martial Art [T'ai-chi Ch'uan]. It is an inborn sensitivity which must be retrained, an innate abililty." [4]

Just as we carry the genes of our mother and father and all the generations before them, so each of us carries Tao itself within our being. The Chinese would say that every living thing is a reflection of Tao. The goal of the "seeker" is to rediscover his or her "original" self, thereby becoming one with the universe and, by extension, one with Tao. The means of fulfilling this quest is the mastering of whatever art one chooses. It makes no difference which art form it is; whether painting, flower arranging, T'ai Chi or something as mundane as sweeping the temple grounds.

T'ai Chi was a martial art particularly receptive to this kind of thinking because it emphasized the internal power within the person. Not brawn or technique, but mind, softness, sensitivity, flow, yielding, and suppleness were a few of the qualities cultivated in T'ai Chi. These ideas, while not Tao itself, reflected the way in which Tao revealed itself in the world.

T'ai Chi and Health

While people choose to learn T'ai Chi for many reasons, for most, the strongest motivation is to improve one's health. This is true in the East as well as the West. For the Chinese, the origins of their medical practices date back to *The Yellow Emperor's Classic of Internal Medicine* in which the balancing of Yin and Yang plays a crucial role in maintaining health:

> "Yin stores up essence and prepares it to be used; Yang serves as protector against external danger and must therefore be strong. If Yin is not equal to Yang, then the pulse becomes weak and sickly and causes madness. If Yang is not equal to Yin, then the breaths which are contained in the five viscera will conflict with each other and the circulation ceases within the nine orifices. For this reason the sages caused Yin and Yang to be in harmony." [5]

The Classic continues in this vein, emphasizing the importance of harmonizing the entire body. According to Chinese medical theory, Ch'i is the body's internal energy or vitality that, when flowing naturally, brings Yin and Yang into harmony. If a blockage occurs in the Ch'i meridians or pathways that nourish the liver, for example, there are bound to be problems with that organ — an imbalance of Yin and Yang. The symptoms could express themselves in many different ways and not necessarily in the area of the liver. As an internal exercise, T'ai Chi, through movement, meditation, and visualization, seeks to open any blockage of the meridians, so that the Ch'i can flow unimpeded and thereby bring the body back into harmony.

Let us return to our T'ai Chi man. As he stands motionless before beginning the form, he is quieting his mind and focusing his Ch'i in the tan tien, just below the belly button. He may employ techniques of visualization by imagining that the Ch'i is golden light, growing and expanding in the area of his tan tien. The underlying principle of this type of meditation is that the Ch'i follows the mind. If he wants the Ch'i to concentrate in his tan tien, then he directs it there with his mind's inner eye. In order to do this, he has probably spent many hours in sitting meditation, practicing the art of directing his Ch'i. After learning to focus his Ch'i in the tan tien, he probably advanced to the stage of guiding it from the tan tien to various points around his crotch, up the spine, over the head, down through the throat and chest, and finally returning to the tan tien. This is called the "small heavenly cycle" or the "microcosmic orbit." Once he becomes proficient at the "orbit," then he can guide his Ch'i at will through the meridians and through his entire body. He need not limit himself to the meridians. He might focus on a particular area or organ that requires healing.

Once our T'ai Chi man begins to move, he can harmonize the Ch'i with his mind throughout the changing flows of each posture. He remains relaxed, open, and loose, not only externally, but internally, so that the Ch'i can flow naturally and freely throughout his body like a great river. He might visualize, for example, that, as his arms float upwards, he sends a continuous golden light of Ch'i from his tan tien, through his arms, and to the tips of his fingers. Moreover, if he were working on self-defense he might imagine that he can project his Ch'i energy outside of the body and onto an opponent. Often the same techniques, with slight modifications, can be utilized for different purposes, like health or self-defense.

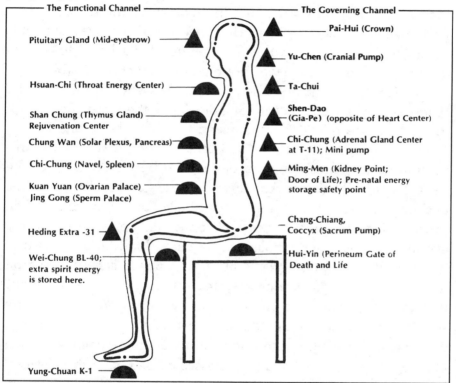

Small heavenly cycle or microcosmic orbit.

When doing T'ai Chi, one must concentrate the mind on the movements in order to perform them correctly — with relaxation, ease, flow, and continuity. This helps to still the mind. The quieter the mind becomes, less tension exists in the body, which promotes the equilibrium of Yin and Yang. When the mind is tranquil yet still alert, the body can function at peak efficiencies.

The implications of this idea are extremely significant for better health.

According to the Fight-or-Flight response, early man often experienced tension such as a threat from a wild beast. His heart and blood pressure rose dramatically as blood was pumped into his muscles and brain, away from his digestive tract. His breathing became faster in order to bring oxygen to the muscles, preparing them to fight or flee. But once the threat was over, his parasympathetic nervous system helped his body to return quickly to normality. He was not burdened by chronic stress.

In Western medicine a new branch has been born with the long name of psychoneuroimmunology. As the word suggests, it focuses on the relationship between the mind/body and illness. Modern Western society is filled tension. For many of us, this tension accumulates day after day until it becomes chronic. We have the same responses to danger or stress as our early cousins, but unfortunately, it is often daily rekindled and maintained. The pressures in the work place may never let up. Chronic stress eventually causes serious illnesses such as high blood pressure, heart disease, ulcers, and many others. Stress seems to inhibit the response of the immune system. There is recent evidence that some cancers are permitted to grow by a depressed immune system that cannot clean out the cancer cells.

The stilling of the mind and the meditative qualities of T'ai Chi counteract the debilitating illnesses caused by chronic stress. From personal experience, I have begun my practice of T'ai Chi in a state of anxiety, agitation or anger and have finished with a totally different attitude. Stilling the mind and focusing on the form create a temporary "time-out" which allows things to settle into perspective, like silt in a stirred-up puddle sinking to the bottom. Once the anger is calmed, it is easier to deal with problems in a composed and clear manner. If our T'ai Chi man had an argument with, say, his wife, we can imagine that, when he returned home, he would deal with their disagreement more effectively than he would have in the heat of the argument. T'ai Chi is a strong antidote for the underlying hysteria of chronic stress.

As a physical exercise, T'ai Chi stimulates the immune system, which of course is essential to stay healthy. The body needs exercise. The Chinese say that if the body does not exercise, it becomes like a stagnant pond that breeds disease. They also say that the hinge on a door becomes rusty and unusable if the door is not opened regularly. There is much wisdom in these sayings. Our immune system does not have a pump, like the heart, to cause its fluids to flow throughout the body and thereby destroy dangerous invaders. The squeezing of the muscles together, something like getting toothpaste out of a tube, is what drives the fluids of the immune system. In other words exercise is absolutely crucial in order to stay healthy.

While there are many forms of exercise that stimulate the immune system, T'ai Chi is unique in its approach. How does T'ai Chi do it? First, T'ai Chi softens and the opens the body which allows all the fluids to flow more freely. Also, the sinking of all the weight of the body onto one leg or the other has a profound impact on the entire body. When done properly, at the end of a half hour or so, one definitely feels that his or her body is getting a workout. One can imagine that the sinking of the weight forces the fluids to flow throughout the body, similar to an air pump that forces air out the hose when you push down on the handle.

In a article in the journal *T'AI CHI,* Dr. Wen Zee, a retired cardiologist and Wu stylist from Shanghai, reported the findings of a study on T'ai Chi and the immune system. [6] The Wu Style Association of Shanghai carefully chose ten people with an average age of 70. The oldest of the group was 93 and the youngest was 56. All of the subjects had practiced T'ai Chi for over 20 years. Four cc. of blood was taken before they began the form, immediately after, and then two hours later. Their study revealed that the "average activating natural killer cells (of the immune system) were higher than in the average young person." Moreover, the amount of killer cells increased after practice and then returned to their previous level after two hours. Dr. Zee admits that his report is "preliminary," yet studies like this are encouraging.

Exercise that stresses intense physical exertion can tear down the immune system. One feels the need to rest afterwards. In contrast, following a T'ai Chi workout, most people feel more energy and a clear sense of physical and mental invigoration. T'ai Chi does not cause the body to be overly stressed and injuries rarely occur. For people who have physical limitations, T'ai Chi can be an ideal way to keep fit without the fear of re-injuring a weakened area, depending of course upon what the problem is.

T'ai Chi can also benefit the sport enthusiast; that is, one who is not hindered by serious, physical limitations. Aside from learning how to better utilize one's powers of concentration, one learns from T'ai Chi certain principles of body mechanics such as — "the power of the body is developed from the legs and controlled by the waist." Not merely the strength of the arms or the shoulders, but total body unity and power are the practical designs of this T'ai Chi principle. If we take the example of a tennis player, we can see how this principle might be learned from the slow pace of the form and then transferred to a player's stroke. When the player hits the ball with his racket, he propels it with the full force and attention of his entire being. In baseball, golf, and boxing as well as in other sports, the athlete's power and concentration are magnified far beyond what is considered "normal."

The world of sports is witnessing the explosion of Chinese athletes breaking world records. This is due, in large part, to Chinese training methods, which are based on traditional Chinese medical practices — from which T'ai Chi comes — as well as to advances of modern, Western ideas in sport. The Chinese have a wide knowledge in both and are not averse to applying them in practical ways.

There are many other ways that T'ai Chi promotes health. Among the elderly, for example, it teaches balance and equilibrium. This instills confidence in their ability to walk without falling and to lead normal lives. Dr. Stephen Wolff of Emory University has been conducting a major study in this regard and his findings are confirming T'ai Ch'i's benefits for the elderly.

T'ai Chi and Eastern techniques of self-cultivation seem tailor-made as methods of self-help for better health and improving the quality of life. But, like most things of value, learning T'ai Chi requires physical exertion, daily practice, and perseverance. Ma Yueh Liang, one of the Grand Masters of T'ai Chi, now over ninety, said that it took him ten years to discover Ch'i and another thirty years to learn how to use it. He was, of course, speaking of the highest levels of T'ai Chi. He added that even one who has practiced only three months can begin to accrue benefits. But one must begin. Your health is your greatest inheritance. Only you can preserve it.

T'ai Chi as a Discipline

Before one can reap the benefits of T'ai Chi, the student must take the learning of it seriously. T'ai Chi is an art that requires discipline, hard work, perseverance, and patience. The students who are most successful are the ones who attend class and practice the form regularly. The ideal criteria for success are completing the form, being able to do it correctly, and finally merging the form and its principles into a totality of mind and movement.

But there is another criterion for success, equally important as the ideal — that each person who brings to bear the best of his or her abilities will also feel and be fortified by the positive effects of T'ai Chi. One does not benefit from T'ai Chi *only* on the basis of how well it is performed. Doing the form and looking good, like beauty, are sometimes skin deep. T'ai Chi is the art of exploring the vast continent that lies untouched beneath the folds of surface appearance.

Mind and effort are powerful components in the T'ai Chi equation, while talent and natural ability are often of secondary importance. The dropout syndrome is all too common where gifted students — whose interest ebbs or who glide along the surface of learning, never fully giving of themselves — suddenly disappear. For some, untamed natural ability lulls them into thinking that they are blessed with a free ride; but there are no free rides in T'ai Chi. The profits to be had are cumulative, over time, and not measured by short bursts of interest here and there.

There are two central aspects of "learning" the form. The first is "horizontal" learning, which is simply memorizing the movements correctly. This includes learning the correct sequence of the postures as well as the correct positioning of the body and its parts.

Many people, young and old, have difficulty memorizing the sequence of the form and the exact character of each movement. It is not a matter of intelligence. They may be able to commit a poem or an entire musical score to memory, but, for some reason, the memorization of movement is excruciatingly difficult for them. From childhood, their memories were encouraged to map out things of the mind while their bodies received little instruction in the sense of learning how to move with "precision." Learning the T'ai Chi form painfully tries their patience and self- esteem. But if they persevere, the vast majority of these people will succeed. Speaking as a teacher, the triumph of the ones who have had to struggle hardest and have had to tap the deepest place of their will to go on is the most gratifying and emotionally uplifting. Frequently, these are the students most likely to stick with T'ai Chi.

Of course learning the sequence of the form is crucial, for, without it, students cannot practice outside of class. But what about doing the form precisely? Is the goal of T'ai Chi to transform its students into machinelike automatons, golems of their teacher's will? Hardly, especially when we consider the important role of spontaneity in T'ai Chi. Learning to do the form in the precise tradition of one's teacher is like a child learning grammar. Before the child can write freely and spontaneously, or even break the rules as most great writers do, the child must first know what the rules are and then use them as a foundation to spring away and create something unique, yet instinctively being able to return to the basics. Then, too, there is something innately valuable, extremely exhilarating, and personally empowering, in learning something pedantically and finally mastering it. When all is said and done, most teachers, even the ones who claim to be teaching the form exactly as their teacher taught it, have changed little things here and there as experimenting with new ideas enriched their understanding. If a teacher's form has remained absolutely unchanged over the years, then he or she is frozen in time and the form is no longer a live and vital thing.

The second aspect of learning the form is "vertical," which means that students begin to engage the principles of T'ai Chi as they practice the form. Vertical learning, for the most part, occurs after learning the form because it is difficult to memorize a new way of moving and, at the same time, apply the "internal" principles of T'ai Chi. For most people who continue with T'ai Chi, vertical learning is the most challenging. It is an important reason why repeating the form day after day is not boring. The idea of "relax", for example, becomes the student's constant companion each time he or she does the form. There is literally no end to how far one can relax (in the T'ai Chi sense).* Students may work on this idea as an integral part of their daily life when, for example, they ride a bus or sit in their office.

Unfortunately, many students never take the plunge into the vertical or 'internal' side of T'ai Chi. They are content to learn the external form well and leave it at that. This is the point that separates the ones who are bound for a deep and nurturing relationship with their chosen art and the ones who are content to stay on the surface, treading water. Just as there are physicians and there are healers, so there are T'ai Chi artists (martial artists) who sink all of themselves into form and people who merely repeat it.

Reaching one's potential in T'ai Chi requires a superb teacher, memorizing the movements, learning the principles, and hard work, in and out of class. It is a daunting challenge to hold postures to the point of painful and shaky muscles and at the same time to strive to be relaxed, while the teacher corrects other students in the hall. From personal experience, the eternal Tao is the last thing on one's mind.** But this training is a necessary part of the process because the student is learning to master his mind and body. This is no simple matter. It is much easier to be a master of something else than it is to master one's self. In the Bhagavad-Gita it is written:

"Restless man's mind is,
So strongly shaken

---

*See the principle of 'Relax' in Chapter 9.
** I am speaking here of one approach to T'ai Chi. Of course, not all T'ai Chi demands such rigorous training. It is clear from various studies that T'ai Chi can be modified for the needs of many different kinds of people. Dr. Steven Wolf's study with the elderly, which we mentioned above, is a good example of this.

In the grip of the senses...
Today I think
The wind is no wilder."

Genuine T'ai Chi offers its students few short cuts. While the form and the basic ideas of T'ai Chi can be learned rather quickly, years are required to grasp its subtleties. In fact most long-time practitioners of T'ai Chi wish that they had a few more lifetimes in which to broaden and deepen their knowledge. Like all art forms, T'ai Chi is an endless path leading toward an un-reachable goal; Wu Chi perhaps, an ideal of perfection egged on by an iron faith in things that cannot be known with certainty, and, when the unreachable is in our grasp, we see the next hori-zon in the distance and we begin again. We grow because we move; we grow because we are still. If we are concerned with "mastery," that is, doing the best that we can, then the art of T'ai Chi must be approached with the unbeguiled eye of purpose and dedication. The process and the moment — all the steps along the way — are important, not merely the goal. In a workshop, Tsung-hwa Jou, a well-known and venerable teacher of T'ai Chi, put it this way: "know yourself, do your best, don't overdo, a little progress each day."

At some undefined point, which is different for each individ-ual, the student begins to 'master' the form and to engage the T'ai Chi principles in a meaningful way. A continuous dialogue bubbles up between mind, body, and T'ai Chi. It is an exciting time, heady with insight and progress, when the hours of hard work begin to pay off. One can feel the easy flow of movement, the strong root, energy coursing through one's body. The form now expresses something deep within and uniquely of the indi-vidual; a blending of art and artist, a fusion of mind and move-ment. At times the self is submerged in the immediacy of the moment and then, newly invigorated and deeply rested, returns to an awareness that the end of the form has suddenly arrived. Now, to simply stand — "no fight, no gain."

Beginning with the Basics –Stance

For whatever reason one chooses to learn T'ai Chi, be it for pleasure, health or self-defense, the student must begin with the very basics. In T'ai Chi this means stance.

One way to illustrate the importance of the T'ai Chi stance is to liken it to the foundation of a house. If the foundation is not built properly, the house will begin to topple and eventually collapse. Similarly, if the stance in T'ai Chi is not strong and properly balanced, the body will be clumsy during the form and topple at the slightest push in push-hands. If you have ever watched or participated in the building of a house, the hardest work is setting a strong and enduring foundation. The more obvious, external aspects of T'ai Chi, such as flow and definition, can be perfected only after a solid and stable stance has been established. The Classics are very clear on this point: "If the timing and position are not correct, the body becomes disordered, and the defect must be sought in the legs and the waist." [7]

The process of developing a stance is the most physically demanding part of T'ai Chi. Students often find themselves struggling and straining, sweating profusely, with sore leg muscles after class. "Is this T'ai Chi," you ask, "is it not supposed to be the art of relaxing, of flow and effortlessness, like swimming in air?" To reach the place where we can truly relax occurs when we have built a strong foundation, that is, when we feel safe and secure.

A favorite story of mine is 'The Three Little Pigs.' They were safe from the big bad wolf and they could sing and dance only in the sturdy brick house of the "sober" brother who built it with the sweat of his brow.

Flow and Definition

Most people who have watched T'ai Chi in a park or on television can easily imagine that there is form and pattern in the movement. What they probably are not aware of is that T'ai Chi is composed of a sequence of movements that is repeated in virtually the same way each time. In that sense T'ai Chi is something like a mantra that is repeated verbatim with little or no change in the words or phrasing. Sometimes the form is done with a different emphasis because the person who is doing the form is working on a specific aspect or principle, such as trying to combine the breath with the movements.

The T'ai Chi form is like the individual frames of a motion picture. If the film is stopped, it is possible to view each frame as a photograph instead of a movie. Load the frames in the projector, speed them up, and they become parts of a sequence that flow together and make sense as a dynamic unity. Each frame is a unique and yet integral part of the whole.

This idea holds true for T'ai Chi. It would be difficult for outsiders to be aware of the unique quality of each posture as well as its parts because what they see is the continuous flow of the form (though some movements, like a punch, are more obvious). Moreover, each posture in the form has a beginning and an end, which must be clearly shown, even though there is absolutely no change in the rhythm.

As a way to encourage an even flow in my T'ai Chi form, one of my teachers pretended that he was holding a camera in his hands. Every time that I changed the form's cadence, especially at the end of a posture, I heard the word "click." The flow should be continuous and consequently hinder the ability of someone to take a photograph.

The problem of flow and definition is that the student is presented with a paradox: definition of movement seems to encroach on the stream of flow and flow tends to decompose the

clarity of definition. What often happens is that the student of
T'ai Chi emphasizes the one at the expense of the other. If the
flow is overly stressed, then the form is expressed as a mush of
abstract movements; if definition is overly stressed, the form
takes on the jerky quality of a beginner learning to drive a car
with a stick shift. Ideally, the form should be performed with both
flow and definition in mind until they blend harmoniously together and yet maintain a sense of separateness. In T'ai Chi both
the trees and the forest are equally important. This is why most
teachers of T'ai Chi institute a two-fold program of "posturing"
where definition of the individual movements is the key element
and "continuity" in doing the form where flow is emphasized.
The result will be that in time the student will naturally combine
flow and definition into a harmonious whole.

These ideas of flow and definition in T'ai Chi conform to the
Chinese view of the universe. Each movement from posture to
posture reflects constant change (Yin and Yang) and represents a
harmonious, orderly and flowing unity. In this respect, T'ai Chi is
clearly a child of Chinese culture. The major difference between
the form of most students of T'ai Chi and the way the universe
works, according to Chinese philosophy, is that most students of
T'ai Chi, of necessity, consciously direct the movements of their
form, initiating them and making decisions as to their content.
This contrasts to what we learned about Chinese philosophy, and
especially from Chou Tun-i who understood movement as a result of something spontaneous, arising out of the emptiness of
Tao.

Accordingly, if the practitioner of T'ai Chi wishes to reach the
highest levels of his or her art, movement must be allowed to
spring spontaneously out of Wu Chi or the emptiness that resides
inside of every human being who is a microcosm corresponding
to the eternal Tao. The T'ai Chi player must surrender the notion
of being the First Cause and allow his or her body to become a

vessel through which the spirit of Tao moves. The form is not performed but rather experienced. We are the moved rather than the mover. This, of course, is the highest level of T'ai Chi.

The Pace of T'ai Chi

Two important questions are often asked by beginning students of T'ai Chi: At what speed should the form be done? And how can T'ai Chi be an effective form of self-defense when its movements are so slow? In the world of T'ai Chi there is no one speed that is universally accepted. In some forms, like the Ch'en style, lightening changes of pace come and go, breaking the usual slow rhythm. Speed is a relative concept and what is slow for one person might be fast for another. The reason that T'ai Chi is taught and performed at a slow pace is to help the students learn the basic principles of rooting, balance, and flow. They also learn to focus and still the mind with a slow rather than fast pace. Moreover, there is nothing wrong in varying the speed of the form in the midst of one complete sequence or from one sequence to the next. This is not recommended for beginners who should learn one pace before they experiment. In class, everyone should strive to follow the teacher's lead.

There are also fast forms of T'ai Chi that have been developed in order to increase quickness and agility. The Ch'en style has a fast form as a complement to the slow one, which is taught to more advanced students. Also, some teachers of the Yang and Wu styles have developed their own fast forms. In the Yang style this appears to have been a recent development. Yang Zhenduo, a member of the Yang family of the fourth generation, observed that "there is no such thing in the the Yang family as fast T'ai Chi." "However," he added, "there might be a teacher whose preference is to teach by practicing the movements faster." [8]

When students ask how can T'ai Chi be used for self-defense because the movements are so slow, one reply is: "we only fight those over ninety years of age." However, there are some teachers like T. T. Liang and Ma Yueh Liang who are over ninety and they can handle themselves quite well.*

The truth of the matter is that T'ai Chi is paced differently when one practices T'ai Chi in a park or when one uses it practically as in the spontaneous demands of self-defense. Different circumstances call for different responses; like the jazz guitarist who practices scales at home and improvises freely on the stage. The T'ai Chi Classics say that if the opponent moves quickly, then one must respond quickly: if he moves slowly then one must follow him slowly. [9] Here is the Yang family's interpretation of these words, which are a clear answer to the use of speed in T'ai Chi self-defense:

> "At present most of my fellow T'ai-chi practitioners understand the art of yielding but do not understand the method of quick response. I am afraid they would fare badly against external stylists. "Speed" means quickness; "slowness" means to be deliberate. If the opponent approaches slowly, I respond with yielding and following. This principle is very clear. If the opponent comes at me with great speed, how can I use yielding? In this case, I must respond by using the method of T'ai-chi "intercept energy" and the principle of "not late and not early?" (timing and technique).[10]

Spontaneity

We might ask how it is possible to be spontaneous and let the spirit of Tao flow within us when we practice the same fixed form and principles repeatedly?

I pushed hands with T. T. Liang when he was over ninety and found him strong as an ox, with the surprising quickness of a much younger man.

Many people associate spontaneity with doing something new or extraordinary all the time, such as visiting exotic places or making unusual friends. Certainly, being open to the possibility of departing from one's own beaten path is a kind of spontaneity. Yet, when the drive for newness becomes a steaming compulsion for "cheap thrills" or a sleep-inducing passion to keep up with each and every passing fashion, it becomes a frozen illusion that merely appears to be generating motion. This kind of superficial spontaneity is something external and does not touch the marrow of one's spirit. It has no magic or the fire to inspire. It arises out of the mistaken perception — an internal hysteria, a core belief that I am a bore; that I must constantly absorb continual and exotic kinds of external stimulus in order to make life interesting.

This idea of external spontaneity also harbors the false notion that we are the same person, from one moment to the next, and that our lives are marked by continuity and substantiality. We are of course the same living beings with a past, present, and future. Yet this is only one way of perceiving reality. It does not account for the internal transformations spurred on by a deep and ongoing process of change that affect us, often dramatically, whether we are aware of them or not. We are constantly being made new! It is something we will never escape until our death, and even then, it could be said, we are being transformed. Each moment that we experience life, however significant or insignificant it may seem, we are becoming something quite different to what we were before.

Let us imagine that we are lying on a bed in a room that is familiar to us. We can look around and see everything in essentially the same way. Or we have the unique potential to focus our awareness; perhaps to hear the sound of a bird whose song was there before but we never heard, to watch the wild flight of a common housefly, or to marvel at the magical play of shadows on the wall as a tree sways in the wind outside our window. A thought or a realization might come that will change our lives forever. We need only to summon the courage to see from within. Our hidden panic can settle down and be transformed into insight and movement from which genuine spontaneity can spring.

Above all, spontaneity hinges on one's internal state of mind; its sensitivity to life, and how it interprets the constant flow of new input. Spontaneity flows from the center outwards, like ripples on the surface of a pond. It is the cultivation of seeing familiar events, like a sunrise which has occurred in nearly the same way for millions of years, in a new light. Spontaneity takes its cue from a child, whose time-frame is "now". In T'ai Chi, spontaneity is bringing to bear all of one's awareness and spirit in order to engage the form fresh each time it is done. There is nothing easy or facile about true spontaneity because, if a person gives all he has, he is vulnerable to make a mistake, to look silly, or to tarnish a carefully cultivated image. Spontaneity is about taking chances. And, within the context of T'ai Chi, nowhere is one's vulnerability more obvious and one's spontaneity more challenged than in the play of push-hands.

Push-hands

Push-hands is another response to the dilemma of spontaneity in T'ai Chi. The form and push-hands appear different externally, but both derive their inspiration directly from the general body of knowledge and principles that comprise the art of T'ai Chi. However, in push-hands, form is eventually forsaken for the play of spontaneous movement. Push-hands is the spontaneous expression of natural movement — whether in yielding to, or in pushing one's partner. As such, push-hands is a dynamic encounter of motion and stillness, creating its own unique and inherent pattern each moment it is played.

Push-hands is a complex art based on the T'ai Chi principles,

The Dynamic Encounter of Motion and Stillness.
By Ossie Ben Porat, from author's private collection

requiring a book of its own to do it justice. A competent teacher of push-hands can lead the student through the maze of difficulties and false-starts that surround it. The teacher/guide is a crucial element of success or failure. As the T'ai Chi Classics point out: "Missing it by a little will lead many miles astray." [11]

For those who have not experienced push-hands, it might be helpful to imagine that two people are standing across from one another in the T'ai Chi stance. Their arms and hands are moving in a circular motion touching at all times in what would appear to be a repetitive pattern; their bodies move to and fro, weight shifting and torsos turning. Gradually the pattern is dropped but the arms, hands, and body continue to move, this way and that. At the same time, each person is seeking to apprehend what the other is up to. All the senses — not just eyes and touch but something within — are engaged. The partners are experiencing an alertness of total body and mind intelligence. Suddenly one partner pushes the other but the second one yields and pushes back, catching the first off-balance who then falls away. After a word or two on what happened, they return to the push-hand's form in order to begin again.

This is one possible scenario of many that might occur in the practice of push-hands. The above sequence need not stop after one yield or push, but can continue on, depending on the skills and stamina of the two partners.

Push-hands can be more conducive to spontaneous movement than the form because, while both should arise out of pure emptiness, the form has a set pattern which the player always follows. In push-hands anything can happen and often does.

The T'ai Chi Form and Push-Hands

The T'ai Chi form and push-hands are entwined in a symbiotic relationship. The form is a tool with which one learns certain principles. Push-hands is the laboratory where one learns how well those principles have been applied. Through the practice of push-hands, the student soon discovers if he or she has truly "embodied" the principles learned from the T'ai Chi form. When students do the T'ai Chi form, it is as if they are living in an ivory tower that separates them from the challenges and realities of the "real" world. Conversely, push-hands provides an instant critique whose lessons, because of their physicality and clarity, are immediate and difficult to ignore. If students only practice the form, due to the lack of feedback, they cannot be certain if they are doing "real" T'ai Chi or, what some have called, "flower T'ai Chi."

Flower T'ai Chi has many of the flowing and graceful qualities of dance. Indeed T'ai Chi has been called "The Dance of the Warrior." But where flower T'ai Chi and genuine T'ai Chi part company is over the knowledge and commitment to the principles. While flower T'ai Chi may look good externally, in practice it lacks the fundamentals, like a strong stance or internal relaxation. A talented dancer may learn the form quickly and perform it well, but T'ai Chi is not a performance. Moreover, push-hands can often be the litmus test of whether someone has internalized the T'ai Chi principles — no matter how well they may appear to have mastered the form.

Despite the fact that T'ai Chi is often described as dance, it is a very different art form. While they share the characteristics of creating a mood through movement, they do not have common goals. The purpose of dance is to express the artistic feelings of the dancer and/or to please an audience. *The purpose of T'ai Chi is to learn certain principles of movement which may lead to martial art applications, better health, a reduction of general tension levels, and ultimately a deeper spiritual, emotional, and physical understanding of one's total being.* Although T'ai Chi is not to be identified as dance, it has been a source of inspiration for a number of contemporary dancers. Many dance and theater schools incorporate T'ai Chi into their curriculum in order to encourage the development of a deeper spiritual and emotional awareness in movement.

The T'ai Chi form and push-hands should not be separated because together they form a complete system. They are based on the same principles. What one learns in the form can be applied and refined in push-hands. By the same token, what works or does not work in push-hands can be brought back to improve one's form. The form can provide a setting where the mind and body are actively engaged in solving a particular problem, or achieving a certain goal. This process is uniquely creative and satisfying. Musicians call it 'woodshedding.'

A scenario for a "woodshedding" project might occur in this way: "A" is practicing push-hands with "B" who pushes "A" rather easily. "A" might have the sense that his root to the ground is not as strong or tenacious as it should be. "A"'s "woodshedding" project would be to focus on his problem of rooting. When he practices the form, he might pay special attention to sinking his weight into the soles of his feet and feeling the connection of his feet and his entire body to the ground. He might also utilize visualization techniques where he would imagine that there are roots, like those of a tree, extending through his legs and feet deep into the ground. He could also visualize his roots as brilliant shafts of golden light, burrowing to the center of the earth and entwining with its hot, molten core; an energy source, like the sun, that strengthens his stability and supplies him with vitality or Ch'i.

Physically, he might assume a low standing-meditation posture with knees bent and weight sinking into his legs, holding it while striving to stay relaxed, in order to toughen the muscles in his legs. In T'ai Chi, it is crucial to pay attention that, while fortifying physical strength, one does not become muscle-tight or constricted. If this occurs, it would be like winning a battle but losing the war. William C. C. Chen, a well-respected contemporary teacher, once said that, aside from his T'ai Chi training, he limited his physical exercise to carrying his luggage to and from the airport.

These are just a few examples of many methods and techniques that one might employ to bolster one's root in the form and push-hands. Then, of course, after strengthening his root, "A" would want to return and push with "B" again to see if his "woodshedding" had helped, or if he needs to take some other approach to the problem.

Sensitivity to One's Partner

By virtue of the fact that we work with a partner, push-hands is a personal relationship. Each participant must relate to the mood and the movements of his partner. Mood and movement often reflect each other. Just as there are ups and downs in every relationship, there are ups and downs in push-hands (sometimes literally). For example, perhaps my partner has had a hard day at the office. His or her anger may explode with a hard, forceful push, which I must yield or neutralize and lead its force into emptiness. At the instant that the push misses, my partner is most vulnerable to a push from me. On the other hand, a mood of anger may be best countered with the softness of a yield. In this case restraint might be the most appropriate response.

Push-hands contains a wide variety of spontaneous pushes and yields. Rather than imposing hardfast rules and techniques on it, the more open one is to the flow of what naturally emerges out of the interchange, the more enjoyable and productive the push-hands experience will be. As long as one is striving to be relaxed, soft, and rooted — three key elements of T'ai Chi — the spontaneous flow of movement will be stirred and awakened in its own good time.

One Teacher's View of Push-Hands

Uncontrolled and unfocused push-hands, as might be imagined, can be a sloppy and unpleasant affair. It can take on the characteristics of Sumo wrestling — though without the skill of the Sumos — where brute force is the name of the game. This is not the idea behind push-hands. Just as there are gold and brass lions, so there are authentic styles of push-hands that adhere to the principles of T'ai Chi, and there are many look-alikes. Even with partners who have push-hands experience, when ego crops up, demanding victory, push-hand can devolve into a wrestling match.

There are four ways to ensure that students grow from the art of push-hands rather than being torn down by it. First, a student should learn the entire form before learning push-hands. This can take a year or more. During this period the teacher can evaluate the student's character. If he seems too aggressive and insensitive for push-hands training, he should probably continue with the form class or take private push-hands lessons until he is ready. Once a student has joined a push-hands class and proves to be unsuitable, he might be encouraged to have a cooling-off period in order to think things over.

Second, at the outset, students should be taught that in push-hands your partner is your teacher. Each student is encouraged to respect the "teacher" dwelling within the other. It does not matter if there is a large gap in levels of competence or experience. Often, one learns the most from pushing with beginning students. Unfortunately, this is often something that some advanced students seek to avoid, but it goes with the territory. The advanced student was once a beginner who progressed because, early on, he or she was graced with the push-hands patience of someone standing on a higher rung.

Third, it is important for teachers to keep students under a watchful eye. When things begin to get out of hand, give the students a break or have them change partners. At the same time, teachers must be sensitive to the fact that good things sometimes come out of a tussle or anger. Because two partners are not conforming to the teacher's conception of what "good" push-hands is does not mean that, in the end, things will not work out. Sometimes a laissez-faire attitude is the best approach. All human relationships, which contain the potential for aggression and bad feelings as well as love and respect, are complex processes with their own unique, natural rhythms. Yet the teacher may have to employ his or her good judgement, intuition, and experience in order to choose the right moment for intervening. The judicious use of Wu Wei separates a wise decision from an iffy one.

The fourth way to release tension that sometimes arises in push-hands is to buoy the general spirit of humor and lace it with a general environment of playfulness. It keeps a push-hands'

class loose and on-track. Most egos wilt in the friendly light of laughter. One good joke will do more for relaxing a push-hands class than ten hours of relaxation exercises. When there is an atmosphere of fun, trust can begin to build between the diverse members of a class. A sense of humor often encourages an élan of "we're all in this together." And, the truth is, no matter how much you know or how good you are, there is always somebody better.

Here is a list called a "survivor's personality" which sums up one way of looking at push-hands:

*Aimless playfulness for its own sake, like that of a child.
*The ability to become so deeply absorbed in an activity that you lose track of time, external events and all your worries...
*A child's innocent curiosity.
*An observant, nonjudgemental style.
*Willingness to look foolish, make mistakes, and laugh at yourself.
*Open-minded acceptance of criticism about yourself.
*An active imagination, daydreams, mental play, and conversation with yourself. [12]

The road to my present attitude about push-hands was neither smooth nor easy. Some time ago, when I was beginning to learn push-hands, I took a workshop which included push-hands practice. One of the teachers was a very strong woman, who was a little larger than myself. She of course was far more experienced in push-hands than I. At this early stage of my development I had read a lot about push-hands and I knew that one was supposed to learn softness and yielding abilities. Yet my direct experience with push-hands partners had been very limited. It seemed to me that "push-hands," as the word suggested, meant "pushing" and that it was related to the T'ai Chi method of self-defense. Thus, at one point I let go with a very strong and powerful push which caught her off-guard, and I managed to push her, although not nearly the distance that I thought it would. My ego blew up like a hot-air balloon and I asked her, "how was that?" She said very calmly, "It was OK if that's what you're interested in."

Her comment managed to dent a little of my density. I knew it was a criticism, but I was not sure exactly why. I justified myself at the time by thinking that perhaps her ego was bruised. The interesting thing is that this episode and her comment never left me. Over the years, through many hours of push-hands practice, it gradually began to sink in. I am now convinced now that anyone who approaches push-hands (or T'ai Chi) for purely ego satisfaction or reinforcement will never understand the art of push-hands.

The reason for this is that there is a built-in mechanism in push-hands that activates as soon as one expresses fear, pride or aggressiveness. I've witnessed this repeatedly. If students approach T'ai Chi and push-hands purely for reasons of self-defense, their minds become fixated on the applications of the movements. This attitude tightens and constricts their way of thinking, which in turn restricts the possibilities of their physical response. Their flow is engineered to run in a predictable current, similar to what a great dam does to a river. This prevents them from learning the key principles of push-hands, yielding and softness; and even more important, they never learn that movement is limited only by the extent of one's imagination.

If students are afraid, they are not open to the relationship of sharing — which admittedly contains intimacy — that nurtures the learning of push-hands. Insecurity inhibits the surrender of one's self to the possibility of making mistakes, and in push-hands one needs to make mistakes in order to learn. One of my teachers reminded me to give myself the freedom to err. The other side of that coin is to be compassionate not only to others, but also to oneself; to forgive oneself when we do make mistakes. Forgiveness is the balm that allows us to begin again, with vigor. Great progress in T'ai Chi only comes out of a willingness to change, a tenacious perseverance and a deep-seated sense of humility. This is a tall order for anyone, yet absolutely necessary.

If a student is full of pride, the teachings of T'ai Chi will not find a place to make a home. There is a famous story about a Zen master who had a meeting with an intellectual. From the outset the intellectual began telling the master all he knew and chattered away without end. The master began pouring tea for them. Soon the teacup was full but the master continued pouring, and the tea flowed onto the table and the floor. The intellectual thought that this was very strange — that the master was either stupid or clumsy. The master only smiled, pouring as he listened. Finally the intellectual pointed out that the tea was spilling. The master said simply: 'I know.' The intellectual was unable to perceive that he was not allowing any room in himself to learn from the Zen master.

The Power of Push-Hands: Two Examples

Over time the practice of the T'ai Chi form in combination with push-hands has a tendency to balance the personality of people in a healthy, non-invasive way. It is healthy because the process is slow and tends to be self-adjusting. If students will persevere during the hard times or the plateaus, they will generally feel much better about themselves for the effort.

A good example of this process was a student called Orly (not her real name). Orly was very tall, thin, and had a fragile quality about her. One feared for her safety; that she might blow away in a strong wind. But she had a stubborn stick-to-itness that it takes to be successful in any field. She learned the form and began to practice push-hands, something that she surely must have willed.

She clearly felt uncomfortable with the aggressiveness of other students, while she herself refused to express any kind of aggression in return. On the surface, her Yin nature, soft and nurturing, clearly suppressed and dominated any Yang fire that threatened to make itself known. Gradually she began to change. I encouraged her to push with me and other students — that is, to really push — to be more aggressive, without losing her focus on retaining her naturally soft and yielding qualities. Not only did she develop more balance and rootedness in her T'ai Chi form, but she also began to radiate an aura of self-confidence. Her push-hands became quite good.

In contrast to Orly, many male students tend to be overly aggressive and incredibly tight; their muscles and joints deprived of natural free-flowing movement from years of misuse and inhibitions. Soon it becomes apparent that they will not grasp push-hands or the T'ai Chi form unless they begin to relax and soften themselves.

In T'ai Chi this does not mean to become soft like a wet noodle, but rather, as the Classics describe it, to be like cotton on the outside and refined steel on the inside. Lao Tzu put it this way: "Know the masculine; cleave to the feminine." [13] In other words, each person must cultivate a balance between the hard and the soft by knowing the source from whence they come. To accomplish this, we must develop a deeper understanding of who we are as individuals; that we are not only men and women, but each person is a unique being composed of infinite varieties and combinations of Yin and Yang.

As one develops rootedness and flexibility in T'ai Chi and push-hands, their benefits are often felt in astonishing and mysterious ways. Carman, one of my students, is a dance therapist, who was working with a violent woman committed to a psychiatric institution. The committed woman was so dangerous to herself and others that a security guard always had to be present when a staff member worked with her. One day, as Carman was trying to elicit a response from her, the woman began to push Carman in an aggressive way. The guard moved in to protect Carman, but she waved him off. She was familiar with this game from her push-hands experience in class. Carman began to yield to the woman's pushes and playfully began to push back. Carman said that she was smiling as she pushed and the woman began to smile in return. For Carman and her client, this playful game of push-hands proved to be a breakthrough and they developed a relationship of trust and warmth that might not have occurred under most circumstances. Push-hands gave Carman not only a way to deal with her fear of the woman, but also provided her with the courage and the means to move from isolation to relationship.

Confucius, Lao Tzu and T'ai Chi

T'ai Chi is not "this" or "that," as Chuang Tzu put it, but rather it is the interplay between the world of the practical and the world of solitude. This idea was very much a part of the Chinese philosophical tradition, especially among the Confucians and Neo-Taoists, for whom the philosopher/king — the man who is both a contemplative sage and a practical ruler — was revered as an ideal.

The question arises: is it possible to understand the character of T'ai Chi more deeply by probing the influence of its most important progenitors, Confucius and Lao Tzu? If the answer is "yes," then what specifically can we learn about the T'ai Chi form and push-hands from them? Do the philosophies of Lao Tzu and Confucius represent a metaphor for a basic conflict in the life of society and of the individual — the need for order and the desire for freedom? How does this conflict of freedom and order play itself out in T'ai Chi? And how is it resolved?

One could argue legitimately that Confucianism, a rigid and

fixed moral system, most influenced the T'ai Chi form, while Taoism, with its emphasis on freedom and spontaneity, left the stronger mark on push-hands. There is no doubt that Confucian morality became a rigid set of rules and was characterized by the unyielding relationships between members of the family, the community, and the government. Similarly, the nature of the T'ai Chi form is one of definitions where postures and transitions are clearly shaped on the authority of the T'ai Chi written and oral traditions. With its rules, form limits freedom of choice and is based on the seal of some greater authority.

Lao Tzu, on the other hand, sought unity with Tao. He believed that Tao could be experienced through its symbols — freedom and spontaneity. For him, although enigmatic and mysterious, only Tao was real. This contrasted to the artificial, man-made relationships that typified Confucian morality. Thus, Lao Tzu wrote that the man who is not aware of his goodness is truly good, while the (Confucian) man who strives to be good is often not good and only foolish. The man who acts simply, naturally, and spontaneously is truly free and good. He lives according to Tao.

From this way of viewing Confucius and Lao Tzu, we could conclude that the T'ai Chi form naturally fits with the Confucian way of thinking and push-hands reflects the freedom and spontaneity expressed by Lao Tzu.

But it is not so simple. There is another way to look at it which is just the opposite; that push-hands was influenced by the ideas of Confucius while the form is actually closer to Lao Tzu.

How is this possible? Push-hands can serve as a metaphor for action in the real world of men and women, which is the Tao of man. Confucius would wholeheartedly approve of this notion. Indeed, to deal successfully with people on a daily basis, one must summon reserves of flexibility and spontaneity moment to moment. A person might have a "pushy" co-worker, for example, who is constantly acting out in an aggressive manner. Depending on what one hopes to achieve, it is possible to devise a strategy to neutralize the aggressive person. One might want to yield and not do anything, hoping that the problem will go away on its own. After all, the *I Ching* and common sense teach that everything is changing all the time. The troublesome person might be transferred or take another job. Or one may want to yield, catch the person off balance, and then push back. If one chooses this alternative, it is important to decide in which direction and with how much force. The ramifications of an aggressive push can reverberate for a long time afterwards.

In this sense of working in the real world, push-hands reflects the vision of Confucius because one is always in a relationship with others. Conversely, the Taoist monk living on the mountain may be as stuck and inflexible as his brethren in the city. He may be unable to change for lack of challenge or stimulus. From the perspective that freedom and spontaneity are only found within, it does not matter where one is or what one does. Hong Ying-ming, a Confucian scholar with Taoist inclinations, distilled this idea into a few fitting words:

> "When machinations cease, then the moon is there and the breeze comes; so one needn't experience the world as an ocean of misery. When the mind is aloof, there are no dust and tracks from the rat race; so why get addicted to mountains?" [14]

In contrast to push-hands, the T'ai Chi form contains a clear element of being separate from the reality of the mundane world. It is the place where the T'ai Chi student retires to his or her "mountain top" to practice the art of self-cultivation, to meditate on the principles of T'ai Chi, to perfect one's spirit and art, and, ultimately, if one so desires, to seek Tao. For some, the mountain top is the most important aspect of T'ai Chi, while, for others, it is the relationship and interchange which occurs in push-hands.

Yet, when all is said and done, the form and the formless belong together, like Yin and Yang or the Chinese ideal of the philosopher-king. Confucius and Lao Tzu represent two sides of the same coin that are found in all cultures; the call to order and the cry for freedom. Perhaps the ideal in T'ai Chi is achieved when the form and the formless merge and seek their own unique balance, easily adjusting to the changing winds of circumstance. One never knows from where the next push will come or what it will feel like, and thus one must live in the spontaneity of each moment. Push-hands is a paradigm of the natural and unpredictable activity of life itself. It cannot be understood unless the student has rooted him or herself deeply into the principles of the form. Yet the form can become static and moribund if not renewed by the dynamic nature of relationship which push-hands offers it.

PART 4

The Eight Principles: Where Culture, Ideas, and T'ai Chi Meet

CHAPTER 9

THE PRINCIPLES OF T'AI CHI

1) The Importance of Mind

The Awakened Mind

The T'ai Chi Classics are rich in references to the role of the human mind. In this they reflect a fundamental feature of Chinese philosophy — that the mind has the potential to control and manipulate both spiritual and physical phenomena of the world. The Neo-Confucian Chu Hsi averred that the "mind is ruler of the entire person," while the Taoists viewed the mind as the nurturer and guide of the internal energy, which could lead to better health and even immortality. The Buddhists believed that, while the mind could ensnare human beings in the web of illusion, it could also be the key to salvation, because the human mind shared a common nexus with the idea of Absolute or Buddha Mind. Although the role and nature of the mind was in dispute among the various religious and philosophical camps, its importance in human affairs — spiritual and mundane — remained above the fray.

To understand the place and the function of the mind in T'ai Chi, we might turn to a Chinese parable that compares the mind to a driver and the body to that of a horse and carriage. If the driver is asleep, the passengers (desires) and the horses (muscles) will argue over which is the best road to take, ultimately leading to a crash of the carriage (skeleton). Only when the driver is fully awake can he safely steer the carriage and its passengers to their destination.

This attitude and response of the driver is similar to the T'ai Chi approach in dealing with the world. If he uses the reigns to guide the horses instead of whipping them and yet knows when a crack of the whip is appropriate, or if he is sensitive to his passengers by guiding them around the ruts in the road, if he knows when to stop and rest rather than pushing everyone to the point of exhaustion, then we could say that the 'driver' is acting wisely and is sensitive to the harmony of the world.

Only the "awakened" mind is capable of this kind of awareness. One of the central goals of T'ai Chi is to cultivate a balanced sensitivity to both the internal and external worlds. *If the mind is not engaged in both a conscious and intuitive way, or, at the very least, moving in that direction, it is clear that one is doing something other than T'ai Chi.* The implications of this idea are absolutely pivotal in understanding T'ai Chi.

Mind and Awareness

T'ai Chi stresses the use of the mind rather than brute strength. One reason for this is that the mind has the capacity to be everywhere simultaneously. In push-hands, for example, one must be extremely sensitive to every movement of one's partner, not just if he pushes on the left side but what he's doing on the right side, not only how he is standing, but also the character of his posture. The mind engages in a kind of peripheral vision that is aware of everything happening at the same time. The human mind not only has the capacity to assess data and determine an appropriate strategy but it also has the potential for intuitive and instantaneous awareness. Because of this, the mind can focus the entirety of one's conscious and unconscious experiences onto the present moment, and, if necessary, devise the optimal response. In Confucianism, Taoism, and Buddhism we can find references to the idea that the human mind can bridge the physical and metaphysical worlds, albeit they reached this idea from different perspectives. The T'ai Chi Classics put it this way:

"Up or down,
front or back,
left or right, are all the same.

These are all i (mind) and not external."* [1]

The mind can "flow like a great river" to which there is no end, or be sensitive to the feel of energy "like reeling silk from a cocoon." It can plumb the depths of the inner self or interpret the events of the outer world, and it can merge the two, so that the information of the conscious and intuitive minds (left and right hemispheres) can be organized into a coherent picture of reality. The possibilities of the awakened or "knowing" mind are limitless because it can merge with a sense of the infinite or Wu Chi, and thus reflect the true reality of Tao.

An example of the knowing mind's potential for sensitivity and awareness was driven home in a beginners' class I was conducting. We were outside in a park and it was getting too dark to continue teaching the form. I asked the students to pair up with partners and that one of the partners should stand behind the other. I instructed the student whose back was to the other to relax and go deeply inside of him or herself. After a few minutes, I asked the other student to gradually move their fist toward the

---

* See, too, our use of the same quote later in the Appendix where it exemplifies the difficulty of reading the Classics without a guide.

back of the first student. On almost every occasion the students were able to detect the first movement of the fist. When we switched roles, the same result occurred. The students were both surprised and overjoyed at their newly-found skill. It would appear that this kind of sensitivity is an innate dimension of all human beings, and requires only the right method and practice to bring it to the surface.

"I" and "Hsin"

One important problem for many students in reading the T'ai Chi Classics arises from the fact that there are two words for mind, "i" and "hsin," that are often used in different contexts. "I" means mind that contains an idea and is in the process of actualizing it. "I" is the active, conscious side of the mind that is somewhat analogous to the Western scientific notion of the left hemisphere of the brain. We find in the T'ai Chi Classics, for example, "The i (mind) and ch'i (breath) are king, and the bones and muscles are the court." [2] Like the parable of the driver, the king directs his court in the way he wishes or believes correct. Thus his ideas are actualized by his subjects, in this case, the bones and muscles, (carriage and horses).

Another example of "i" is when you are driving a car and you want to stop. The "i" of the mind tells the foot to press on the brake.

"Hsin," on the other hand, means heart, consciousness or mind. In Confucian literature "hsin" had a negative connotation of being weaker than "i" because it was strongly influenced by the emotions. [3] According to Zen sources, in contrast, "hsin" (Kokoro in Japanese) meant "the mind of a person in the sense of all his powers of consciousness, mind, heart and spirit...." [4] "Hsin" is the name for the internal process that occurs when all the forces of the mind — intuitive, emotional and spiritual — combine to give birth to an idea out of a meditative or reflective state. While "i" seeks the actualization of an idea in the physical world, "hsin" is often both the source of that idea or represents the activity of the mind in the process of internal alchemy. This is made clear in the T'ai Chi Classics:

"It is said "First in the hsin (mind),
then in the body."

The abdomen relaxes,
then the ch'i (breath) sinks into the bones.
The shen (spirit) is relaxed
and the body calm.

It is always in the hsin." [5]

From this we see that frequently the directing work of "hsin" is the internal work of manipulating the Ch'i in the body.* Hsin can also contain the meaning of a certain quality or attitude. In this context "hsin" might be best translated as 'heart.' He has the heart (hsin) of perseverance or the heart of great courage.

Despite the occasional and apparent confusion of "i" and "hsin," what is important here is that we understand the seminal role mind plays in the art of T'ai Chi. This important idea should be a constant companion in one's studies.

The Mind and Self-Cultivation

One clear example of the importance of mind in Chinese thought is found in Neo-Confucianism. The key to understanding

---

Sometimes "hsin" is used in a similar way to "i," "The hsin (mind) is the commander," which is something like the king directing his court.

the Neo-Confucian concept of self-cultivation is that the mind controls and directs the body. Chu Hsi put it this way:

"...the mind is the master of the body and it is unique without a duplicate. It is the host, and not a guest. It is the commander and not a receiver of commands." [6]

The Neo-Confucians viewed the mind as a helpmate and a companion in the search for apprehending the true nature of the universe. Unlike the Taoists or the Buddhists, Neo-Confucians encouraged the use of logic and reason as tools for uncovering truth.

These Neo-Confucian ideas of the primacy of the mind played a crucial role in the principles of T'ai Chi. Only when the mind is actively engaged as the "commander" of the body, is one truly performing T'ai Chi. Cheng Man Ch'ing employs the above quote from Chu Hsi by asking, "Is the host at home?"* [7] Professor Cheng explains that the "host" is the heart/mind which functions in a dual capacity of being both "wise" and the governor of the body's internal energy.** In essence Professor Cheng is saying that the "host" (mind) must be in charge of the body's functions and not the other way around. *In the realm of self-cultivation, both external and internal, the mind must be the master of the body. Externally the mind directs the physical movements of the body while internally it guides the Ch'i and ensures that the proper transformations occur, that is to say, the*

---

* Cheng quotes it from a Ch'an Buddhist source. It is possible that Chu Hsi borrowed the quote from the Buddhists or that Professor Cheng is mistaken in his source. Most likely it comes from Buddhism.
** In Chinese traditional medicine the heart governs the jen meridian.

three treasures — Ching to Ch'i to Shen.

Another example of the primacy of the mind is located in the T'ai Chi Classics which state that "the hsin (mind) is the commander." [8] Again, this is almost a direct quote from Chu Hsi. The idea that the mind is master has a long tradition in Chinese thought and can be found in the writings of the great Confucian Scholar, Mencius (371-289 BCE), who wrote: "The will is the leader of the vital force, and the vital force pervades and animates the body." [9] Here, will — which is one aspect of the conscious mind — is given a primary role in the area of self-cultivation.

The Mind as Ruler

That mind is compared to a ruler or king is certainly no accident. In the Chinese scheme of the universe the emperor had a special and exalted role to play which was similar to the role that mind plays in the T'ai Chi Classics. In ideal circumstances the emperor ruled in a way that ensured the security and well-being of his people. He was the mediator between Heaven and earth, both the leader of the people and the people's representative before nature. It was his role to guarantee that there was harmony between Heaven, earth and man; the trinity on which the cosmos was based.

The way in which the emperor ruled — morally, politically and economically — determined the fate of his people as to the decrees in heaven and the quality of life on earth. Only he could perform the appropriate rituals and sacrifices, and delegate the proper authority to his officials and representatives who ruled the land in his name. In his person the thoughts, perceptions, and feelings of the people found their outward expression. Thus the emperor embodied the "mind" of his people. Just as the emperor protected, guided, and provided stability for his people, so the human mind in T'ai Chi fulfills the same function for the individual.

The mind is the unifying source of each human being's component parts. From the Taoist perspective, for example, it guides the Ch'i to the tan t'ien, and eventually transforms it into Shen. As the mind gradually develops greater sensitivity, an acute awareness emerges that is "inner-directed" because the mind can know itself, and "outer-directed" because it can know someone else. According to the T'ai Chi Classics, by practicing the form each day one can know himself; by practicing push-hands one can know others. [10]

The movements of T'ai Chi strive to achieve stability and harmony because they are unified by the mind's conscious awareness and direction. Like the conductor of a symphony orchestra who brings together all the instruments under his or her direction and creates a harmony of wills, so the mind fulfills the same role by integrating harmoniously one's thoughts, perceptions, and emotions with the physical dimension of the body. This is what Chu Hsi meant when he said: "The mind is the ruler of the *entire* person."

But what occurs if the mind cannot serve as the stabilizing force of the body and psyche? The body becomes awkward and debilitated, and an unstable mind precipitates the individual's loss of one's psychic center, which in turn could, and often does, effect the body's language. The term coined by R. D. Laing "The Divided Self" is appropriate in our analogy of the emperor to the mind. If the emperor is of two or more minds, he will be unable to lead his people with a unified policy that is workable or that they can understand. Instead of peace and harmony, chaos will reign. In psychological terms Laing explains the loss of one's center in this way: "However, when the 'centre' fails to hold, neither self-experience nor body-experience can retain identity, integrity, cohesiveness, or vitality...." [11] This is a perfect example, on the level of the individual, of the old saying: "United we stand, divided we fall."

There is another important connection that can be made between the emperor and the mind. Earlier we spoke about the traditional Chinese belief that the ideal emperor was both a sage and a ruler; that he was a moral and just person who spent time in meditative introspection while also dealing with the mundane affairs of state. Accordingly, we could understand "hsin" as the mind which is more passive and out of which grow the seed-ideas to guide the individual, while "i" is the more active aspect of mind which works to actualize and put into practice those ideas. "Hsin" is the quiet mind of the sage who is a seeker of truth while "i" is the practical mind of the ruler who puts the insights of "hsin" to work in the world.

No matter what level you are on, in T'ai Chi the conscious mind is the key that unlocks the door to greater wisdom and understanding.

Mind and No-Mind

The importance of the "controlling mind" has to be offset by the paradox inherent in the learning process in which one also strives for spontaneity. This paradox is reminiscent of the ideological conflict in Buddhism of whether it is more efficacious to follow the path of sudden or gradual enlightenment. In Buddhism the former eventually won out in the form of Ch'an Buddhism. In contrast, the T'ai Chi Classics, as well as most teachers of T'ai Chi, follow the gradual approach. Yet, by emphasizing control, principles and a gradual process of growth, a learning pattern is established which is hard to break. If one wishes to do T'ai Chi in an effortless and flowing way — which, at the deepest level, means union with Tao — at some point the logical, conscious mind must surrender its power and drive-to-control.* Like most

---

* *Interestingly, the two native Chinese religions -- Confucianism and Taoism -- stressed control and manipulation far more than Buddhism which was rooted in Indian culture.*

entities who have tasted power, it is not always willing to do this.

One solution devised by the Ch'an (Zen) Buddhists to cope with this problem was the ingenious technique of the *koan*. In T'ai Chi it was less easy to deal effectively with this conflict because one is learning a form with specific postures in a fixed sequence. Moreover, because T'ai Chi is rooted in the practical considerations of self-defense, techniques of boxing also had to be learned and experimented with. In both the form and self-defense, not only were students required to perform movements in the "real" world, for example, in push-hands or in sparring contests, they were constantly building on what they had learned. In this respect there was a logical structure built into the learning process. One could only move on when they had achieved a certain level of proficiency, which was determined by the teacher.

Thus, for T'ai Chi, sudden enlightenment was an impractical goal. Only at the very highest levels of the art could one experiment freely because he or she had already learned and "embodied" the principles of T'ai Chi. If the *koan* was the way of Buddhism to attain enlightenment, then various techniques, like push-hands, became T'ai Chi's response to the paradox of mind and no-mind, in the search for freedom and spontaneity.

2) Intentionality

Definition

Intentionality in T'ai Chi relates to the quality of one's state of mind, as it is reflected in one's attitude, will, and character. Here we are speaking of mind as "hsin" rather than "i." In T'ai Chi and push-hands the ego is a constant impediment to growth and improvement. By employing the idea of intentionality, we are endeavoring to limit the influence of the personal ego and to train the human spirit, pruning and honing its rough edges.

In *Zen in the Art of Archery*, Herrigel's teacher points out the importance of the archer's spirit: "Your arrows do not carry," observed the Master, "because they do not reach far enough spiritually...It does not depend on the bow, but on the presence of mind, on the vitality and awareness with which you shoot." [12]

An important part of intentionality is the way one approaches the practice of T'ai Chi, which encompasses everyone from the beginner to the master. In certain traditional schools of karate, it is customary for teachers who have reached the highest level of black belt to don the beginner's white belt. This is symbolic that, despite their great skills, they still approach their art with a beginner's mind as they "practice" its basic skills and techniques. It points to the direct influence of Zen Buddhism on the martial arts, where one must see the world anew at each moment.

The Quality of the Mind

The quality of beginner's mind is linked to the question of character and patience. Far too many students are only interested in finishing the form and moving on to the next stage. They have no patience for the process — which requires much perseverance — and seek only some instant, and perhaps, illusory goal.

Most teachers encourage their students to focus on the quality of their T'ai Chi. If a beginning student performs the first movement with the proper intentionality, it is much better than a student who knows the whole form and does it out of habit and boredom.

But how can a person do the same movements day in and day out, and remain fresh and vital in relation to the form? This is not an issue of doing the external movements correctly, but more a problem of the inner spiritual renewal in daily practice (as we pointed out in Chapter 8). One of the interesting characteristics of T'ai Chi is that you never know what will happen once you begin the form. Your mind may wander to something that happened a few minutes before, or you may experience the exhilaration of understanding a movement in a new way. You may experience nothing at all.

I once took a class with a well-known Rabbi who said something that has never left me: "true spirituality can only follow after delayed gratification." Daily practice often contains much delayed gratification in that it can be hard work, somewhat boring, and monotonous, without any sense of personal accomplishment or reward. It is much easier to turn on the television or to lie down on the couch instead of practicing T'ai Chi. Yet daily practice is the cloth that polishes the diamond. Without it, the pristine clarity of one's spirit is hidden by dirt and grime that builds and becomes encrusted with time. The student who succeeds in turning the drudgery of daily practice into a challenge or play will be the one who masters his or her art. Some even come to love the experience of practice itself. It is said of the great basketball player, Larry Bird, that he was often shooting baskets hours before practice and that he was usually the last one to leave the court.

A favorite question of beginning students is "Where will all this hard work lead me?" The concern implied here reflects a natural wish for a guaranteed result, similar to what one would receive with the purchase of a car or vacuum cleaner. But just as in life there are no guarantees, it is also true in T'ai Chi. Moreover the fact that there are no guarantees can help to build character. The student who studies T'ai Chi must find a well-spring of trust, intuition, and even faith inside of him or herself in order to keep going. This is the attitude of "hsin" or heart; the promethean courage of perseverance.

Intuition is important because, despite the fact that the student cannot clearly state why he is continuing with T'ai Chi, he has an inner sense that this is the right path for him. There is also an element of surrender to the teacher because, if a teacher is qualified, he is probably in the best position to know the needs of the student. Surrender, trust, and faith are, by any measure, positive characteristics of spirituality. The answer to the student's question is that you'll know when you get there and hopefully, by then, you won't care.

Spontaneity and Effortlessness

In all Eastern art forms, as in T'ai Chi, there is no goal to attain. If you have a goal in mind, based on the emotional need to succeed, it is highly unlikely that you will achieve it in the way that you had hoped. In Zen terms, something happens, but that "something" occurs outside of the person's ego and beyond, or despite, his or her rational mind. In *Zen in the Art of Archery,* which has many striking parallels to the art of push-hands, its author, E. Herrigel, asks the Master a crucial question as to how the arrow is shot:

'One day I asked the Master: "how can the shot
be loosed if 'I' do not do it?"
"'It' shoots," he replied.
"I have heard you say that several times before,
so let me put it another way: How can I wait
self-obliviously for the shot if 'I' am no longer there?"
"'It' waits at the highest tension."
"And who or what is this 'It'?"
"Once you have understood that, you will have
no further need of me. And if I tried to give
you a clue at the cost of your own experience,
I would be the worst of teachers...." [13]

And then, when 'it' finally shoots, the master says:

"...you are entirely innocent of this shot. You remained abso-

lutely self-oblivious and without purpose in the highest tension,
so the shot fell from you like a ripe fruit." [14]

Herrigel had to release the arrow "unintentionally." This "effortless" shot took years of hard work to achieve, which is the paradox, the Gordian knot, that is not untied, but cut through by "seeing" intuitively into the heart of the matter.

The notion that "it shoots" is very similar to the idea in push-hands that "it pushes." The best pushes often come in the midst of push-hands when there is absolutely no plan or strategy; you are playing push-hands and suddenly the "it" pushes. These pushes are generally smooth and extremely powerful yet they do not hurt the person being pushed. Instead of a clash of two energies, or force against force, the "clean" push merges with the energy of the one being pushed and sends him flying.* The clean push is an exhilarating sensation for both individuals. Interestingly enough, the T'ai Chi Classics liken the push to the art of archery:

"Store up the chin (internal strength)
like drawing a bow.

Mobilize the chin
like pulling silk from a cocoon.
Release the chin
like releasing the arrow.

One has to be very careful with this kind of push and I immediately catch the person by the arms to protect him from injury. In some T'ai Chi schools the students work with mattresses against the wall.

To fa chin (release energy),
sink,
relax completely,
and aim in one direction!" [15]

But the "it pushes" moment does not come right away. There is a process that most students naturally undergo in which their analytical faculties ride roughshod over their intuitive mind. This is generally a substantial period of time when the student analyzes each movement, whether it be push or yield, trying to integrate these new ideas into their repertoire of offense and defense. It does little good for them to be told that it takes far longer for the message to reach the brain and return, than it does for the fight/flight response of the sympathetic nervous system — which only has to reach the spine before returning to the limbs as an order to push or to yield.

As logical as this process is, it is usually acknowledged by the more science-minded students only to be promptly forgotten! We in the West are both beneficiaries and prisoners of our educational system which is geared to the logical, left-hemisphere side of the human mind. Apparently, as Herrigel's archery master observed, every student needs to go through the experience of long hours of pushing until suddenly, and unexpectedly, "it pushes."

Push-hands and Intentionality

For beginners, one important problem in push-hands is that its practice seems so vague and imprecise, lacking clear-cut rules. They often feel lost and inadequate. Yet teachers know that push-hands is a process that the students have to go through. They can be guided to feel what push-hands is like, but ultimately they must practice until the art of push-hands becomes natural like the falling of a ripe fruit from the tree. Push-hands, like the

T'ai Chi form, involves the "doing" rather than too much talking or intellectualizing. In this respect it is similar to "not overly talking" about Zen, which Master Wuzu observed is like trying to find fish tracks in a dry river bed.

Though the parallel of Zen archery and push-hands is compelling, there is an aspect of push-hands which makes it radically different. In contrast to the art of archery or the T'ai Chi form, in push-hands we are working with a partner. The totality of the push-hands experience is composed of two separate individuals who make up a dynamic and unified whole. The implication of this is that the push-hands experience tends to be more unpredictable and less easily controlled than if a person is working alone. Not only does each partner have to deal with the spontaneous movements of the other, but also in push-hands we are always changing partners, which adds a new dimension of unpredictability, because each person has his or her own unique style.

The nature of push-hands is one of competitive cooperation in that one needs a partner, and cooperates with him or her, while being focused on one's own development. For many practitioners, the goal of push-hands is to perfect the art rather than to overcome an opponent. If competition enters into it at all, it is with oneself rather than one's partner.*

One method that resembles push-hands in the West is the "havruta" system in Jewish institutes of learning called "Yeshivas" where the din of two partners in the study room can be heard for blocks away. The two "havrutas," like partners in push-hands, are engaged in a dynamic dialogue over an oral and written text. Each person is using his counterpart as a sounding board for the validity and truth of his ideas in comprehending the text.

---

* It should be noted that push-hands tournaments have recently become more popular, where competition between participants is often fierce.

In contrast, partners in push-hands are communicating on both the physical and emotional levels as well as speaking to each other. Good push-hands is the sharing of ideas and energy of two individuals who wish not only to improve their physical abilities but are also seeking to comprehend the way energy works in their bodies. Consequently, after a successful push or yield, the two partners usually discuss what happened and how the push or the yield might be improved next time, or if there are other alternatives to what happened. Good push-hands has within it the intention to create an environment in which each partner learns from the experience.

Summary

Ultimately, intentionality is a vision that can lift the student from seeing life as being dull and commonplace to one that is alive with miracles. The incisiveness of intentionality is like a mental laser cutting away the cataracts of the mind.

Nowhere has the power of intentionality become more apparent than in sports and in cancer research. In Russia it has been shown that athletes who put as much as three-fourths of their energy into visualizing the winning performance do much better than those who put more time on physical preparation. It has also been discovered that some people who are seriously ill with cancer can reduce the pain of their symptoms and some can even effect a cure through visualization.[16]

In T'ai Chi, as in probably every field of human endeavor, intentionality is a necessary ingredient for success. Not that each student divines a clear vision of what they are seeking in the beginning. But, with the help of the teacher — who should provide an example of excellence — prodigious hours of effort, one's own inner vision, and a hunger to live fully, intentionality will gradually work its magic. The old ways of habit will give way to new vistas that lie waiting to be discovered.

3. The Idea of Ch'i

We have already discussed many aspects of how Ch'i was understood in traditional Chinese culture (see chapter 6, Neo-Confucianism). Now we will focus on the nature of Ch'i as it appears in T'ai Chi and the Classics.

Ch'i and the Alchemical Process

Earlier we spoke of the power of visual imagery, which led to enhanced performances by athletes or to the healing of cancer patients. For the Chinese, this visualization process was understood in terms of mobilizing the Ch'i. According to this view, Ch'i was a tool which followed the directions of the mind, like the hammer in the hand of a skilled smith. Because it was seen as a source of healing and of extraordinary physical power, Ch'i was often spoken of in terms of miracles and wonders.

At the beginning of the T'ai Chi Classics, from a section traditionally attributed to Chang San-feng, it states:

"The Ch'i (breath) should be excited,
the shen (spirit) should be internally gathered." [17]

Gathering the spirit, according to the Yang Lu-shan, means summoning a meditative state of "stilling the mind." Once the mind is stilled, then one can begin the process of circulating the inner energy, Ch'i, and the alchemical process commences. Exciting the Ch'i in the Classics does not mean merely the inhaling and exhaling of the breath, but it also suggests that the individual's bodily "Ch'i vibrates with (the Ch'i of) the air." According to Cheng Man Ch'ing, there are three types of Ch'i at work in the inner alchemical process:

"First, within the body there is the Ch'i of the blood. It is the most fundamental and maintains the body temperature at 37° C.

Second, outside the body there is the air which enables the breath to reach the tan-t'ien. The tan t'ien is the "sea of Ch'i" and the storehouse of sexual energy. If one cultivates Ch'i for a long time and directs the breath to the tan-t'ien, this causes the sexual energy to be heated and to be transformed into Ch'i. This is the third kind of Ch'i. It is called Primordial Ch'i. This Ch'i not only permeates every membrane of the body, but can penetrate into the bones." [18]

By storing and mobilizing the Ch'i through the practice of meditation and movement, T'ai Chi can bring to bear the healing and strengthening qualities of Ch'i to improve the way in which the body functions. Once the Ch'i of the tan-t'ien is heated through breathing techniques and meditation, then the Ching, or sexual energy, is transmuted into a refined Ch'i (vitality) which can then be guided around the groin area and up the spine to the top of the head where the the Ch'i sinks into the bones and the spine. During this journey, it is transformed into Shen or spirit and the individual achieves a heightened degree of awareness and natural movement. Again from the T'ai Chi Classics:

"When the Ching shen (spirit) is raised,
there is no fault
of stagnancy and heaviness.
This is called the suspended headtop." [19]

The above description is the essential nuts and bolts of the alchemical process which finds its roots in Taoist meditation practices. T'ai Chi was born and nurtured in an atmosphere where these particular notions about meditation were common and accepted. They were readily available and easily integrated into the slow, internal character of T'ai Chi. Moreover, Ch'i provided an explanation of the tremendous power generated by T'ai

Chi masters, despite the fact that T'ai Chi differed from the other martial arts by virtue of its slow, soft movements. The idea was that, with the breathing techniques and the Ch'i traveling up the spine, one tapped of the energy of the entire universe, which could be directed through the arms, hands, and fingers. Thus, T'ai Chi derives its power not from purely martial arts techniques, or from mere physical abilities, but, most importantly, from the primordial Ch'i of the universe. This is the way in which devotees of T'ai Chi traditionally viewed and explained the excellency of their art.

Taoist Meditation Techniques in the West

The question naturally arises: how important are these Taoist meditative techniques to the practice of T'ai Chi? There are many ways of looking at the problem. If the Westerner is interested in Eastern thought, or the background of T'ai Chi, they should at least be familiar with these techniques.* Generally speaking, most Westerners have little connection or understanding of Taoist meditation techniques, and much can be gained from T'ai Chi without them. Moreover, there are some teachers, like Cheng Man Ch'ing, who took a more natural approach in cultivating the Ch'i. He believed that by practicing T'ai Chi with the proper focus and breathing techniques — as opposed to an over-emphasis on manipulation — the Ch'i would circulate naturally and effortlessly without the dangers of injuring the body or one's psychic stability. [20]

Another side of the question is whether it is possible to separate an idea, or a way of life, or a religion from its cultural milieu

---

See Mantak Chia, Awakening the Healing Energy Through the Tao or Dr. Yang Jwing-Ming, The Root of Chinese Chi Kung. If one wants to explore and experience these methods, it is advisable to do so only under the direction of a qualified teacher.

and transplant it to another culture. As far as this relates to individuals, exiles or emigres generally do not accustom themselves totally to foreign soil and often cling to people or groups who have a similar cultural background. In Israel, for example, Anglo-Saxons tend to associate with other Anglo-Saxons or Russians with Russians, although usually not exclusively. What often happens to these emigres is that they basically remain a part of the culture they come from and at the same time begin to adapt and adopt aspects of their new culture. Something novel and unique grows out of the cultural synthesis, which can have both positive and negative results.

This could well be the fate of T'ai Chi, which has undergone great changes in the last hundred years or so, even in its native environment in China. There is no telling what the West's influence will be with its rigorous scientific tradition. Yet we can speculate that the Taoist meditation techniques of circulating and transforming the Ch'i are probably much too exotic for most Westerners to easily accept or have the inclination to practice, although there will be small groups, guided by qualified teachers, who will practice and benefit from it.

Other positive aspects of T'ai Chi, like the strengthening of the body or reducing stress, for which there is both a tradition in the West and an on-going demand, are far more likely to find a home. Cultures tend to borrow from other cultures to the extent that it suits their needs and biases, and T'ai Chi is likely to follow this pattern.

As for the idea of Ch'i itself, it can be a useful way in understanding how people can manipulate their bodies' internal energy for positive results. But the use of Ch'i is not the only way. We could improve our abilities in push-hands by meditating and visualizing the optimum performance like the Russian athletes of whom we spoke earlier. We may even learn from a child.

Dr. Bernie Siegel tells the story of a young child who had a terminal brain tumor. [21] He used the idea of rocket ships from a video game, "flying around in his head, shooting at the tumor." After a few months the tumor was gone. In the world of a child rocket ships destroyed the cancer. For others, focusing the Ch'i may be the answer. The bottom line is that the creative interplay of mind and body need not be confined to this or that tool or philosophy within a particular cultural context.

Breath and T'ai Chi

When considering the possible role of Ch'i in the West, it might be useful to return to the original root of the word, which simply meant "air" or "breath." We not only need to breathe in order to stay alive, but the way we breathe can make a difference in the quality of our lives. Most Eastern traditions connect the meditative state to some technique of controlling the breath. They have well understood that the breath opens the gate to the tranquil mind. If we are to engage the mind and intentionality in our T'ai Chi practice, then some form of breath control is required.

Cheng Man Ch'ing suggests that there are four words to describe the way one should breathe in T'ai Chi: "thin, long, quiet and slow...like drawing the silk from a cocoon." [22] This type of breathing does not seem so difficult to achieve and yet, from personal experience, it is hard to put into practice. We lead such busy lives, taking care of "business" or the family, that we hardly have time "to catch our breath." As an antidote to this loss of one's life (and this is meant literally), each beginners' class of mine starts with a sitting or standing meditation and an emphasis on breathing. The breath should be similar to what Cheng Man Ch'ing described in the above quote. It takes most people a long period before they can breathe both deeply and quietly. If an individual is able to breathe in the correct manner, and has learned to perform each movement of the T'ai Chi form correctly, he or she will have taken a large step in laying the foundations of becoming skillful in T'ai Chi.

4. Relax

A Story

Some years ago, my wife and I were traveling in Minnesota and found ourselves close to the town of St. Cloud. It was here that Master T. T. Liang, one of the first Chinese teachers and authors to introduce T'ai Chi to the West, had supposedly retired. At the time he was over ninety. I called him on the phone and asked if I could attend a class. He graciously invited me to come that same evening. When I arrived, I found only him awaiting me and I was fortunate to receive about two hours of personal instruction. As an illustration of the ability to relax, he told me the following story.

According to Master Liang, at some point early on in his long martial art's career, he heard of a T'ai Chi master who did not teach and lived high in the mountains not far away from where Liang lived in China. One day Master Liang journeyed to the area where the old master lived and asked him to share some of his great knowledge. The T'ai Chi master refused, saying that he did not teach any more. Master Liang decided to goad him into teaching. Master Liang said that he did not believe that he was really a great master of T'ai Chi. Then Master Liang proceeded to show the old man his T'ai Chi form. The old master said that what Liang did wasn't bad. Then he stood and adopted the posture, "Golden pheasant stands on one leg." (see figure 1)

Master Liang told him quite honestly that he saw nothing special in that. The old master asked Liang to feel the muscles of the leg on which of all his weight was resting. Master Liang said that he was astounded by the old master's leg because the thigh and calf muscles were totally relaxed, soft as cotton.

This story demonstrates just how important the idea of relaxation is in the art of T'ai Chi. We can hardly imagine someone in any other discipline, East or West, standing on one leg, his muscles still soft, in order to demonstrate how relaxed he is!

Definition

For the Chinese, the idea of relax (sung) does not correspond to our idea of relaxation as, for example, sitting on a couch and drinking beer, watching television, or going out to dinner with friends. By the same token, it has nothing to do with what we commonly call relaxed like someone who has "collapsed" from exhaus-

Figure 1. Golden pheasant stands on one le

tion. Often in T'ai Chi we see people doing the form who have mistaken a collapsed posture for being relaxed. *In T'ai Chi 're-lax' means that the person is using only the correct muscles for the desired movement. The muscles are activated to their maximum efficiency with no more tension than is necessary to fulfill the task required while the rest of the body remains in a relaxed state of alertness.* Relax also means an inner softening of the tendons and blood vessels, so that the body has virtually no tension, except for what is needed to move efficiently. One of the secrets in achieving such a state of relaxation is the ability to assume a balanced body posture.*

---

* *This will be discussed later in the chapter.*

Sources of the Concept of Relax

One of the main sources for the Chinese idea of relax comes from Lao Tzu and his notion of Wu Wei. As mentioned earlier, Wu Wei literally means 'no action,' not in the sense of doing nothing, but rather of not doing anything that would contradict the laws of Tao. Returning to our analogy of the coach driver, he represents the epitome of Wu Wei in that he guides the horses at the right speed, knows when to slow down, how to follow the road, and to care for his passengers. He responds to the needs of the moment. By virtue of being in total harmony with the natural flow of Tao, he drives in a spontaneous and effortless manner. *The Tao Te Ching* puts it this way: "Tao abides in non-action [Wu Wei], Yet nothing is left undone." [23]

Confucius also accepted and taught the idea of Wu Wei with respect to the example of a certain ruler: "The Master said, 'If there was a ruler who achieved order without taking any action, it was, perhaps, (the legendary emperor) Shun. There was nothing for him to do but to hold himself in a respectful posture and face due south.'" [24] The idea here is not to reduce the ruler to a kind of silly caricature, but rather to allow the forces of nature to take their natural course. Emperor Shun struck a balance by being the center around which all things could focus and thus not swing out of control.

Generally in Chinese thought "natural" man and his inclinations are to be trusted as opposed to "calculating" man with malice aforethought. In Ch'an Buddhism, too, we find that the right action is the one that is truly free and spontaneous in the sense that Lao Tzu used Wu Wei, or as in the story of the Zen master who carried the woman across the swollen stream. As one Zen master put it: "In Buddhism there is no place to apply effort. Everything in it is normal — you put on clothes to keep warm and eat food to stop hunger — that's all."

The key to comprehending the old man's ability to stand on

one leg while maintaining soft and relaxed muscles grew out of a belief that only the practice of T'ai Chi could actualize the following ideas of Lao Tzu:

"The softest thing in the universe
Overcomes the hardest thing in the universe.
That without substance (like water) can enter
where there is no room.
Hence I know the value of non-action (Wu Wei)." [25]

T'ai Chi and Learning to Relax

T'ai Chi offers the tools by which we can learn to relax. Concurrently, by practicing the form, one gradually strengthens him or herself both physically and emotionally. From a health perspective, relaxing the body and mind reduces the stress that is felt by nearly everyone in modern industrialized society. Stress can bombard us from many directions; pressures of family and work, a death in the family or just being lonely. Fear and anger can shape our bodies and the way we walk or talk. We are told, for example, to "shoulder" our responsibilities. Learning how to relax — to let our stressed-out bodies find their natural shape, to soften ourselves by knowing when to yield, to allow the ideas of Wu Wei find a place in our lives — is a major step in improving the quality of everyday living.

From a self-defense perspective, relaxing the body internally allows all the joints to open up. This work occurs especially in the form where one employs the mind intuitively to soften and open the joints in conjunction with physical movement. Through this process of opening the joints, and relaxing the muscles and sinews, all the blocks that have restricted our freedom of movement gradually begin to dissolve and one's energy begins to flow freely — in Chinese terms — through the body's meridians. When one is soft and yielding, he can "know his opponent" while possessing the potential to discharge explosive energy that is not only muscular but also the result of Ch'i. Recalling the idea of water, it can be placid, as in a pond, or a raging torrent breaking through and crushing anything that stands in its way. Water can also have the quality of endurance, like drops dripping on a rock, gradually wearing it away.

According to Lao Tzu, that which is stiff and hard is dead or dying while that which is soft and supple is vital and alive. [26] In T'ai Chi the process of learning to relax is thus choosing to be a "disciple of life."

There is a story of a student who asked his teacher: "what is the most important concept in T'ai Chi?" The teacher replied, "Relax." Another student continued the conversation by saying, "So relax in T'ai Chi is like the root of Western Religion: 'Love your neighbour as yourself'." "Yes," he answered, "but how can love flourish if you're uptight? Love requires openess in order to grow."

So how does one go about learning to relax in T'ai Chi? Another story is told of a student who asked the T'ai Chi master: "How do I relax?" The teacher answered: "Don't have tension!" "But how do I get rid of tension?" "Relax the mind," said the master. "But how do I relax the mind?" The teacher replied, "don't have tension." The class laughed and began work on the form once more.

Here, the individual's will must guide the body until "it falls into place," and relax becomes second nature, something like the ripe fruit falling. One learns to relax by the process of "doing" T'ai Chi and very little comes of talking about it. However, especially in the West, not talking at all about the principles of T'ai Chi can leave the student bewildered and frustrated. What works in the East where students learn through imitation cannot be simply grafted onto Western minds. Cultural differences are real and must be taken into account.

Laughter is one of the most important tools in getting people to relax, as we discussed in relation to push-hands. There is the well-known story of Norman Cousins who was dying of a terminal illness. As a therapy, he began to read funny books and watch Marx Brothers movies. He recovered. Dr. Bernie Siegel reports that after a laugh, "All the muscles are relaxed, including the heart — the pulse rate and blood pressure temporarily decline. *Physiologists have found that muscle relaxation and anxiety cannot exist together....*" [27]

The French poet Hugh de Berze said it well: "...for he who is angry and gloomy and melancholy may well lose paradise, and he who is full of joy and gaiety can well gain it, so long as he keeps himself from sin." [28]

If T'ai Chi doesn't have an aspect of fun, then that person should probably seek some discipline that does. Moreover, if someone is unwilling to surrender the tension of his or her body armor and unwilling to be vulnerable, then perhaps T'ai Chi is not for them. Life affords a plethora of possibilites to choose from. One should seek whatever discipline or art resonates with his or her personality and needs.

5. Balance

The Importance of Balance

One of the most serious problems for the elderly in our society is that of losing their balance, falling and, as a result, being seriously injured. Infants in contrast fall many times, usually without serious injury, as they learn to walk. It might be suggested that one reason the former are often injured and the latter not is due to the soft, supple body of the infant. Lao Tzu asks us: "Can you be as a new-born babe?" This quote serves as the prototype for softness and relaxing in T'ai Chi.

There is a close link between softness and balance. It is important to understand that the more relaxed one's body is — that is, in softness and pliability — the easier it is for the body to find its natural center of balance. The relaxed body allows for the limbs to subtly sink inwards and thus reach a quicker and more genuine state of homoeostasis.

In the case of toddlers they are establishing patterns of communication between the intuitive mind and body, enabling them to move and perform quite remarkable feats of agility that a few days before seemed impossible. As people age and often grow more sedentary, they begin a slow process in which the pattern of communication between the mind and body breaks down. Accordingly, it is generally more difficult to teach the movements of T'ai Chi to older adults. They cannot easily translate what they have heard and seen into physical movements. This problem of communication is often accompanied by a weakening of memory. This loss of communication can eventually lead to tragic results where even the simple task of walking becomes a dangerous adventure.

Through T'ai Chi it is possible for the elderly to gradually re-awaken the natural communication of body and mind, which can re-establish a general state of balance and stability, and restore a sense of self-confidence. To one degree or another, most people take for granted their bodily balance which is naturally seeking homoeostasis. *T'ai Chi offers all people an improvement in their sense of balance, whether it be an athlete of great physical abilities, or an average person simply walking down the street.*

Recently a student told me that her tennis game had dramatically improved, which she attributed to her learning T'ai Chi with its emphasis on balance and body unity.

Another student, a devotee of basketball, explained that his defense had become "sharper" because of T'ai Chi's idea of "previous energy." He felt the offensive player's direction before he actually moved.

Definition of Balance

In general terms balance is a stable condition that implies an equal distribution of weight or the proper relationship of one element or part to the others. One can be balanced emotionally, for example, when the various parts of his or her personality express themselves at the appropriate moment in the right amount, let's say, of love or of anger. When a person is in balance, we think of them as steady and stable and able to carry out his or her tasks in life with authority and confidence. People can also be in balance physically when they are able to perform the basic tasks in everyday life with grace and clarity.

On a more subtle level balance implies the harmony of the "whole" person — spiritual, emotional, and physical — like a musical chord that is made up of many individual notes.

There are many kinds of wholeness, depending on the individual. We all walk, to one degree or another, to the beat of a different drum. My movements on a balance-beam, for example, would be less graceful than a gymnast with natural ability and years of experience in his sport. In push-hands I might also fare a little better with the same gymnast. *In the real world balance and harmony are the dynamic experience of one's being in nature, each moment, seeking to accommodate new and often opposing circumstances. Whether we are aware of it or not, our innate sense of balance is our negotiator of the unknown. How well this innate sense is finely tuned, internally calibrated and functions, determines in large part how smoothly our lives run.*

Cultural Sources of Balance and Harmony

As we have seen, the idea of balance and harmony is deeply imbedded in Chinese thinking. In *The Yellow Emperor's Classic of Internal Medicine* balance is a key concept in the Chinese view of health. When the person's body is out of balance in regard to Yin and Yang, the Ch'i is prevented from circulating naturally and the result is illness. According to this view, the body is constantly seeking a natural balance with the forces inside and outside of itself. The role of the physician is merely to facilitate this process.

The Chinese way of health provides us with good examples of balance, and is familiar to Westerners due to the influence of acupuncture and massage. The idea of balance and harmony is the thread that literally weaves together the Chinese cultural tapestry.

Historically, next to *The Yellow Emperor's Classic of Internal Medicine*, the most important source for the Chinese concept of balance and harmony was the *I Ching* and it in turn influenced Confucius' "doctrine of the mean" (Chung Yung). The "doctrine of the mean" not only exerted a seminal impact on Neo-Confucianism, it also influenced Taoism and Buddhism and formed a bridge between the various systems of thought. The "doctrine of the mean" stressed the relationship between human nature and the Tao of Heaven; that a person could best live up to his or her potential by emulating the natural way of balance and harmony which is the way of Heaven. In the "doctrine of the Mean" it is put this way:

"Before the feelings of pleasure, anger, sorrow, and joy are aroused it is called equilibrium (chung, centrality, mean). When these feelings are aroused and each and all attain due measure and degree, it is called harmony. Equilibrium is the great foundation of the world, and harmony its universal path. When equilibrium and harmony are realized to the highest degree, heaven and earth will attain their proper order and things will flourish." [29]

In the classical sense balance (equilibrium) meant a state of mind before one is influenced by emotions ("pleasure, anger, sorrow, and joy..."), a state which is "objective and impartial" while harmony implied one's state of mind "when emotions arise yet are still moderate." [30]

And what are the characteristics of the sage who follows the "doctrine of the mean?"

"Therefore the superior man maintains harmony [in his nature and conduct] and does not waver. How unflinching is his strength! He stands in the middle position and does not lean to one side." [31]

While Confucius here is speaking of harmonious patterns of a person's nature and his or her moral attributes, the idea of balance and harmony extended to all facets of Chinese life.

T'ai Chi and Balance

Both the moral and physical dimensions of balance and harmony are pivotal in understanding T'ai Chi. There are stories about a student who wishes to study with a particular teacher and is accepted or rejected on the basis of his character references, including the status and background of his family. In traditional Chinese society these factors were considered crucial in determining how well a particular student would fit in.

In one of his talks to his class, Cheng Man Ch'ing explained that the most important point of the "doctrine of the mean" is the idea of balance, and that its influence on T'ai Chi is extremely significant. To be successful in T'ai Chi, he explained, *"has nothing to do with strength and has all to do with balance."* [32] This statement can be understood in terms of developing a sense of moral and physical balance, because, for the Chinese, the one goes hand in hand with the other.

In the T'ai Chi Classics it states, "Don't lean in any direction," — which is practically a direct quote from Confucius — and "stand like a balance." [33] The idea here is that the spine, representing the meeting-place between Heaven and earth, remains "plumb erect." Man's straight spine and his strong stance signify the principle of balance and harmony which unifies the trinity of Heaven, earth, and man. (see figure 2) Practitioners of T'ai Chi focus on the Tan T'ien because it is the center of the waist, and it "controls" the motion. This focus allows the individual to realize both balance and harmony in his or her movements.

Figure 2.

Awareness of our center enables us to move with confidence, authority and grace. The opposite is also true: that being unaware of one's center can lead to clumsy and awkward movements. To lose one's center is to be constantly in search of oneself.

Depending on the circumstances, the search for balance and harmony can be positive in that it can lead to a deeper self-awareness. On the other hand, in the case of the elderly who are merely trying to walk from one place to another, it can often result in broken bones that are difficult to mend. The work of developing balance in T'ai Chi can thus mean something quite different to various kinds of people, depending on their circumstances and priorities. T'ai Chi can and should be adapted to the needs and circumstances of the students.

In T'ai Chi the ideal of the practitioner is to be able to move in perfect balance and harmony from the center of gravity, the tan t'ien. Because one is constantly moving in the form and in push-hands, change is always occurring. What T'ai Chi is trying to nurture is the natural homoeostasis in an individual that brings about a harmonious and balanced adjustment to new circumstances. In T'ai Chi, as in life, we are constantly exposed to transitions at which time we are the most vulnerable. By knowing mainly intuitively but also intellectually where our center is, transitions can become the most interesting and exciting experiences of our lives. Great movement arises out of a calculated risk that becomes so internalized as to be natural to both the mover and the moved.* In sports, like gymnastics or ice skating, innovations are constantly being introduced that a few years before no one thought possible and now have become commonplace in the repertoires of almost all of the competitors.

The notion of keeping the spine *plumb erect* in T'ai Chi has its counterparts in other body therapies of the West, most notably the Alexander Technique and Feldenkrais work.**

From a T'ai Chi perspective, one must keep the Wei-lu point (bottom of the tailbone) and the spine straight in order to maintain one's central equilibrium. But there are other benefits than just keeping the body's central equilibrium. The straight spine allows the "transmuted Ch'i" to flow naturally and unobstructed to the top of the head which is beneficial from the perspectives of both Taoist meditation and martial arts.

In the T'ai Chi Classics Shen is compared to "a cat about to catch a rat." [34] The cat maintains its total awareness on its prey, and does not move. It waits for the rat to make the first move, at

---

* A great example of this is the soaring dunk of Michael Jordan.
** The word plumb is derived from the way a plumber determines whether a vertical line of a pipe is straight. He uses a string with a weight and allows it to fall with gravity. This is similar to the image of the string of pearls.

which time the cat is so fast that it appears to move first and thus catches the rat. In T'ai Chi we call this "previous energy" and it is used in push-hands to anticipate the movement of one's partner. "Previous energy" only works when one's awareness is honed to a high level which, according to the Classics, requires a straight spine and a suspended headtop.

From the point of view of maintaining good health, central equilibrium with a straight spine is also crucial. With the straight spine the body "sits" on the powerful muscles of the legs instead of being held in place by the smaller muscles of the back, which must then constantly struggle against the pull of gravity. Without proper alignment there is pressure on the lower back muscles which leads to lower and upper back pain. When we speak of a straight spine, we are not asking people to straighten their spines in an unnatural way through force or to affect an aethestically pleasing posture. In T'ai Chi the image often used for the "plumb-erect" spine is that of a string of pearls being held from the top of the head, and being allowed to hang in a natural way. At the same time the waist sinks into the hip joint and legs. The purpose of this posture is to facilitate the circulation of energy so that it flows naturally through the spine and counterbalances the effects of gravity.

Proper posture is important in maintaining health in both the East and the West. According to Cheng Man Ch'ing, "any curvature in the body (he was speaking of the spine and head) will increase with age." [35] As mentioned earlier, he recommended to his students that they should imagine the top of their heads hanging from a skyhook in order to develop a sense of the head and spine being in alignment. This is also similar to the image of the head and spine hanging downwards like a string of pearls.

One of the most obvious signs of aging is the curved spine or the head that tilts forward. Even the young suffer from these problems, which are sometimes hereditary, but often the result of poor habits like sitting in front of a computer and leaning forward towards the screen.* I have many people in my classes who suffer from poor alignment of the head and spine and most complain of sore and aching backs. One of the most precious gifts that T'ai Chi can offer its practitioners is a deeper awareness of sitting, standing, and walking with straight spines; necks and heads that are balanced, relaxed, and thus in harmony with the entire body and the force of gravity.

But a word of caution is in order here. The spine should not be forced into an alignment that seems "correct," according to a teacher or some external concept. Each person is an individual and, as such, the relationship of spine and head to the lower body is often unique. If the teacher tries to force balance and harmony, it can lead to catastrophic results. The forced integration of body parts can cause painful flareups in any number of places in the body which at first might seem totally unrelated. Any kind of "shock treatment" is totally foreign to the principles of T'ai Chi. Thus the image of the string of pearls hanging downwards is a way of gently nudging the body to find its own intuitive balance. Sometimes I utilize my hands to adjust the body of a student or suggest they look in the mirror in order to see how they are standing. *Where the teacher has to manipulate the student's posture, the rule of thumb is less rather than more!*

6. Rootedness

The Natural Roots of T'ai Chi

Human beings naturally associate the idea of rootedness with our physical connection to the land and the soil. In the Bible, Adam, the first man, was created by God from the soil of the

---

I know this problem well and am constantly working on sitting straight. If you have this problem, you probably tried to improve your posture while reading this.

earth. Similarly in T'ai Chi a common image of rootedness is that of a tree whose roots descend deep into the earth's soil. This image extends to the practitioner who "sinks into the ground" with invisible roots, so that, after many years of practice, he or she can actually feel as though they were connected deeply in and with the earth. A tree is generally thought of as being immovable by the forces of nature due to its burrowing roots, strong trunk, and yielding branches. The combined qualities of strength and yielding allow the tree to survive in the strongest of winds. As already mentioned in the chapter on Neo-Confucianism, the word "Chi" of T'ai Chi means, among other things, "root" or "source."

This strong connection to the earth — that of developing rootedness — is a potential source of increasing one's sense of balance and harmony. The opposite is of course true: without a sense of being rooted, a person's life can easily become aimless and destructive.

When a person does not have a strong root, he can be easily thrown both physically and psychologically. He cannot survive the strong winds of change and is often blown about like a leaf on a stormy day. In push-hands, for example, someone who is not strongly rooted to the ground will be easily knocked off his stance. This may be applied to life in general in that people must "know where they stand" in order to remain in their place. Like the tree with roots deep into the ground, rootedness implies strength of purpose because one is connected to the land on which he lives or to the historical soil from which he grew. One can afford the luxury of being relaxed in the sense of being self-confident, only after he has developed a strong root.

Spiritual Rootedness

Rootedness can also be thought of in a spiritual sense that relates to cycles and their movement — to use the Chinese terms

— from Yin to Yang and back to Yin again, constantly changing in the dynamic flow of creation and destruction, life and death. Spiritual rootedness does not necessarily imply immovability; the kind of vertical inflexibility that the roots and trunk of a tree can suggest. Rather, being rooted spiritually can be understood as inner fluidity. It lends one the ability to return to his or her "basic nature," which implies tranquility, wherein lies the essential harmony and balance of the universe. In his typically poetic fashion Lao Tzu describes spiritual rootedness in this way:

> "Attain utmost emptiness
> Maintain profound tranquility.
> All things are stirring about.
> I watch their cycle.
> Things flourish, and each returns to its root.*
> Returning to the root is called tranquility;
> This is what is meant by returning to one's basic nature.
> Returning to one's basic nature is called constancy.
> To understand constancy is called enlightening.
> Not to understand constancy is blindly to do
> unfortunate things." [36]

According to Lao Tzu, the natural order of things is that everything has a cycle that eventually returns to its root or source. Because the true sage is always connected to his spiritual root, he has the possibility of returning to his root and his basic nature at will. In that respect he never leaves his root no matter what he does, even if he is called on to administer the affairs of state. If he can perform his duties "morally," as Lao Tzu goes on to explain later, it will enable him to communicate with heaven, which is "to be in accord with Tao." Being "in accord with Tao"

---

* *In Feng and English's translation "root" is rendered as "source".*

is tapping into Wu Chi or emptiness and, to Lao Tzu's mind, is the ultimate mystical experience.

Returning to one's basic nature and one's root engender the qualities of balance and harmony. In this sense rootedness and balance are inseparable, the latter made possible by the existence of the former.

Lao Tzu is saying that rootedness is not merely a physical place that we are connected to. The image of the tree is only one way to think about rootedness. Rootedness is the ever-present source or center of our being, whether we are flying in an airplane or standing on the ground. We need only to connect. Chuang Tzu wrote that: "when the wise man grasps this pivot (another word for Chi of T'ai Chi), he is in the center of the circle, and there he stands while "Yes" and "No" pursue each other around the circumference." [37]

The idea that being rooted is something internal was driven home to me while watching Boris Becker play tennis on television. At one point in a very exciting match, he flew into the air to hit an almost impossible shot that represented the epitome of balance and coordination. His body was in an almost vertical position and had none of the obvious signs of rootedness. Then he put the other hand down to catch himself, somehow jumped up and whirled around to return another volley, which was a winner. It was clear to me that as Becker flew in the air, he carried within himself an internal root which allowed him to keep his poise and concentration under the most difficult of circumstances. The development of that internal root undoubtedly came from countless hours of practice and competition on the court, enabling him to literally stretch himself to the limit and still maintain his "natural" balance.

Rootedness in T'ai Chi

To develop a root in T'ai Chi, most teachers begin with teaching the students how to do the form correctly, as well as introducing techniques of standing meditation. In the Yang form there is an emphasis on the separation of weight which is one way of establishing a strong root. "The motion," according to the T'ai Chi Classics,

> "...should be *rooted* in the feet,
> released through the legs,
> controlled by the waist,
> and manifested through the fingers." [38]

Through the T'ai Chi form, the idea is to teach the body to develop a firm base of support and the ability to move from one place to another in a unified and harmonious way. The feet, legs and waist must move as one unit or the position and timing will be off. If a student has a problem moving harmoniously, "the defect must be sought in the legs and waist." [39]

While doing the form or standing meditation, the student should allow the weight of the body to sink into the soles of the feet, so that the weight is evenly balanced on the floor. In push-hands one of the keys to acheive a good push is to allow the weight to sink into the soles of the feet as one begins to push. This is not as easy as it sounds because often students of T'ai Chi will "hold" the weight in their knees or ankles, which can cause undue stress and/or damage. Moreover, many beginning students float upwards as they try to push their partner. The weight must sink freely downwards to the floor or earth, with no impediments, in order to foster a truly strong root, which is also the key to a powerful push. After a period of time, it is often possible for students to feel as though their feet were glued to or sunk into the ground, while the upper body has the soft yielding character of a weeping willow. *Rootedness allows one to focus his or her energy, whether the goal be a push in push-hands, finding the right wife or husband, or whatever direction one wants his or her life to take.*

One way to develop a strong root in T'ai Chi is through "posturing" which is a combination of standing meditation and the T'ai Chi form. One chooses a particular posture from the form (in the Yang style, the weight distribution is almost always 70% on the front leg and 30% on the back leg or 100% on one leg or the other) and holds it in a relaxed manner, checking both the external and internal alignment and making adjustments as needed. A qualified partner can be very useful in helping with the external alignment, while a mirror is the second-best alternative. Simultaneously, one works on the internal balance by cultivating a relaxed sense of inner awareness and a slow and easy rhythm of breathing. In an article on posturing, Lenzie Williams explained that "Posturing allows for a kind of metaphysical balancing of Yin and Yang (body and mind), what your mind is thinking or intending, and what your body is actually doing." [40]

On a physical level, one allows the body parts to fit together in the proper balance and alignment, like the colors in a kaleidoscope turning and falling to form a balanced and colorful design. When the proper alignment is attained, the weight can sink into the soles of the feet and a strong root can be cultivated. If the body is not in proper alignment, the weight is held in the lower back, which can cause muscle stress and back pain. Lacking the proper alignment, one could stand in a T'ai Chi position and "posture" until the end of time and not make much progress.

A woman recently visited my school in Jerusalem and complained that she was easily pushed off her center in push-hands even though she practiced the form everyday. When I pushed with her, I discovered she was right. She was not rooted well in her stance. When the class did some "posturing," I could nudge her off balance literally with one finger. Moreover, her body was slightly off in its alignment and her stance was too narrow for her size. Being off just a few inches is as good as a mile when it comes to developing the proper balance and rootedness.

The T'ai Chi Classics speak of this problem: "the upright body must be stable and comfortable to be able to support (force from) the eight directions." [41] If one cannot "be stable and comfortable" to support a reasonable amount of force, then he or she must return to the drawing board to uncover the reasons why.

In the Taoist concept of circulating the Ch'i, rootedness is important because it is one way of tapping the natural energy (Ch'i) of the earth. When the weight is dropped to the soles of the feet, one should imagine that it sinks through the Bubbling Well-Spring, a point that is found at the bottom of the feet, and continues into the ground. One should also imagine that the mind is focused on the bottom of the foot with the intention of relaxing it. Simultaneously, as the weight sinks downwards into the bottom of the foot, it causes the sole to spread a little wider, which opens the Bubbling Well-Spring even more. When this point opens and becomes connected to the ground, the Ch'i begins to bubble up from the earth and fills the body with energy much like the way roots of a tree take the energy of the soil and transform it into sap which nourishes the tree. On the deepest level, one's root is not merely a physical connection to the earth that is advantageous for push-hands, or one's health. Rather, it is a metaphor for becoming one with mother earth and her offspring, so that the destruction of nature's forests, for example, is literally a violation of one's own spiritual and physical being.

7. Change and Changelessness

The Unity of Yin and Yang

It should come as no surprise that change, the dynamic interplay of Yin and Yang, plays an integral role in T'ai Chi as it does in Chinese society as a whole. One could no more think of extracting Yin and Yang from Chinese religion and philosophy than excluding logic from Western science, or leaving out the yeast when baking bread. For the Chinese, Yin and Yang represented the fundamental, cyclical rhythm of the universe; for example, like the turning of one season into another. As we learned from the Neo-Confucians, Master Chou in particular, all movement arises from Wu Chi, or emptiness. When movement reaches its peak (active = Yang) or its nadir (passive = Yin), it begins a process of "reversion" which means that any change will eventually bring about its opposite result. Here, Chuang Tzu summarizes the nature of Yin and Yang:

"The perfect Yin is majestically passive.
The perfect Yang is powerfully active.
Passivity emanates from the Earth.
Activity proceeds from Heaven.
The interaction of the two forms a harmony
from which all things are produced." [42]

From Chuang Tzu, a Westerner might think that "perfect" Yin or "perfect" Yang represent two opposing poles that actually exist in reality. From personal experience in class discussions about Yin and Yang, students often describe woman as Yin or passive while man is Yang or active. These are "loaded" terms which can lead us far astray in understanding the profound meaning of Yin and Yang. There is no such thing as complete Yin or complete Yang. Each woman and man is composed of his or her own unique combination of Yin and Yang. For the Chinese — and this is important to remember — Yin and Yang are conceptual and complementary descriptions of movement and change in the universe. Yin and Yang are never thought of as being separate, one from the other, or as a unit of one, but rather they compose

two variable and ever-changing parts of the whole which constantly seek equilibrium.

Yet, paradoxically, in the midst of change stands the concept
of changelessness; for example, like the unending cycle of the
seasons. There is a center, the pivot that Chuang Tzu speaks of,
where the sage can find Tao: at rest Tao is changeless, yet out of
Tao emerge Yin and Yang that are always changing.

The example of "T'ai Chi Walking"

On a practical level, one way of introducing novice students to
the concept of changelessness and change is with a simple exercise called "T'ai Chi walking." The students are asked to take a
T'ai Chi stance which is a comfortable length, one foot in front
of the other at shoulder width. The weight distribution is approximately 70% on the front leg and 30% on the back leg. (See figure 3)

The front leg is pointing directly ahead while the back leg is at
about a 45 degree angle. What is changeless in the exercise is
that the spine and head remain vertical at all times with the ceil-
ing and the floor. What is constantly changing is the weight distribution which shifts back and forth from 70-30 to 100% on the
back leg and back to 70-30.* When the weight shifts to 100% on
the back leg again, the front leg (that was pointing straight ahead)
turns to a 45 degree angle and the weight slowly shifts on to it,
(see figures 4 and 5) so that the back leg can step forward to
become the front leg (see figure 6) and the weight shifts to 70-30
once again. (see figure 7) From here the exercize repeats itself.
Sometimes we simply shift the weight back and forth a few times

---

* Since nothing can be totally Yin or totally Yang – because that
would imply an absolute separation -- the empty leg, while having
no weight on it, still has substantiality because energy is flowing
through it. In this sense it is not totally empty.

Figure 3.   *Figure 4.*

Figure 5.   *Figure 6.*   *Figure 7.*

in order to emphasize the awareness of different weight sensations before moving on to the other side.

Before doing the above exercise, I explain the basic idea of Yin and Yang, telling the students that Yang is associated with fullness and Yin with emptiness. When the weight is 70% on the front leg, it is more Yang than the Yin back leg, which is supporting only 30% of the weight. As the weight shifts to the back leg (which was more Yin), it gradually becomes the "Yang" leg while the front leg, which is nearly totally empty, becomes the "Yin" leg.

There is one more crucial aspect of this exercise that the students need to know. They should imagine that their legs are tube-like and that the tubes are connected through the waist so that the weight can flow freely from one leg to the other. I suggest the image of their weight flowing like liquid that passes from one leg to the other, something like an hour glass in which the salt flows from the top side to the bottom. From this image the unity of Yin and Yang, which is just as important its separation, is learned.

Through T'ai Chi Walking, students experience the changes of Yin and Yang in a practical and genuine way. Along with their minds and their imaginations, they are learning the meaning of Yin and Yang, change and changelessness, through their bodies. The use of visualization, or other meditation techniques, that do not in some way incorporate body-learning, can often mislead students into thinking they understand and can perform some physical action when, in fact, they only comprehend it conceptually. When the body can do what the mind knows, the student has learned and understood on a profound level.

This technique of walking is a simple version of the way the weight shifts from one leg to the other in the T'ai Chi form itself. As one becomes more advanced, his or her understanding of Yin and Yang should also progress. Emptiness and Fullness, Yin and Yang, can also be understood in terms of energy. In every movement of the form there are parts of the body which are more Yin and parts that are more Yang. Here, a knowledge of self-defense — the applications of the postures in an offensive or defensive sense — is helpful. Making use of an earlier example to explain flow and definition, if we could take a movie of the entire form and examine it frame by frame, we should be able to identify the Yin and Yang parts of the body in each movement, according to energy-flow, weight distribution, and/or purpose.

Change and Practical Applications

Another example of the interplay of Yin and Yang in the form is the way in which we are always changing from offense to defense and back to offense, or the way we are constantly and simultaneously yielding and attacking. As the Classics observe: "Yin and yang mutually aid and change each other." [43] Because Yin and Yang never exist in a vacuum and are complementary parts of the whole, when Yang becomes full, it retreats and changes into Yin, and when Yin reaches its peak, it tranforms into Yang. Thus, we should not think of these changes of Yin and Yang as separate actions like a cadence, for instance, 1) strike, 2) block, 3) strike, or any combination of the two, similar to a musical score that has a particular beat in, say, 4/4 time. Yin and Yang — yield, block or strike — must flow into one another spontaneously and instantaneously like the liquid weight flowing through the tubes that we described above in T'ai Chi Walking. (see figures 8,9,10)

Perhaps more than any other martial art, T'ai Chi emphasizes the *quality* of change in its approach to movement. In contrast to the horse stance of Karate, for example, where the weight is evenly distributed on both legs which makes for a solid strong stance, the T'ai Chi Classics warn against taking such a posture: "Sinking to one side is responsive; being double-weighted is sluggish (stagnant)." [44] The movement must be quick, light and nim-

*Figure 8. Left hand is yang
(forceful), right hand is yin (soft)*

*Figure 9. As left hand
blocks low, right hand
begins to move forward
to push.*

*Figure 10. Right hand
now finishes forcefully
with a push, left hand
becomes soft and waiting.*

*The energy has circled up the left arm and
around the shoulder to the opposite hand.*

ble. In T'ai Chi there is a clear preference for movement and response to the changes occurring outside the individual. T'ai Chi would have us be the river rather than the rock. But within — the place of changelessness — the Classics tell us to "be still as a mountain." [45] Once again we find the idea that the most efficacious movement grows out of tranquility.

In practical terms push-hands represents the grand teaching tool of Yin and Yang, where teachers and students alike discover how well they've learned the lessons of T'ai Chi Ch'uan. In push-hands the flowing interaction of Yin and Yang is brought into play because the most effective movement arises spontaneously out of emptiness, or Wu Chi, and evolves into an endless array of possibilites that are limited only by our imaginations. In describing the importance of change in T'ai Chi, Yang Cheng-fu, the great master of Yang family T'ai Chi, put it this way:

"The meaning of the T'ai-chi symbol lies
in the mutual production of yin and yang,
the complementary exchange of hard and soft,
the thousand changes and ten thousand transformations.
This is the basis for T'ai-chi Ch'uan.
Push-hands is the embodiment of
the T'ai chi symbol." [46]

For Yang Cheng-fu, push-hands meant becoming the changes, and not merely knowing about them intellectually or technically. There is no time to think and then change in the ardor of action. One must develop a profound sensitivity to the slightest touch and be prepared, in the same moment, to push or yield again. One of my push-hands teachers, Lenzie Williams, once told me that his best pushes always came spontaneously after he had yielded his partner's push. The Classics confirm this by stating, "empty the left whenever a pressure appears, and similarly on the right." [47]

If you can yield to your partner's push or pushes, often that renders him slightly off balance and vulnerable to the lightest touch. In yielding, one must always maintain his or her center and root, which is an important aspect of changelessness in the midst of change.

Previous Energy

The idea of changelessness within — despite the action occurring outside oneself — gives rise to another important quality of push-hands. This is called "previous energy," which was mentioned earlier, and basically means knowing what my partner is going to do before he does it. In other words I move before he does and my changes "fill him with wonder."

The basis for the concept of "previous energy" is found in the famous treatise by Sun Tzu called *The Art of War*:

"So it is said that if you know others and know yourself, you will not be imperiled in a hundred battles; if you do not know others, but know yourself, you win one and lose one; if you do not know others and do not know yourself, you will be imperiled in every single battle."[*][48]

Sun Tzu is generally understood to mean that knowing others is to have good intelligence as to the capabilities and designs of the opponent's armies. The same is true in push-hands on the individual level, although "previous energy" also contains the idea that, ideally, one can know his opponent not only by the

---

* When it says in the T'ai Chi Classics that doing the form every day is the way of knowing oneself while push-hands is the way of knowing others, this is a clear reference to Sun Tzu. [49]

lightest touch but also intuitively sense the opponent's intentions. Sun Tzu was speaking to other soldiers and officers, but his wisdom resonates in the play of push-hands.

In order to cultivate this kind of "previous energy," one must be able to listen and discern the intentions of one's partner. This means cutting out all the static of disconnected thoughts and conversations that go on in our minds, most of the time, so that we can receive a clear reception. Through meditation and relaxation techniques, we can gradually quiet the internal noise which is the first step in developing "previous energy." The next step is to cultivate a sense of inner quiet, which will gradually come of its own. It cannot be hurried. This inner quiet must then be brought to bear in the play of push-hands in order to intuit the intentions of one's partner. This generally involves a long, though often satisfying, journey of intention and practice.

T'ai Chi may emphasize the soft, but no one said it would be easy.

Summary

Growing up in the heartlands of America, I often heard people say: if you don't like the weather, wait a few minutes and it will change. People in the West are generally well aware of the changes in nature, although they do not call them, "Yin and Yang." What the Chinese did was to make change an integral part of the way they viewed the universe which led them to create the highly sophisticated yet very simple concept of Yin and Yang. The Chinese saw that change is circular and that one kind of change is rooted in what seems to be an entirely different kind of change. The Chinese understood change as a process of becoming or, we might say, de-becoming, which is the essence of the dynamic relationship of Yin and Yang. Along with the notion that movement emerges out of emptiness, the principle of change and changlessness reflects a crucial root paradox and truth in Chinese thought.

When one does genuine T'ai Chi, he or she, if so desired, can play out these truths on the spiritual and physical planes. Of course everyone in T'ai Chi struggles with the imperfections of the body when compared with the ideal of what the mind perceives as possible. Sometimes, out of pure frustration, one feels like calling out to the cosmos, "any spare change!" At these low points the accomplishments and encouragement from a sympathetic T'ai Chi master or a master teacher can inspire students to achieve far more than they ever dreamed of, demonstrating again the pivotal role of an experienced and authentic teacher. Yet, however good the teacher is, he or she cannot do the student's work. As the well-known Chinese saying goes: a teacher can only point towards the moon, but the student must reach for it himself.

8. Flow and Continuity

Sources of Flow and Continuity

T'ai Chi reflects the notion of change in Chinese thought, as well as the quality of that change which is "flow" and "continuity." The Chinese viewed the motion of the universe in terms of a dynamic rhythm and cyclic unity where Yin and Yang, the creation of life, its ultimate decay and rebirth, the four seasons, and the Five Elements were a "cosmic dance" that revealed its own patterns and order without the need or benefit of a choreographer.

Behind the changes is, as Lao Tzu suggests, "The great Tao (that) flows everywhere, The ten thousand things depend upon it; it holds nothing back." [50] While Tao can never be defined in ultimate terms due to the poverty of mind and language, he goes on to "describe" it as "a river flowing home to the sea." Thus flow is a key concept in understanding the quality of Tao.

China is a land rich in reserves and reservoirs of water. It is not difficult to understand why the image of flowing rivers had such a powerful impact on the Chinese mind. The meridians of the body along which the Ch'i flowed were often likened to rivers or canals. In order to maintain one's health, these meridians or "channels of Ch'i" needed to be kept open so that the Ch'i could "flow" freely through them, thereby nourishing the entire body.

It is natural that the image of a river is often used to describe the flowing quality of T'ai Chi. In the T'ai Chi Classics, for example, it is said that "Ch'ang Ch'uan (T'ai Chi Ch'uan) is like a great river rolling on unceasingly." By picturing the image of water as we do the form, our movements inherit the characteristics of softness as well as fluidity. Someone who does the form well suggests the intangible and transient quality of liquidity, yet with the smoothness and buoyancy of mercury. Cheng Man Ch'ing put it this way:

"...you must move as if moving with
water, or moving the water as you
move...when you kick, you must kick
as if you were pushing the water away." [51]

On one lofty level, the form symbolizes the "cosmic dance" of the universe, in which the ten thousand things are created through movement. The quality of that movement can be thought of as flow rather than something jerky and out of control. Flow connotes the idea of unity in which all things naturally grow out of what precedes them. It also suggests the idea of something contained, especially when we think of a river which is contained by its banks. Thus flow implies the idea of continuous and orderly movement in which all the visible parts are subsumed in the idea of the whole. This quality of wholeness and flow often engenders a sense of eternity in the eyes of the beholder.

Developing Flow in T'ai Chi

In order to express these ideas, the T'ai Chi form—and especially the Yang style—is usually performed in a continuous flow, at the same speed or rhythm, where one maintains a consistent height throughout. There are no stops or starts once the form begins and no movement that is not smooth and even. As the Classics state: "In motion all parts of the body must be light, nimble and strung together," and "Let the postures be without breaks or holes, hollows or projections, or discontinuities and continuities of form." [52]

The form suggests a sense of symmetrical containment in which all the mind's concentration and body's parts have merged into one continuous stream. Internally, the Ch'i should be flowing naturally and unimpeded through the meridians and the internal power known as "Chin" should become one unit. To see someone doing T'ai Chi well is to see someone who is neither fish nor foul but swimming effortlessly in the air with feet on the ground.

What conveys the sense of organic unity is the concentration of mind, the harmonious coordination of the body, the rounding of the movements and the limbs themselves, and the cyclical nature of the form itself.

Ideally, when a person initiates the form, his or her mind should be quiet, serene and focused. While this is often difficult to achieve, it is important that when one begins the form, he or she must strive to empty the mind as much as possible and to seek the place of Wu Chi that dwells within each of us. In accordance with Master Chou's Diagram of the Supreme Ultimate, one should allow the movement to flow naturally out of the tranquil place of Wu Chi, with minimal outside control or direction. The spontaneous arousal of movement will become more "natural" with time and will occur with increasing frequency.

However, what works for an experienced teacher might not

work for someone else. Once, in an experiment with one of my classes, I asked the students to begin the form only when they felt the movement inside of them, rather than directing the movement in a conscious way. Two of my students remained frozen in the beginning posture as the rest of us finished at various intervals. It was unclear to me whether they were on their way to beginning the form, or simply and irrevocably stuck. I was confronted with the decision of continuing the class with or without them. Finally I concluded the experiment and asked the two to rejoin the class, despite the fact that they had not moved! When I asked them what had happened, they explained that they had not experienced the "natural arousal of movement."

These exceptions apart, the basic idea of the spontaneous arousal of movement is an important one in the form as well as in push-hands. If we are to understand push-hands as the embodiment of Tao, as Yang Cheng-fu suggested, we must then learn how to yield or to push in a spontaneous way, since, by definition, spontaneity is the nature of Tao.

The question remains: how does one move from a position of being generally programmed against change to one of spontaneity? First of all we must recognize that *we are programmed* and that change in one's life is generally a process rather than a mighty leap (although mighty leaps are possible if risky.) In the form and in push-hands, as in life, we can respond naturally and spontaneously only when we have learned to listen to Tao that dwells inside of each and every one of us. This process of learning to listen is precisely why T'ai Chi is called the Supreme Ultimate. On this level, Lao Tzu exhorts us not to hear with the ears, but to listen with the intuitive mind. [53] To rephrase an old saying: the right hand "knows" what the left is doing.

Getting back to basics, the key to learning flow is in the legs. In T'ai Chi Walking, for example, many beginning students find that they cannot step forward and shift their weight from one foot to the other in a flowing, graceful manner. This is a relatively easy exercise to perform, assuming that the person has no serious physical or psychological handicaps. The reason for this problem is that the legs of most people are simply not strong enough to hold the body in a comfortable; upright position as they move. Interestingly enough, there is a Chinese saying that old age and disease first come through the legs. One of the first prerequisites of T'ai Chi training is the process of strengthening the legs. Many teachers emphasize separating the weight on one leg or the other (100%) and holding the posture for short periods, gradually lengthening the time.

While stepping forward, backwards or sideways, confidently and effortlessly, is very important in developing flow, one must also be able to coordinate the upper body and limbs so that they move as one unit. In the Yang style T'ai Chi there are two important rules that foster unity of the body, which in turn give rise to the sense of flow and continuity. The first is that all the movement comes from the waist and ultimately the tan t'ien, which is the center of the waist.

Physically this means that one could draw a straight line downward from the nose, through the center of the chest, through the navel, and through the genitals all the way to the floor. When the body turns in the form, that line always remain straight.* (see figures 11,12)

The result of this line is to create a physical alignment where the shoulders are always directly over the hips. The body should not twist so that the navel points one way, while the chest and shoulders, which are able to turn farther, move out of alignment.

The limiting factor is the waist which has a smaller turning radius than the upper body. When the torso truly flows as one

---

There are a few exceptions to this rule.

*Figure 11. Incorrect: the
body is twisted.*

*Figure 12. Correct: the
body is properly aligned.*

unit, there is no sense of awkwardness.

The idea of unity is repeated in push-hands where one soon learns not to "over-compensate" by turning the shoulders too much to the right or left, which, if it occurs, leaves one in a very vulnerable position.

T'ai Chi Mind and Emotions

In T'ai Chi, the quiet mind, which causes the Ch'i to sink into the Tan T'ien, plays the same role as the commander on the battlefield. A confident and successful commander must be acutely aware of what is happening in all places, at all times. As we quoted earlier, he must know what is happening to the left, right, up, down, and back, in order to win the day. Like Emperor Shun, who needed only to face south, the commander is the fulcrum for his soldiers. Moreover, a good commander never allows his emotions to overwhelm him. In push-hands, even though the body turns one way or another it remains unified and balanced because its "commander" remains clear-headed and decisive. This ensures the proper flow and continuity of body and mind. There are no surprises because the mind is everywhere at once and can quickly adjust the body according to the demands of circumstance.

William C. C. Chen, a well-known teacher, observed that, if the form is done "slowly, smoothly, and uninterruptedly," with flow and continuity, the Ch'i will sink to the tan t'ien like tea leaves, sinking to the bottom of the tea pot after being properly heated.* [54] He explained that the Ch'i can still rise if the person

---

* In Chinese yoga practices, the Ch'i should sink to the Tan T'ien until called upon where it is released in an orderly and flowing manner according to one's needs. If the Ch'i is flying around wildly, it is understood that the individual has lost his or her center.

is not careful to do the form slowly and calmly. To do the form hurriedly, without flow and continuity, would lead to disturbing the tea leaves — the Ch'i — causing them to rise to the top of tea pot.

We can also understand Chen's analogy as referring to the way the emotions can rise up out of control. If you have ever had a busy day, for example, where time is limited and you are running from one thing to the next, one small incident can set off an explosion of anger.

T'ai Chi is an educational experience that not only works on the body but also on the emotions, which, as we learned from the "doctrine of the mean," must be in harmony. If one does not do the form in a calm and relaxed manner, the negative emotions that this generates can be a symbol and/or a cause of a loss of control, anger and irrationality which, on an individual level, or, for a "commander" of an army, could spell disaster. The famous Chinese General, Zhuge Liang (3rd century CE.) explained why culture must be valued over military preparedness (here "culture" has the Confucian meaning of taming one's emotions):

"If you put victory first, you will surely
get beaten later; if you start out with
anger, you will surely regret it later.
One day's anger can destroy your whole life.
Therefore a superior man is stern
but not ferocious: he may get angry, but
not furious; he may worry, but does not
fear; he may rejoice, but is not overjoyed." [55]

Timing

Another way of developing flow and continuity is connected to the notion of "timing." In sports, as in push-hands, timing is one important key to success. In push-hands if one does not yield or push at precisely the right moment, usually the technique will not work. Even the most powerful push can be yielded successfully if the timing is correct.

It often happens that students will avail themselves of a losing position and ask the inevitable question: now what do I do? The answer is that it is already too late for this round; the student must find the appropriate response, at the right moment and, for now, he must give up and start again. Nevertheless, many of the greatest moments in push-hands come at the very instance of greatest vulnerability and desperation where somehow the one being pushed manages to save himself and turn the tables on the pusher.

In the T'ai Chi form there is a subtle way of working on timing which simultaneously develops flow and continuity. When we perform a posture in T'ai Chi, usually there are many parts of the body moving at the same time. These body parts must begin and end their movement together, though often the distance to be covered is considerably different for each body part. Because we learn to perform these complicated movements, slowly and consciously, the T'ai Chi form becomes an educational process rather than a test of will between the body and mind, which if the latter occurs, often ends in anger and frustration. Even those who conceive of themselves as being awkward will hopefully benefit and be able to move in a more harmonious and flowing manner by understanding T'ai Chi as a lesson and a process. In T'ai Chi many an ugly duckling has grown up to be a swan.

One such movement is "Crane Spreads Her Wings." After the "Shoulder Stroke" (the preceding movement), the weight shifts on the right leg and then the body turns to the left. (see figures 12, 13, 14) The right hand has a long distance to go from the right leg to the height of the forehead while the left hand has a relatively small distance to cover from the chest to the left leg, and the left leg has an even smaller distance to go. (see figure 15)

Figure 12. Shoulder stroke.

Figure 13. Weight shifts to right leg.

Figure 14. Body turns to left.

Figure 15. The movement of all body parts must begin and end together.

All this must occur after the waist turns to face the left. Learning to coordinate a complex movement like this takes lots of practice and concentration. One must be aware of a wide range of body parts, from the head to the left foot, calculating their speed and course while standing on the right leg.

While "Crane Spreads Her Wings" is one of the more complicated postures, it serves to illustrate the point that the form teaches students to move different parts of the body at varying speeds. But, just as important, they must move these parts in a harmonious way; that is to say, all the parts must begin and end together smoothly, without any stops. If a person can learn to perform the entire T'ai Chi form while expressing flow and continuity of this kind, there is a reasonable chance that most people can develop a modicum of flow and grace in T'ai Chi as well as the ability to translate this knowledge into everyday life. Even the greatest athletes have handicaps and limitations with which they must cope and overcome. One of Tai Chi's most important gifts is that it can serve as a paradigm which one uses to live a fuller and healthier life. T'ai Chi is not an end in itself, but a tool to be used for the owner's benefit.

The idea of flow and continuity is very important in push-hands where one must react to the sometimes rapid-fire and the often unpredictable flurries of a partner. In push-hands we generally do not utilize the straight-ahead push, like that of the 100-meter sprinter. If you miss on that kind of a push and/or your partner senses what you are about to do, you can find yourself in a very vulnerable position. Push-hands is more likely to have the flowing "give and go" of a basketball player where the ability to change direction instantaneously means gaining that "extra step." In push-hands that "extra step" is being able to change from Yin to Yang and back again without any loss of momentum. As soon as we feel a push on one side, it empties and the other side is ready for a strike. Like the legs in T'ai Chi walking, where empty and full are connected through the groin area, in push-hands the entire body is linked together and becomes empty or full as the need arises. Chen Wei-ming explains the flowing qualities of Yin and Yang in T'ai Chi thus:

> "From beginning to end it is continuous
> and not broken. It is circular and
> again resumes. It revolves and has
> no limits. The original Classics say
> it is 'like a great river rolling on
> unceasingly,' and that the circulation
> of chin is 'like pulling silk.' They
> all talk about being connected together." [56]

The Line and the Circle

Another aspect of flow is its direction. When one is attacking, the body adopts a linear attitude towards one's partner. In contrast, when one is on defense, the body takes on a rounded quality in order to protect itself. In nature roundness is characteristic of defense or protection, for example, an egg or the round belly of a pregnant woman. If one pushes or strikes something round, or if an egg is dropped, the point of the circle being struck is supported by all points of the circle's surface that are equal distance from the center. Something round is less likely to break than something linear.

In push-hands or in self-defense, being able to change instantly from a linear motion to a circular one or vice versa, with flow and continuity, is a valuable lesson to learn from T'ai Chi. In general the form has a rounded quality (Yin) to it, yet one must not forget its linear (Yang) side. In this context there is an enigmatic statement in the T'ai Chi Classics: "In the curve seek the straight..." [57] This statement may be understood as meaning that within every circle, there are numerous straight lines. (see figure 16)

If one can discover and then push (or strike) through one of these straight lines to the center of the circle and out the other side, the push has a good chance of being successful. If, however, the one being pushed can conceal those straight lines or change them within his or her rounded defense, the pusher will have a difficult task in dislodging his partner. Moreover, the one who conceals those lines can also instantly transform them into linear strikes.

Figure 16.

The roles of the partners should be constantly changing, according to what "spontaneously" occurs in the dynamics of their relationship —like the Yin and Yang of the Tao itself. Therefore in offense one must not only seek the straight in the curve but also the reverse. In defense one must seek the curve in the straight. The rule of thumb in T'ai Chi is not only change but also flow, agility, linearity, and roundness.

T'ai Chi: the Never-Ending Idea

Flow and continuity were very much a part of Chinese society: day followed night and returned to day, seasons followed one another in a cyclical motion, Yin followed Yang and Yang would return again. "Returning," according to Lao Tzu, "is the motion of the Tao." Linear time, on the other hand, suggests a beginning and an end, where in-between the stopping and the starting up again there is a break in the flow.

The T'ai Chi form represents the cyclic way of viewing the world in which the flow of the form could conceivably continue indefinitely if it were not for the limited stamina of all human beings. Most T'ai Chi forms begin and end with a specific posture, often called "preparation." Theoretically the form could continue forever since one merely begins again from the "preparation" posture. However, doing the form in a cyclic manner, as we often do, does not in any way imply that we experience the form in exactly the same way. Just as one Spring will be different from the one before and after it, so each time we do the form, it changes, either from intention or of its own nature.

The idea of the form being ongoing and never-ending, without any break of flow or continuity, is one that can be integrated into one's life. Just because one stands up at the end of the "formal" T'ai Chi form does not mean that his or her T'ai Chi need come to a halt. If anything the opposite is true. One should bring the ideas of T'ai Chi principles, including those of flow, into one's everyday experience. Thus, not only the form itself is cyclical but the periods of time between doing the form also represent cycles. One never stops doing, or even trying to do T'ai Chi. Once a student reaches a certain level of competency, T'ai Chi is as natural as walking down the street or standing at a bus stop. T'ai Chi is kept vibrant and alive by the regular physical and mental repetition of its principles, at all times and in all places. The artist remains an artist despite the fact that he or she works during the day as a lawyer or a truckdriver. This is the nature of an artist. There is also the art of law and the art of driving.

The T'ai Chi form itself contains a strong tendency to make the movements circular instead of linear. The circle implies the idea of infiniteness and eternity precisely because there is no point where one can say it begins or ends. A good example of the way the form teaches circularity is from the punch, which is one of the most linear movements of all the postures. (see figures 17, 18, 19)

Figure 17. Linear punch.

*Figure 18. The punch
becomes circular.*

*Figure 19. Withdrawing in
preparation to push.*

After the punch, the fist gradually opens and its linear direction is transformed into a circle which swings to the left and then withdraws in preparation for the next movement. In this way the body's movement retains its momentum. If the punch were to be withdrawn along the same projectile from which it came, it would remain linear, thus breaking the energy cycle, if only for an instant. This kind of linear punch of its very nature suggests a finiteness, a beginning and an end, in the process of re-cocking the arm. The T'ai Chi Classics describe the linear punch as having "breaks" (in the energy) and therefore being "finite." [58]

One of the most important lessons T'ai Chi is trying to teach — with, say, the example of the circular punch — is that: just as Tao flows on, with no beginning or end, always returning, so human beings can experience the same sense of limitlessness in their movement and their lives. This of course is a clear illustration of how Chinese religious and philosophical ideas were reflected directly in the concrete reality of doing the T'ai Chi form.

AFTERWORD

In the process of writing this book, two notions concerning the nature of the universe profoundly influenced my practice of T'ai Chi, as well as the way in which I view the world. These two notions are inextricably bound together, the one flowing from the other.

The first is the idea — which was developed and clarified by the Neo-Confucians — that the world of forms (T'ai Chi) grows out of emptiness or Wu Chi. This is an intriguing question for the student of T'ai Chi. The heart of the matter is: what is the primary source of movement? One could argue that Wu Chi is both empty and not empty, for within its emptiness there exists the *potential* for movement and by connecting ourselves to this potentiality through the quiet mind, the universe moves through us. In this way we are shaped into a vessel through which spontaneous and natural movement can flow. Taking this idea a step further, we can speculate that all artistic creavity of any depth arises out of the emptiness of Wu Chi. One Chinese source for this idea was clearly illustrated in Chuang Tzu's story of the woodcutter and the bellstand.

This idea, however, is not solely Chinese. While watching the 1992 Barcelona Olympic games, I noticed that athletes frequently took a few moments to seek a quiet refuge within themselves before facing the challenge and the pressure of performing their speciality. I was particularly impressed by the 100-meter sprinters who demanded absolute quiet as they readied themselves at the starting line. If something broke their concentration, any one of them could raise his hand at which time they all stood up and the process of settling into the starting blocks began anew. It seemed clear to me that one of the most dynamic events in athletics, the 100-meters dash, exploded out of the quiet of apparent emptiness.

This idea is also expressed in what is probably the most widely accepted scientific theory of how the universe was created — the "Big Bang." In its bare essentials the "Big Bang" theory states that the world of forms, as we know it, resulted from a huge explosion of matter and energy. Before the "Big Bang" — and this causes much confusion — most scientists believe that nothing at all existed, neither space nor time, or even the matter and energy that exploded.* If this pre-Big Bang emptiness sounds something like Wu Chi, I would agree. Our minds can comprehend an expanding universe of forms, but logic is stopped cold before the vacuous wall that separates both scientist and layman from grasping Wu Chi intellectually. To step beyond requires imaginative speculation, a mystical inclination and perhaps a religious faith. Only the quiet, meditative mind can glimpse and intuit the realm of Wu Chi, which, as Lao Tzu observes, is the *"unfathomable* source of ten thousand things."

These examples are all variations on the same theme: that movement and creativity are born of emptiness which is generally thought of as a state of tranquility and stillness. One might argue that there are various states of quiescence; and not only the profoundly philosophical one that Wu Chi implies. The gym-

---

* *There is much speculation on this basic theory which is beyond the scope of this particular discussion.*

nast who concentrates before a performance, for example, is merely doing so for her composure. Yet if we look carefully at the root meaning of the word "composure," we find a compelling connection between quiet and creativity. To compose is to create and the "composed" person is one who is both calm and self- possessed. Clearly calmness and creativity have an undeniable link.

This connection of tranquility and movement has had major implications for my practice of T'ai Chi. Before the research and writing of this book I understood that both calmness and movement were important in T'ai Chi and I cultivated them, more or less, separately. What is new for me is that I am in the process of integrating them as a way of uncovering the true source of my movement. In this way the quiet mind takes on a greater significance or role because it is the nexus between the source of creativity and creativity's manifestation in the world.

T'ai Chi is a tool with which to better understand creativity in everyday living. One need not retire to a mountain in order to cultivate a quiet, meditative mind and thus live a more full and insightful life. The mountain is inside of you or, as Huanchu Daoren put it, "so why get addicted to mountains?"

The second idea, which is unquestionably linked to the above discussion, is that all things in the universe are intertwined and interconnected. The Chinese believed that this is so because all things evolved from the same source which they called Tao. When one investigates the nature of Tao thoroughly and deeply with a calm and intuitive mind, it is possible to understand that the universe is a whole indivisible unity. As the Moslem poet Kabir wrote, "When the eyes and ears are open, even the leaves on the trees teach like pages from the scriptures."

Most, if not all, religious and artistic traditions contain a strong belief, often mystical, that the universe is one. St. Francis of Assisi or Walt Whitman come to mind; both being kindred souls who saw everything as a living unity and held out a vision that was sensitive to and encompassed the entire universe.

There is a wonderful story about Rabbi Abraham Isaac Kook (1865-1935), the first Chief Rabbi of Israel (then Palestine), as told by Rabbi Aryeh Levin. One afternoon the two rabbis took a stroll in the fields near Jerusalem. On the way Rabbi Levin picked a branch or a flower. He relates Rabbi Kook's reaction:

> "Believe me: In all my days I have taken care never to pluck a blade of grass or flower needlessly, when it had the ability to grow or blossom. You know the teaching of the Sages that there is not a single blade of grass below, here on earth, which does not have a heavenly force (or angel) above telling it, Grow! Every sprout and leaf of grass says something, conveys some meaning. Every stone whispers some inner, hidden message in silence. Every creation utters its song (in praise of the Creator)." [1]

When I first read the story about Chou Tun-i's refusal to allow the grass around his home to be cut, I did not grasp its deeper meaning. Later, as I studied his Diagram, the reason for his refusal became clearer. Like Rabbi Kook, he believed that, in the scheme of things, everything had a purpose and therefore dignity; that everything was alive and interconnected. To inflict needless pain on anything, a blade of grass or a rock, contradicted his belief system as a man deeply aware of the universe's oneness. Organic and inorganic things were made of the same substance as he was, and thus their pain was his pain.

In the Bible Moses is apparently not allowed to enter the Land of Israel because he strikes a rock instead of telling it to give forth water as God commanded. There are many commentaries on why the punishment was so severe for what seems to be a relatively minor offense. Could the reason be that a man of Moses' spiritual level, who should have been sensitive to the pain of the rock, chose to cause needless pain out of anger as an act of rebellion against God and nature? The degree of one's awareness is often the measure of one's responsibility.

One of my most profound T'ai Chi experiences occurred during a visit to Berkeley, California, the place where I first studied T'ai Chi. I was sitting with my daughter, who was about 4 years old, during the Bar Mitzvah of a friend's son. She was getting restless so we decided to visit a nearby park. While we played together on the swings, there was a class of T'ai Chi in progress, which included a group doing push-hands. What held my attention was not the teacher or the students but rather an old Chinese gentleman, probably in his seventies, who was standing in meditation with his eyes closed in front of a large tree. He stood that way for at least a half-hour or so until we left. I felt that he was in a deep communion with that tree, that his roots sank deep into the ground like the tree's sucking up the earth's nutrients, that his veins flowed freely like the sap of the tree, and that he was not separate from that tree as an other, but rather their communion was a relationship of, as Martin Buber put it, "I and Thou."

Often when I do T'ai Chi or standing meditation, I first prepare myself by thinking of that stranger whom I never met and yet has exerted such a powerful influence on my life. There are many others like Rav Kook, Master Chou, Walt Whitman and Lao Tzu, known and unknown, and of course my T'ai Chi teachers Benjamin Pang Jeng Lo, Lenzie Williams and Ken Cohen. For me, T'ai Chi, among other influences, has opened the door to a world "beyond" ordinary reality. I often feel blessed for its presence in my life.

Personally one of the happiest moments in T'ai Chi is when winter is over, and we can move our classes outside to a park. Our T'ai Chi takes on a new character as it resonates to the rhythms of spring. In contrast, one of the most difficult moments is when the weather grows inclement and we must return indoors. Yet even in the studio, closed off from the immediacy of nature, each time we begin the form, a memory is engaged that summons the summer stirrings of my inner self. The fact remains that T'ai Chi has become a bridge not only to an intimate relationship with nature but to a total, life experience which reminds me daily that I am composed of the same material as, and forever bound to, everyone and everything in the universe.

THE WRITTEN AND ORAL TRADITION OF T'AI CHI CH'UAN

Historical Background

L ong before human beings learned to read or write, there was an oral transmission which formed the basis of most ancient spiritual and artistic traditions. Knowledge was transmitted from teacher to student in an unbroken chain whose origins were lost in time or the source being attributed to a mythological figure or god. Even today, among primitive tribes, in the Amazon jungle, for example, the knowledge of a medicine man would have been passed on to him by his teacher and he will pass on to his apprentice for the benefit of the tribe. The method of transmission is usually by the spoken word or subtle gestures and the doing of the task under the guidance of his or her teacher. The pedagogical tool is memorization in which the apprentice is required to know by heart every detail of each procedure. A lost step in religious or medicinal process could spell catastrophe for the tribe.

With the introduction of writing into a culture, detail memorization of the written texts remained the major pedagogical tool to retain knowledge, at least in the early years of study. In Greek and Jewish institutes of learning before the Common Era, students were taught to memorize the material and to recite it out loud; it was understood that comprehension would come later as the student matured. For Greek students, it was the work of Homer to be memorized; for Jewish students, it was often the entire Bible and large portions of the Oral Law which were eventually written down. In China students learned the Confucian Classics by heart as well as being required to compose essays in their precise styles. Confucius himself was viewed as the ideal teacher who interpreted the Classics for his students, calmly answering their questions as to the proper way to conduct their lives. He exemplified the confluence of the oral and written traditions in the person of the teacher.

The common denominator of these diverse cultures — Greek, Jewish and Chinese — was the role of the teacher whose task was to fill in the spaces between the lines. He was often the guardian and transmitter of both the written and the oral traditions. He was responsible for ensuring that the traditions remained pure, that not one word was added or subtracted from the written tradition, and that only qualified students reached the higher levels of study. He often represented the mechanism of change, in that he interpreted the oral tradition, according to novel circumstances.

In many cultures, after the ancient oral tradition was written down, a new kind of oral tradition grew up around it which was essentially an interpretation of or commentary on the written tradition. While the written tradition could be read by anyone who knew the language, its meaning remained hidden and required a teacher who was intimately familiar with both the oral and the written. Only the initiated could reveal secret knowledge to the uninitiated.

T'ai Chi and the Oral Tradition

Although of much later vintage, the oral tradition of T'ai Ch conforms to this general pattern. Benjamin Pang Jeng Lo, a well-known contemporary teacher of T'ai Chi and translator of the T'ai Chi Classics into English, describes the relationship of T'ai Chi to the outside world in this way:

> "In China martial arts are shrouded with a misty curtain. T'ai Chi too, used the "closed door" teaching method, i.e., total secrecy; or the "half-closed door," in other words, people knew what T'ai Chi was, but they didn't know the method. In either case, the transmission was directly from grand-teacher to teacher, teacher to students. But for those standing outside the door, the content was mysterious." [1]

The teacher was a bridge for the student to pass over to the other side, from novice to initiate. The teacher could also be a barrier to someone he deemed unworthy. In the early days martial arts were often taught in a Taoist or Shao Lin (Buddhist) temple under the watchful eye of a priest or in the home of a master. In the example of T'ai Chi, its transmission became a family or clan affair and, as such, it is no surprise that the three main styles of T'ai Chi today — Ch'en, Yang and Wu — are known by their family names. Just as every family has its well-kept secrets hidden in the attic, so these T'ai Chi families kept their knowledge and interpretations under wraps. The students were often the sons, daughters or members of the extended clan. If an "outsider" was accepted as a student due to unusual circumstances, as was the case of Yang Lu-shan, it was likely that he would become an adopted member of the family; a combination of T'ai Chi apprentice and domestic servant, which was his way of repaying the master for teaching him.

Teachers and Students: East and West

The relationship of student to teacher in T'ai Chi, as in almost all spiritual, religious and martial traditions of the East, was one of deep respect and honor and was modeled on the Confucian example of clear and strict lines of authority. Based on the family model, the teacher was often viewed by the student as a father figure and his fellow students as "brothers." Discipline was sharp and demanding; the student giving himself over, in fact, surrendering his will to that of his teacher. It was not merely that the teacher knew more than the student. Rather he held a position of being a respected elder in a hierarchical society. This meant that the younger generation, his students, regarded him with a humble awe bordering on reverence. This respect grew out of his position as "father-teacher" as well as a surety on the part of the student that, as a great martial artist, his teacher also held the power of life and death in his hands.

The idea of respect and obedience was enshrined on the family altar of ancestor worship and very few in China were free from its grip. Moreover, the T'ai Chi master represented the "embodiment" of both the oral and written traditions. One movement, one word, one touch could contain a thousand words of wisdom, written or spoken, and the student ultimately knew that, if he had chosen well or if he had been the chosen one, his best chance to learn the secrets of T'ai Chi came from hard work and commitment to his teacher. It was unusual for a student to shop around for a better or different teacher unless unique circumstances arose such as a severe clash of personalities, or the student had learned all that the teacher had to offer.

Perhaps nowhere is the cultural gap between China and the West so apparent as in the relationship between student and teacher. In the West it is a source of pride that knowledge is available to anyone who seeks it (at least in theory). This reflects the widespread commitment to democractic values; students are encouraged to be skeptical of their teachers and their learning, to question everything, and to arrive at their own conclusions. In

China, however, T'ai Chi was usually taught by imitating the movements of the teacher with little or no talking or questioning. In the West students expect a coherent explanation and the reasons for what they are doing. For most Westerners, it would be very difficult to study T'ai Chi with a teacher using only the traditional Chinese method. The positive side of the Western approach is that people are not deceived so easily by half-truths and myths. On the other hand, people can become so skeptical that they find it difficult to believe in anything at all.

Due to this skepticism, when people in the West turn their attention to a religious or spiritual tradition, they often only read the written word, which is readily accessible to all, and miss out on the "living" oral tradition — the interpretation of what they are reading. They thus absorb the tradition on a literal and horizontal level only and lack the depths of the oral dimension. Moreover, the status of the teacher has been lowered in the West, in comparison with the East, so that even when students are fortunate to hear words of insight from an outstanding teacher, they are either too skeptical or blase to probe their meaning, or in an indignant state of shock because the language of a genuine tradition is so far from their everyday reality.

The Tradition of Wisdom Literature

The very best wisdom literature in both the East and West fuses philosophy and poetry. A few words say much, evoking a multitude of meanings and images. One of the great examples of Chinese wisdom literature is Lao Tzu's *Tao Te Ching*. It is written in such a way that one can never be sure that he or she has totally understood the concise, enigmatic phrases and rhetorical sleight-of-hand that turns common sense upside down. For example:

"Give up sainthood, renounce wisdom,
And it will be a hundred times better for everyone.

Give up kindness, renounce morality,
And men will rediscover filial piety and love.
Give up ingenuity, renounce profit,
And bandits and thieves will disappear." [2]

For Lao Tzu, Tao is something dark, mysterious and enigmatic. It is deceptively simple and yet difficult to grasp, something like a mist that one feels but cannot contain. Lao Tzu's wisdom and style require the guidance of a teacher and the perspective of an oral tradition in order to clarify his ideas and insights. Indeed the Chinese produced a plethora of commentaries on his work.

Lao Tzu profoundly influenced the style and content of Chinese thought throughout the ages and his mark can be seen in Sun Tzu's *The Art of War*, the Chinese masterpiece of military strategy which provided a model for the T'ai Chi written tradition. It could be said that Sun Tzu's treatise did for the military what the T'ai Chi Classics spelt out for the individual in the realm of self-defense. Push-hands, for example, becomes far more intelligible when viewed from the perspective of Sun Tzu's military strategy. Just as Lao Tzu's philosophy could be enigmatic, so too could Sun Tzu's advice on military matters. For example:

"So in the case of those who are skilled in attack,
their opponents do not know where to defend.
In the case of those skilled in defense,
their opponents do not know where to attack. [3]

If we compare this statement with the following advice from the T'ai Chi Classics, we can see immediately the similarities:

"If the opponent rises up I seem taller;
if he sinks down, then I seem lower;

advancing, the distance seems
incredibly longer; retreating, the distance seems
exasperatingly short." [4]

Both of these statements require a tradition and teachers in order to clarify their meanings. If one does not learn the techniques of strategy from a competent teacher, for example, it will be impossible to put even the finest martial tactics successfully into practice. The student's knowledge will be confined to book learning and theory, never seeing the light of day. The student will remain an armchair general or only pushing the arm of a chair instead of that of a fellow student.

The Importance of the Oral Tradition

Before the twentieth century there is little doubt that the major vehicle for the transmission of T'ai Chi was the oral tradition. The Classics themselves confirm this:

"To enter the door and be shown the way,
you must be orally taught.
The practice is uninterrupted,
and the technique (achieved) by self study." [5]

However, "self study" here could suggest that the reading of the Classics themselves and the practicing of what one has been orally taught are the primary means of being *fully* initiated into the T'ai Chi tradition. In practice it probably meant both.

There were a number of reasons why the oral tradition was emphasized. First of all, it seems that T'ai Chi was developed in the countryside, away from the main centers of learning and education. Without question the vast majority of Chinese, who were peasants and urban workers, had no opportunity for anything but a rudimentary education. Literacy was the privilege of the relatively small upper and middle classes.* But the fact that someone was illiterate did not rule him out as having the potential to be an outstanding martial artist just as many great boxers in the West are not known for their intellectual skills.** A boxer may bring a lively intelligence to his fighting skills and never have had the opportunity or the inclination to study their art from a book. In that situation, it would be particularly important that he have access to the oral tradition, which is to say, a very good teacher.

As evidenced by reading the T'ai Chi Classics, some of the early masters of T'ai Chi certainly combined both a literary and a martial knowledge of traditional Chinese Classics, like the *Tao Te Ching* and *The Art of War*. Most of the pioneers in T'ai Chi were probably not scholars, but more likely semi-literate men of action out of both necessity and vocation. This fact is borne out with some of the great masters of T'ai Chi even into the twentieth century. Douglas Wile points out that Yang Cheng-fu "was not a scholar" and that his first and second books were probably written and compiled by two of his students, Cheng Man Ch'ing being one of them. [6]

In various periods of Chinese history, too, the educated classes were specifically not encouraged to develop a fighting or military spirit. One of these periods was about the time that Chang San-feng lived.

"In the thirteenth century...boxing, wrestling, fencing, polo, archery, and football were only practiced by army officers and

---

* *Unfortunately, even today when the literacy rate has increased substantially, many people, East and West, who practice T'ai Chi, are unfamiliar with the Classics in an intimate way.*
** *Mike Tyson is an excellent recent example of this. His mentor was Gus D'mato who was famous as a teacher and the man who trained Mohammed Ali.*

soldiers. There was a sharp contrast...between the games of physical prowess and of skill which were enjoyed by the common people, and the aristocratic games of the scholar class: chess, calligraphy and literary composition. Skill in the use of arms was rare and not encouraged. This was why it was chiefly from among the uneducated and the peasants that men with a military vocation arose, and that swashbuckling types were recruited." [7]

As a rough and tumble martial art, T'ai Chi, in the early days, tended to attract the man of action rather than the scholarly type.* The very act of learning T'ai Chi involved the "doing," a physical exertion that meant sweat, pain and bruises. One also had to be prepared psychologically for the boxing challenges that could arise if a reputation for fighting skill was established. Martial arts were often socially unacceptable to the upper classes, who were generally the most literate. The fighting arts were not viewed as a viable or attractive activity by those who preferred the library or the salon to the practice hall.

This was not always true, however. Yen Yuan (1635-1704) was an example of a Confucian scholar who concluded that classical Chinese culture was "practical" in its nature. He established an academy of learning whose curriculum included the subjects of military strategy and martial arts along with astronomy, history and mathematics. Throughout its development, in different historical epochs, T'ai Chi would attract men who combined the world of thought and the world of action, modeled after Sun Tzu and famous statesmen-generals like Zhuge Liang and Liu Ji.

---

*It is important to remember that in the beginning and continuing into the 20th century, T'ai Chi was thought of primarily as a fighting martial art. And for many, this is still the case.

Aside from the fact that the nature of the martial arts involves doing rather than reading, there was also a practical problem that encouraged the growth of the oral tradition. Until recent times, China had a large illiteracy rate. The upper and middle classes could afford to send their children to school while the poor urban and peasant class, which represented the vast majority of Chinese, received almost no education at all. As a counterbalance, China had a rich oral literary tradition which was told and retold by poets, playwrights and puppeteers in the marketplace. Most Chinese of all classes were familiar with these histories and legends of the past. Even the lower classes were accumstomed to receiving their limited educations from the oral tradition. It was natural for students of T'ai Chi to look to their teachers and the oral tradition for knowledge of their art. Thus, a lively tradition of stories and tales grew up around T'ai Chi, a few of which were retold in the previous chapters.

Some scholars have suggested that the written word was less important than the oral tradition because of the primitive level of the printing press in China. This does not seem to be borne out by the facts. According to the historian Jacques Gernet, while the invention of typography was a great leap forward for Europe where only a few hundred letters were needed for any one text, it did not have the same significance for a culture whose language possessed a wealth of signs to write its language. "The superiority of Western printing," writes Gernet, "only asserted itself slowly and did not become incontestable until mechanized methods were developed in the nineteenth century." [8] Until then, the Chinese method of block printing efficiently and cheaply produced books on a level equal to and surpassing what was being printed in Europe.

Perhaps the most important reason for the emphasis on the oral tradition over the written one was the need for secrecy. The student who was taught orally often had only bits and pieces of the puzzle, which could take years to assemble into a coherent whole. In that time a teacher would have the opportunity to judge his character and determine if he was worthy of the complete teaching.

Then, too, there were teachers who, for various reasons, did not want their students to know more than they did. In China, as in the rest of the world, fame of one's martial arts prowess could be translated into financial gain at the expense of the original teacher. As a consequence, many great martial artists tended to keep their secrets under wraps, like family jewels, lest some unworthy steal them away.

An excellent example of this danger is the story* of how the T'ai Chi world came to possess the secrets of the Yang family. Stuart Avle Olson recounted the story in his journal, "The Bamboo Tablet": [9]

"It seems that in the late 1920s and early '30s a man named Chen Yen-lin, a rich merchant, was a student of Yang Cheng-fu. On one occasion he asked to borrow Master Yang's family notes to study during the evening. Master Yang agreed to allow this as long as the text was returned the next day. But it seems that Mr. Chen had hired seven transcribers who spent the night copying the text. In 1932 Mr. Chen published this work as his own, which of course infuriated the Yang family. I (Olson) heard this story from Master T. T. Liang, who in turn heard it from one of his teachers, Master Cheng Man-Ch'ing, who heard it from Yang Cheng-fu himself."

---

*Some well-known teachers have questioned the veracity of this story. Whether true or false, it is a clear example of how difficult it is to separate truth and fiction years after the event took place when the participants are no longer alive. Despite its controversial status, this story has found a place in the annals of T'ai Chi's oral tradition.

This story is an excellent example of the oral tradition becoming part of the written tradition. What he does not add here is that the theft encouraged the Yang family to publish its own version of their oral tradition. This episode, while having its negative, ethical implications, would be to the benefit of T'ai Chi students world-wide. Moreover, the way in which Olson heard the story is an excellent example of how the oral tradition is transmitted.

In sharp contrast to what we learned previously — that Yang Lu-shan taught openly — here it appears that the Yang family guarded its deepest secrets closely. There are those who claim on the basis of this story that Yang taught a popularized version of T'ai Chi to the public while retaining the pure traditon for his family and his closest students. This dualistic approach — of teaching openly and retaining one's secrets — often raises problems for T'ai Chi students who are uncertain whether or not they are receiving the complete tradition. Cheng Man Ch'ing, for one, tried to allay his students' fears by stating that he taught everything he knew and held nothing back, which, at the very least, suggests that such a problem existed.

In truth, being told the greatest secrets is of no use without a mentor to steer the student in the right direction. Usually the best that one can hope for is that the knowledge of secrets will help to keep one on the right track and perhaps provide some short cuts. A good teacher will try to guide the student so that his pupil will not make the same mistakes that he did and waste precious time. But one thing should be clear: there is no substitute for hard work, which is the unavoidable path to embodying all that T'ai Chi has to offer.

Patience is another virtue when nurturing the seeds of knowledge. Often one will be told something by his teacher or will read something in the T'ai Chi Classics that suddenly becomes crystal clear many years later. Some knowledge — the best kind — percolates in the hidden corners of our consciousness; like the locust that hibernates in the ground for seventeen years until it bursts out to see the light of day.

The Ascendancy of the Written Tradition

It is not uncommon for "oral" traditions to be written down and still be called the oral tradition. In Judaism, for example, the Oral Law was written down and embodied in the Talmud, which comprises one of the basic texts of the Jewish religion. Yet even though it was written down, the Talmud is still known as the "Oral law," being an amalgam of law, tradition and legends. In the same way that Olson heard the above story, one rabbi or scholar could support his point of view by stating that he heard it from his teacher, who in turn had heard it from his teacher, who saw the event occur. In this way the oral tradition lends the aura of personal authenticity that is not easily disputed.

Oral traditions were often written down in a fixed form at a particular time because that period was experiencing social and/or political instability. Devotees of their tradition feared that it might be lost forever, if not written down. This was certainly the case of the Talmud and very well might have been on the minds of those T'ai Chi masters who committed their knowledge to the written word. As pointed out earlier, China was often undergoing difficult and insecure periods in which life and property were in constant danger from human as well as natural disasters.

As the popularity of T'ai Chi increased in the twentieth century, the demand for more knowledge about it mushroomed. Thus, to satisfy this need, many more books were written about T'ai Chi. Among those satisfying this demand were no doubt some individuals drawn by the possibility of achieving fame and fortune. This was probably a factor in the theft of the Yang family notes.

This century has also witnessed the rise in literacy and therefore the publishing of more books than in the past, which also contributed to the availability of the written word. Not only were the T'ai Chi Classics published, but all kinds of commentaries and interpretive works on them, or about T'ai Chi in general, have found their way into the written word and now comprise what could be described as the "larger" written tradition, with the Classics occupying the center.

The Necessity of a Teacher

Yet, just because the principles were written down and accessible to all who could read them did not mean they were easily understood. For example:

"Up or down,
front or back,
left or right, are all the same.

These are all i (mind) and not external.

If there is up, there is down;
if there is forward, then there is backward;
if there is left, then there is right." [10]

A person who is experienced in T'ai Chi may have some idea of what these words mean; for the novice, the above quote might as well have been written in Moon-script. For most people it is extremely helpful to have a teacher/mentor, who can initiate the student into a tradition which has an interpretation of the T'ai Chi Classics and its principles. Otherwise, the student is walking around in the dark, bumping into things that seem familiar but never really knowing where he or she is.

Oral traditions — whether spoken or written — often contain secrets within secrets, with their own language, logic and unique interpretations. The ideas expressed in the tradition might seem obvious to the outsider but actually the true meaning is meant to be hidden from the uninitiated. This is true of the Talmud, for example, where, even if the student learns Aramaic — the language of the Talmud — it is no guarantee that he or she will grasp the inner meaning of the text or the interpretation that a particular tradition and its teachers have projected onto it.

Indeed some points are so obvious to the people on the inside of a tradition that they seem shocked when someone outside its cultural context asks a question regarding something fundamental. I once questioned Benjamin Pang Jeng Lo as to the meaning of the word "one" in the following passage from the T'ai Chi Classics: "Although the changes are numerous, the principle that pervades them is only one." It was a passage that had puzzled me for years. In reply to my query he said, "Tao," as though it were obvious. For someone like Lo, Tao is an accepted and integral part of his Chinese culture — something like the virgin birth for a believing Christian or the Divine Origins of Mosaic Law for an observant Jew — and is not easily accessible or obvious to someone from outside. After his answer many ideas and thoughts I had had about the Classics became clearer. This is a good example of what the Classics mean when they say one must be orally taught. While the written tradition can spark the right questions, often the answers can come only from an eminently qualified teacher of the oral tradition.

The Legitimacy of the T'ai Chi Classics

It is appropiate at this juncture to consider the warning of the scholar Douglas Wile who has been instrumental in translating many important T'ai Chi books into English:

"The few existing written documents, however charming, are grossly contradictory and there is not a single detail of record or recollection which is not the subject of bitter scholarly debate. No two genealogies are congruent and there are at least three completely different definitions of even such basic terms as "internal system" (nei-chia). Even the dates and activities of twentieth century figures are inconsistent in various sources." [11]

Bearing Wile's warning in mind, we can proceed in telling the most popular version of how the T'ai Chi Classics were found. This tradition suggests that it was a "historical accident" that we have the T'ai Chi Classics at all. Apparently an old manuscript was found in a salt shop in the 19th century and was passed on to Wu Yu-hsiang who was a student of the Ch'en family and Yang Lu-shan. Wu showed it to the latter who recognized it as "genuine" and interpreted it for Wu. Wu later wrote "Expositions and Insights," which became a recent addition to the Classics and was generally accepted by students of T'ai Chi. Susan Foe, one of the translators of the Classics, observed that Yang and Wu "made the Classics the literary foundation of their teachings and founded schools which survive to the present day." [12] The Yang and Wu schools of T'ai Chi have been extremely influential in the 20th century, spawning many great teachers and variations of their T'ai Chi forms.

The fact that the T'ai Chi Classics were found in the 19th century, in a salt shop, is not so far-fetched as it first might appear. If we think of two relatively recent discoveries in the West — the Dead Sea Scrolls and the Genizah in Cairo — the sudden finding of the Classics is altogether credible. What is less believable is that the early "authors" actually wrote what they are credited with. The first of the classics, for example, is attributed to Chang San-feng. The style is not at all what one would expect of a Taoist immortal. There are only two lines that suggest any connection to Taoist yoga techniques:

"The ch'i (breath) should be excited,
the shen (spirit) should be internally gathered." [13]

One would expect an elaboration of T'ai Chi in the context of Taoist yoga from someone like Chang San-feng who was well-versed in this area. The treatise itself reads like that of a master who understood the basics of Chinese culture and the physics of movement. Apparently the reason that this work was attributed to Chang San-feng was that there was a note attached to it which stated: "This classic was left by the patriarch Chang San-feng of Wu Tang Mountain. He desired the whole world to attain longevity, and not only martial techniques."

In China, as well as in other cultures, it was not unknown for writers to credit a famous person as the author of their work in order to enhance its value and authority. The Biblical book, *Ecclesiastes*, for example, was attributed to King Solomon, though most scholars believe that it was written at a far later date.

The Way to Proceed

It is clear that, at some point, a student of T'ai Chi should be introduced to the Classics. Most books on T'ai Chi have some of the Classics quoted in them along with the author's interpretation (see bibliography). One of the most reliable books in English is *The Essence of T'ai Chi Ch'uan* in which the Classics are arranged chronologically and in poetic form. It reads smoothly and clearly and allows for time to ponder the salient ideas of the texts. The concise treatises in this little book represents what might be called the "true" written tradition. The texts presented are generally accepted by most authorities as containing genuine and profound insights into T'ai Chi, although there is much scholarly dispute as to authorship and dates. As Wile points out, these issues may never be authoritatively and finally decided. Furthermore, this translation of the Classics contains almost no interpretation (as much as this can be said about any translation), except for a brief glossary of terms at the back, while the introductory sketch offers some historical background.

But the student need not limit him or herself to one translation or commentary. By comparing translations and commentaries, one can cull the insights and experience of numerous teachers. Fortunately T'ai Chi can claim a rich treasure of great teachers of all styles, past and present. The next step for a student is to find a commentary, like Wile's book of the Yang family's secret transmissions, or Lo and Inn's translation of Cheng Man Ch'ing's *Cheng Tzu's Thirteen Treatises on T'ai Chi Ch'uan*. Books like these commentaries gradually become "classics" in their own right. Fortunately, for the English speaking public, there are a number of translations of important commentaries on T'ai Chi.*

What cannot be stressed enough is that there is no substitute for a teacher who knows both the written and the oral traditions and who can guide the student in a step-by-step process to a deeper understanding of the art of T'ai Chi. One must find a mentor and choose well in order to be initiated into the inner circles of T'ai Chi. T'ai Chi cannot be learned from books or ancient manuscripts alone, nor will television videos be of much help. A deep experience of T'ai Chi means going back in time and adopting, as far as is possible, the model of the medicine man or woman and their apprentice. It requires a hands-on experience, initially *doing* much and talking, or even thinking, little. One must give the "critical mind" a rest and *temporarily* suspend one's judgement. Later, there will be time to evaluate the experience of the teaching. If this is not done, one experi-

---

* *The most extensive mail order house for books on T'ai Chi is Wayfarer Publications. For more information, see* T'AI CHI *(journal) in the bibliography.*

ences mainly the process of the critical mind at work and not the profound relationship that can be kindled betweeen teacher and student.

In the beginning, T'ai Chi necessitates memorization of movement, not unlike the methods of teaching in the ancient academies of China, Greece and Israel. It means approaching the teacher and the art with the deepest respect and purpose and, simultaneously, with a clarity of mind that recognizes magic and mystery as a legitimate part of all ancient traditions.

It is helpful if beginning students can nourish an inner confidence that things will sort themselves out in time, (which they usually do). Patience and trust are qualities that students must develop if they hope to have a fruitful encounter with traditional forms of learning. When students fully give of themselves to a teacher and the spirit of the tradition, in return, the gesture is abundantly rewarded.

The tradition of T'ai Chi is alive and flourishing, like a great tree rooted deep in the ground. Its students are the branches and leaves, growing and evolving in new ways, the same and yet different from what grew the season before. Only by a mature commitment can students come to know, express, and finally claim their full inheritance of the written and oral traditions that comprise T'ai Chi Ch'uan.

CHRONOLOGY OF CHINESE HISTORY

Dynasties	Approximate Dates	Men and Events
I. Legendary Period	(ca. 2852-2197 BCE)	
		Fu Hsi, Shen Nung, and Huang Ti's *The Yellow Emperor's Classic of Internal Medicine* (thought to be of a later period)
II. Primitive Dynasties	(2197-221 BCE)	
Hsia	(1994-1523)	Casting of Bronze
Shang (Yin)	(1523-1027)	Oracle Bones of Yin
Chou	(1025-256)	The idea of the all-powerful god, Shan-Ti declines Feudal system falls Time of Confucius, Lao Tzu, Chuang Tzu
Warring States Period	(ca. 403-221)	The great writings: *Tao Te Ching, The Analects of Confucius, The Art of War, I Ching* (compiled in its final form)
III. Ancient Dynasties	(221 BCE-618 CE)	
Chin	(221-207 BCE)	Great Wall of China is built Book burning
Han	(207 BCE-220 CE)	Development and unification of Yin and Yang and Five Elements Theories from ancient sources Confucius deified Growth of Taoism

Dynasties	Approximate Dates	Men and Events
Han cont.		Buddhism introduced (2nd century CE) Hua T'o and Tao Yin exercises Revolt of two sects of religious Taoism
Three Kingdoms	(220-265)	Religious Taoism recognized as an official state religion
Chin (Tsin)	(265-420)	Seng-chao's Immutability of Things (Buddhism) Ko Hung, Taoist alchemist
North and South	(420-589)	Bodhidharma, founder of Ch'an Buddhism and Shao Lin health and self-defense exercises
Sui	(589-618)	
IV. Medieval Dynasties	(618-1279 CE)	
T'ang	(618-905)	Fa Tsang and the Flower Garland School Ch'an Buddhism flourishes (Northern and Southern Schools)
Five Dynasties	(905-960)	Buddhist persecutions Beginnings of Neo-Confucian philosophy
Sung	(960-1279)	The Neo-Confucians: Chou Tun-i, Chang Tsai, and Chu Hsi The idea of Ch'i becomes fully developed
Yüan (Mongol)	(1280-1368)	Chang San-feng, legendary founder of T'ai Chi Ch'uan

Dynasties	Approximate Dates	Men and Events
V. Modern Dynasties	(1368-1911 CE)	
Ming	(1368-1644)	Wang Tsung-yueh, T'ai Chi's link to its founder The T'ai Chi of the Ch'en family is developed
Ch'ing (Manchu)	(1644-1911)	Yang Lu-Shan, founder of Yang style T'ai Chi and his descendants Wu style T'ai Chi T'ai Chi Classics found (19th century)
VI. Republic of China	(1912 CE-)	
Sun Yat-sen	(1912) First Republic	The ongoing popularization of T'ai Chi:
Yuan Shih-kai	(1912-1916)	
Chiang K'ai-shek	(1927-) Second Republic and Taiwan	
Mao Tse-tung	(1949-) Third People's Republic	T'ai Chi's beginnings in the West (1960s-), due in large part to the early ties of the West to Taiwan and the immigration of teachers like Cheng Man Ch'ing, Da Liu and T.T. Liang The Communist state begins to encourage T'ai Chi as a health practice – The Peking 24 is introduced, as a simplified style of T'ai Chi

FOOTNOTES

Chapter 1

1. Veith, The *Yellow Emperor's Classic of Internal Medicine*, p. 9.
2. Ibid., p. 97.
3. See Da Lui's *T'ai Chi Ch'uan and I Ching* and Cheng Man Ch'ing's Cheng Tzu's Thirteen Treatises on T'ai Chi Ch'uan, Treatise Three, p.30.
4. Chang Chung-yuan, *Creativity and Taoism*, p. 62.
5. Sun Tzu, *The Art of War*, Trans. by T. Cleary, p. 27.
6. Lao Tzu, *Tao Te Ching*, Trans. by Feng and English, Ch. 31.
7. *The Analects of Confucius*, Trans. by James Legge, p. 254.
8. Ibid., p. 198.

Chapter 2

1. Chan, W. T., *A Source Book in Chinese Philosophy*, p. 245.
2. *The Essence of T'ai Chi*, edit. by Lo, Inn, Amacker and Foe, p. 31.
3. Ibid., p. 38.

4. Ibid., p. 27.
5. Smith, Robert, *Chinese Boxing*, p. 36.
6. Chang Chung-yuan, p. 139-140.
7. *The Jerusalem Bible*, Genesis, Ch. 2, v. 7, p. 2.
8. Needham, Joseph, *Science and Civilization in China*, Vol. 2, p. 273.
9. Chan, W. T., p. 244.
10. *Tao Te Ching*, Trans. by Feng and English, Ch. 2.
11. Kaptchuk, Ted, *The Web That Has No Weaver*, p. 8-11.
12. Chan, W. T., p. 247.
13. Ibid., p. 248-249.
14. Veith, p. 115.
15. *Sunflower Splendor*, ed. Wu-Chi Liu and Irving Lo, p. 32-33.
16. Thomas, Dylan, *Collected Poems*, p. 10.
17. *The Jerusalem Bible*, Ecclesiastes, ch. 3, v. 1-4, p. 877.
18. Capra, Fritjob, *The Tao of Physics*, p.160.
19. Blofeld, John, *Gateway To Wisdom*, p. 17.
20. Capra, *The Tao of Physics*, p. 194.
21. Chan, W. T., p. 249.
22. Ibid., p. 245.

Chapter 3

1. Creel, H. G., Confucius And The Chinese Way, p. 135.
2. *The Analects of Confucius*, Book vii, ch. 20, p. 201.
3. Ibid., Book xi, ch. 11, p. 240.
4. Chang, Chung-yuan, p. 23.
5. Creel, p. 1.
6. *The Analects of Confucius*, Book xii, ch. 5, 253.
7. Yang, C. K., *Religion in Chinese Society*, p. 244.
8. Cheng, Man-jan (Cheng Man Ching), *Lao Tzu: "My words are very easy to understand,"* p. 79.
9. Tao Te Ching, Translated by R. Wilhelm, p. 11.

10. Chang, Chung-yuan, p. 23-24.
11. *Tao Te Ching*, Trans. by Richard Wilhelm, p. 1-2.
12. Creel, p. 195 and Needham, p. 35-36.
13. *Tao Te Ching*, Feng and English, ch. 1.
14. Ibid., ch. 21.
15. Cheng, Man-jan, *Lao Tzu...*, p. 34.
16. *Tao Te Ching*, Feng and English, ch. 14.
17. Ibid., ch. 14.
18. *Tao Te Ching*, Wilhelm, p. 72.
19. *Tao Te Ching*, Feng and English, ch. 42.
20. Needham, p. 478.
21. Chang, Chung-yuan, p. 211, (author's italics).
22. *The Essence of T'ai Chi*, p. 31.
23. *I Ching*, trans. by Richard Wilhelm, Intro., p. xxxviii.
24. Ibid., p. xxxiv-xxxv.
25. Fung, Yu-lan, *A History of Chinese Philosophy*, Vol. 1, p. 392.
26. Tao Te Ching, Feng and English, ch. 12.
27. Ibid., ch. 48.
28. Ibid., ch. 49.
29. For a general overview of the concept of Jen, *see* W. T. Chan, p. 788-789.
30. Fung, Yu-lan, Vol. 1, p. 226.
31. *The Way of Chuang Tzu*, trans. by Thomas Merton, p. 103-104.
32. *Tao Te Ching*, Feng and English, ch. 2.
33. Ibid., ch. 2.
34. Fung, Yu-lan, Vol. 1, p. 239.
35. *Chuang Tzu*, trans. by Burton Watson, p. 34-35.
36. *The Way of Chuang Tzu*, Merton, p. 154.
37. Chan, W. T., p. 178.
38. Ibid,. p. 179.
39. *The Way of Chuang Tzu*, Merton, p. 60.

40. Cheng Man Ch'ing, *Cheng Tzu's Thirteen Treatises...*, p. 77-78.
41. *Chuang Tzu*, Watson, p. 27.
42. Ibid., p. 121.
43. *The Way of Chuang Tzu*, Merton, p. 52.
44. Ibid., p. 53.
45. Ibid., p. 153.
46. Chang, Chung-yuan, p. 129.
47. See Rowley, *Principles of Chinese painting*.
48. *The Way of Chuang Tzu*, Merton, p. 111.
49. Ibid., p. 109.

Chapter 4

1. Fung, Yu-lan, vol. 2, p. 240.
2. Chan, W. T., p. 337.
3. Fung, Yu-lan, *A Short History of Chinese Philosophy*, p. 3.
4. Yang, C. K., p. 282-283.
5. Chan, W. T., p. 425.
6. Dumoulin, Heinrich, *Zen Buddhism: A History*, p. 64.
7. Day, Clarence Burton, *The Philosophers of China*, p. 107.
8. Chan, W. T., p. 345.
9. Capra, *The Tao of Physics*, p. 77, author's italics.
10. *The Essence of T'ai Chi Ch'uan*, p. 54.
11. Ibid., p. 89.
12. Ibid., p. 89.
13. *T'ai Chi Touchstones: Yang Family Secret Transmissions*, trans. by Douglas Wile, p. 109.
14. *The Essence of T'ai Chi Ch'uan*, p. 89.
15. Ibid., p. 32.
16. Cheng Man Ch'ing, *Cheng Tzu's Thirteen Treatises...*, Trans. by Benjamin Pang Jeng Lo and Martin Inn, p. 60.
17. Suzuki, D. T., *The Awakening of Zen*, p. 29.
18. Hoover, Thomas, *Zen Culture*, p. 47.

19. *Dialogues of Plato*, p. 80.
20. Chang, Chung-yuan, p. 13.
21. Suzuki, D. T., *The Zen Doctrine of No Mind*, p. 17.
22. Ibid., p. 22.
23. Clark, Ronald, *Einstein...*, p. 115.
24. Fung, Yu-lan, Vol. 2, p. 399.
25. Leggett, Trevor, *Zen and the Ways*, p. 82.
26. Chang, Chung-yuan, p. 43.
27. Chen, Wei-ming, *The T'ai Chi Ch'uan Ta Wen*, p. 21.
28. *Cheng Man-Ch'ing's Advanced T'ai-Chi Form Instructions....*, trans by Douglas Wile, p. 11.
29. Suzuki, D. T., *The Awakening of Zen*, p. 30.

Chapter 5

1. Blofeld, J., *Taoism; The Quest for Immortality*, p. 90.
2. Thompson, Laurence G., *Chinese Religion*, p. 18.
3. Yang, C. K., *Religion in Chinese Society*, p. 28.
4. *Chuang Tzu*, Trans. by Burton Watson, p. 11.
5. Fung, Yu-lan, *A Short History...*, p. 3.
6. *The Encyclopedia of Eastern Philosophy and Religion*, p. 79.
7. Cheng, Man-jan, Lao Tzu..., p. 1.
8. Fung, Yu-lan, Vol. 1, p. 175.
9. Fung Yu-lan, *A Short History...*, p. 219.
10. *The Secret of the Golden Flower*, Trans. by Richard Wilhelm, p. 17.
11. Ibid., p. 17.
12. *The Essence of T'ai Chi Ch'uan*, p. 66.
13. *Tao Te Ching*, Feng and English, ch. 76.
14. Ibid., ch. 25.
15. Gernet, J., *A History of Chinese Civilization*, p. 210.
16. Capra, *The Tao of Physics*, p. 114.
17. Needham, Joseph, vol. 1, p. 33 quoted in.

18. Cheng, Man-jan, *Lao Tzu...*, p. 12.
19. *Tao Te Ching*, Feng and English, ch. 10.
20. Blofeld, J., *Gateway to Wisdom*, p. 12.
21. Blofeld, J., *Taoism...*, p. 180.

Chapter 6

1. *Tao Te Ching*, Feng and English, ch. 28.
2. Bruce, J. P., *Chu Hsi and His Masters*, p. 23.
3. *I Ching*, trans. by James Legge, Appendice III, p. 373.
4. *The Essence of T'ai Chi Ch'uan*, p. 21.
5. Ibid., p. 44.
6. Cheng Man Ch'ing, *Thirten Treatises...*, p. 89.
7. Bruce, J. P., p. 134.
8. Chan, W. T., p. 464-465.
9. Bruce, J. P., p. 139.
10. *The Essence of T'ai Chi Ch'uan*, p. 31.
11. *Tao Te Ching*, Feng and English, ch. 1.
12. *The Essence of T'ai Chi Ch'uan*, p. 32.
13. Chan, W. T., p. 638.
14. Chang, Carsun, *The Development of Neo-Confucian Thought*, p. 261.
15. Chan, W. T., p. 463.
16. Kaptchuk, p. 4.
17. Chan, W. T., p. 463.
18. Bruce, J. P., p. 102.
19. Kaptchuk, p. 35-36.
20 *The Encyclopedia of Eastern Philosophy and Religion*, p. 69.
21. Capra, Fritjof, *Uncommon Wisdom*, p. 170-173.
22. Needham, J., Vol. 2, p. 484.
23. Cheng Man Ch'ing, *T'ai Chi Ch'uan...*, trans by Beauson Tseng, p. 6.
24. Chan, W. T., p. 590.

25. Chang, Carsun, p. 178.
26. Da Liu, *T'ai Chi Ch'uan and Meditation*, p. 20.

Chapter 7

1. Cheng Man-Jan, *Lao Tzu...*, p. 28.
2. *Tao Te Ching*, Feng and English, ch. 48.
3. *Sunflower Splendor*, p. 96.
4. Siou, Lily, *Ch'i Kung*, p. 5.
5. Cooper, J. C., *Chinese Alchemy...*, p. 110.
6. Waysun Liao, *The T'ai Chi Classics*, p. 9.
7. Cheng Man Ch'ing, *T'ai Chi Ch'uan*, trans. by Beauson Tseng, p. 9.
8. Feldenkrais, M., *Body and Mature Behavior*, chapter 8.
9. Genesis, 1:26.
10. Gernet, J., *Daily Life in China...*, p. 105.
11. Chen Wei-Ming, *Tai Chi Ch'uan Ta Wen*, p. 15.
12. Cheng Man Ch'ing, *T'ai Chi Ch'uan*, trans. by Beauson Tseng, p. 5.
13. Smith, R., *Chinese Boxing*, Appendix A, p. 113-114.
14. Chen Wei-Ming, *Tai Chi Ch'uan Ta Wen*, p. 13.
15. Huang, Wen-Shan, *Fundamentals of Tai Chi Ch'uan*, p. 61.
16. *T'ai-Chi Touchstones...*, Translator's Note.
17. Ibid., p. 153-154.
18. Ibid., p. 100-101
19. *The Essence of T'ai Chi Ch'uan*, p. 35.
20. Ibid., p. 87.
21. Smith, R., *Chinese Boxing*, p. 42-43.
22. *Tao Te Ching*, Feng and English, ch. 78.

Chapter 8

1. *T'ai Chi Touchstones...*, p. 136.
2. Goldsmith, E., *The Way...*, p. 97.

3. Stevens, John, *Abundant Peace...*, p. 112.
4. *T'ai Chi Touchstones...*, p. 104.
5. Vieth, p. 108.
6. Zee, Dr. W., "The Mechanism of Healing in T'ai Chi," *T'AI CHI*, April, 1994, vol. 18, no. 2, p. 26-27.
7. *The Essence of T'ai Chi Ch'uan*, p. 21.
8. "An Interview with Yang Zhenduo," *T'AI CHI*, August, 1990, Vol. 14, no. 4, p. 4.
9. *The Essence of T'ai Chi Ch'uan*, p. 32.
10. *T'ai Chi Touchstones...*, p. 119.
11. *The Essence of T'ai Chi Ch'uan*, p. 40.
12. Siegel, B., *Love, Medicine and Miracles*, p. 164-165, from a list compiled by Al Siebert.
13. *Tao Te Ching*, ch. 28.
14. Huanchu, Daoren, *Back To Beginnings*, p. 131.

Chapter 9

1. *The Essence of T'ai Chi Ch'uan*, p. 22.
2. Ibid., p. 65.
3. Chan, W. T., p. 274.
4. *The Encyclopedia of Eastern Philosophy and Religion*, p. 183.
5. *The Essence of T'ai Chi Ch'uan*, p. 46.
6. Chang, Carsun, p. 271.
7. Cheng Man Ch'ing, *Thirteen Treatises...*, p. 41.
8. *The Essence of T'ai Chi Ch'uan*, p. 44
9. Chan, W. T., p. 62.
10. *The Essence of T'ai Chi Ch'uan*, p. 82.
11. Laing, R. D., *The Divided Self*, p. 162.
12. Herrigel, E., *Zen in the Art of Archery*, p. 80.
13. Ibid., p. 76.
14. Ibid., p. 77.
15. *The Essence of T'ai Chi Ch'uan*, p. 53.

16. See Siegel, B., *Love, Medicine and Miracles*.
17. *The Essence of T'ai Chi Ch'uan*, p. 19.
18. *Cheng Man Ching's Advanced T'ai-Chi Form Instructions...*, p. 16-17.
19. *The Essence of T'ai Chi Ch'uan*, p. 47.
20. Lowenthal, Wolfe, *There are no Secrets*, p. 98.
21. Siegel, B., p. 154-155.
22. Lowenthal, W., p. 98.
23. *Tao Te Ching*, Feng and English, ch. 37.
24. *The Analects of Confucius*, Lun-yu, 15.4.
25. *Tao Te Ching*, Feng and English, ch. 43.
26. Ibid., ch. 76.
27. Siegel, B., p. 144.
28. Dawson, C, *Religion...*, p. 157.
29. Chan, W. T., p. 98.
30. *Mastering the Art of War*, Trans. by T. Cleary, p. 13.
31. Chan, W. T., p. 100.
32. *Full Circle*, Vol. I, no. 4, p. 3.
33. *The Essence of T'ai Chi Ch'uan*, p. 33 & 38.
34. Ibid., p. 59.
35. Unpublished classnotes, Jan. 7, 1973.
36. Cheng Man-jan, *Lao Tzu...*, Trans by Tam Gibbs, p. 65.
37. *The Way of Chuang Tzu*, compiled by T. Merton, p. 43.
38. *The Essence of T'ai Chi Ch'uan*, p. 21.
39. Ibid., p. 21.
40. *T'AI CHI*, Dec , 1988, Vol 12, no. 6, p. 10.
41. *The Essence of T'ai Chi Ch'uan*, p. 55.
42. Fung, Yu-lan, Vol. I, p. 179.
43. *The Essence of T'ai Chi Ch'uan*, p. 38.
44. Ibid., p. 38.
45. Ibid., p. 54.
46. *T'ai Chi Touchstones...*, p. 97.
47. *The Essence of T'ai Chi Ch'uan*, p. 34.

48. Sun Tzu, *The Art of War*, p. 82.
49. *The Essence of T'ai Chi Ch'uan*, p. 82.
50. *Tao Te Ching*, Feng and English, ch. 34.
51. *Full Circle*, Vol. I, No. 4, p. 13.
52. *The Essence of T'ai Chi Ch'uan*, p. 19 & 20.
53. *Tao Te Ching*, ch. 12 & 14
54. Smith, B., *Chinese Boxing*, p. 77.
55. *Mastering the Art of War*, p. 58, my emphasis.
56. *The Essence of T'ai Chi Ch'uan*, p. 89.
57. Ibid., p. 53.
58. Ibid., p. 89.

Afterword

1. Raz, Simcha, *A Tzaddik in our Time*, p. 108.

Appendix

1. *The Essence of T'ai Chi Ch'uan*, p. 14.
2. *Tao Te Ching*, Feng and English, ch. 19.
3. Sun Tzu, *The Art of War*, trans. by T. Cleary, p. 104.
4. *The Essence of T'ai Chi Ch'uan*, p. 34.
5. Ibid., p. 65.
6. *T'ai Chi Touchstones...*, Translator's Note.
7. Gernet, J., *Daily Life in China...*, p. 152.
8. Gernet, J., *A History of Chinese Civilization*, p. 332-336.
9. *The Bamboo Tablet*, Summer/Fall, 1992, p. 1.
10. *The Essence of T'ai Chi Ch'uan*, p. 22.
11. *T'ai Chi Touchstones...*, Translator's Note.
12. *The Essence of T'ai Chi Ch'uan*, p. 9.
13. Ibid., p. 19.

BIBLIOGRAPHY

Bamboo Tablet (journal), published by Stuart Alve Olson, Minn. & Calif.

Binger Gerhardson, *Memory and Manuscript, Oral Tradition and Written Transmission in Rabbinic Judaism and Early Christianity,* C. W. K. Gleerlup Lund Ejnar Munksgaard, Copenhagen, 1961.

Blofeld, John, *Taoism: The Quest for Immortality*, Unwin Paperbacks, London, 1979.

Blofeld, John, *Gateway to Wisdom*, Shambhala, Boulder, 1980.

Bruce, Joseph Percy, *Chu Hsi and His Masters*, reprinted AMS Press, New York, 1973.

Capra, Fritjof, *The Tao of Physics*, Third Edition, Expanded, Shambhala, Boston, 1991.

Capra, Fritjof, *The Turning Point: Science, Society and the Rising Culture*, Flamingo, London, 1982.

Capra, Fritjof, *Uncommon Wisdom*, Fontana, London, 1989.

Castaneda, Carlos, *The Teachings of Don Juan: A Yaqui Way of Knowledge*, Penguin.

Chan, W. T., *A Source Book in Chinese Philosophy*, Translated and Complied by W. T. Chan, Princeton Uni. Press, 1969.
   The most important source book on Chinese philosophy in English.

Chang, Carsun, *The Development of Neo-Confucian Thought*, Bookman Asso., New York, 1957.

Chang, Joland, *The Tao of Love and Sex: The Ancient Chinese Way to Ecstasy*, Dutton, New York, 1977.

Chang, Chung-yuan, *Creativity and Taoism, A Study of Chinese Philosophy, art, and Poetry*, Harper Torchbooks, New York, 1970.
   A fascinating study of Chinese philosophy and its influence on the arts.

Chen, Wei-Ming, T'ai Chi Ch'uan Ta Wen: Questions and Answers on T'ai Chi Ch'uan, trans. by Benjamin Pang Jeng Lo and Robert W. Smith, North Atlantic books, Berkeley, Calif., 1985.
   One of the senior students of the Yang family poses the questions that every T'ai Chi student should want to know, and then answers them.

Cheng Man-Ch'ing,* *Cheng Man-Ch'ing's Advanced Tai-chi Form Instructions with Selected Writings on Meditation, The I Ching, Medicine and the Arts*. compiled and trans. by Douglas Wile, Sweet Ch'i Press, Brooklyn, 1985.
   The master of five excellencies — art, poetry, calligraphy, medicine and T'ai Chi — Professor Cheng was a gift to western students of T'ai Chi. His ideas are a must for the serious student.

Cheng, Man Ch'ing, *Cheng Tzu's Thirteen Treatises on T'ai*

There are several standard ways of spelling T'ai Chi or Chinese names in English. But none that everyone follows. I am following spelling of each author.

Chi Ch'uan, trans. by Benjamin Pang Jeng Lo and Martin Inn, North Atlantic Books, Berkeley, Calif., 1985.

Cheng Man Ch'ing, *Master Cheng's Thirteen Chapters on Tai-chi Ch'uan*, trans. by Douglas Wile, Sweet Ch'i Press, Brooklyn, N. Y., 1984.

Cheng Man-Ch'ing, *T'ai Chi Ch'uan: A Simplified Method of Calisthenics for Health and Self Defense*, trans. by Beauson Tseng, North Atlantic Books, Richmond, Calif.,1981.

Cheng Man-jan (Cheng Man Ch'ing), *Lao Tzu: my words are very easy to understand*, trans. by Tam C. Gibbs, North Atlantic Books, Richmond, Calif., 1981.

Clark, Ronald W., *Einstein: The Life and Times*, Avon Books, 1972.

Chuang Tzu, Basic Writings, trans. by Burton Watson, Columbia Uni. Press, 1964.

Chuang Tzu, The Inner Chapters, trans. by A. C. Graham, Unwin Paperbacks, 1986.

The Way of Chuang Tzu, compiled by Thomas Merton, New Directions, 1969.
  My favorite stories of Chuang Tzu compiled and introduced by one of my favorite modern authors, Thomas Merton.

Cleary, Thomas, see *Vitality, Energy Spirit; Mastering the art of War; and Sun Tzu, The Art of War.*
  A prolific translator who pens fascinating introductions.

Confucius, *Confucian Analects, The Great Learning and The Doctrine of the Mean*, trans. by James Legge, Dover Pub., N. Y., 1971.

Cooper, J. C., *Chinese Alchemy, The Taoist Quest for Immortality*, Sterling Pub., New York, 1990.

Cooper, J. C., *Yin & Yang, The Taoist Harmony of Opposites*. The Aquarian Press. Wellingborough, Northamptonshire, 1981.

Creel, H. G., *Confucius and the Chinese Way*, Harper Torchbooks, New York, 1960.

Crompton, Paul, *The T'ai Chi Workbook*, Shambhala, Boston, 1987.

Da Liu, *Tai Chi Ch'uan and I Ching*, Perennial Library, New York, 1978.
    One of the great masters who is in his nineties and still teaching in New York. His ideas on T'ai Chi and Chinese philosophy are veryimportant for the western student.

Da Liu, *T'ai Chi Ch'uan and Meditation*, Arkana Books, London.

Da Liu, *Taoist Health Exercise Book,* Links Books, 1974.

Dawson, Christopher, *Religion and the Rise of Western Culture*, Image Books, Garden City, N. Y., 1958.

Day, Clarence Burton, *The Philosophers of China, Classical and Contemporary*, The Citadel Press, 1978.

Dumoulin, Heinrich, *Zen Buddhism: A History*, trans. by James W. Heisigand and Paul Knitter, Macmillan Pub., N.Y., 1988.

The Encyclopedia of Eastern Philosophy and Religion, Shambhala, Boston, 1989.

The Essence of T'ai Chi Ch'uan: The Literary Tradition, trans. andedited by Benjamin Pang Jeng Lo, Martin Inn, Robert Amacker and Susan Foe, North Atlantic Books, Richmond, Calif., 1979.
    This book should be the bible of T'ai Chi students.

Feldenkrais, Moshe, *Awareness Through Movement: Health Exercises for Person Growth*, Penguin, 1972.

Feldenkrais, Moshe, *Body and Mature Behavior: A Study of Anxiety, Sex, Gravitation and Learning*, Alef Ltd., Tel-Aviv, 1980.

Full Circle (Journal), Rocky Mountain T'ai-chi Ch'uan Foundation, Boulder, Colo.

Fung, Yu-lan, *A History of Chinese Philosophy*, trans. by Derk Bodde, 2 vols., Peiking, Hen: Vetch, 1937.
   An indispensible history by one of China's greatest modern philosophers.

Fung, Yu-lan, *A Short History of Chinese Philosophy*, edited by Derk Bodde, The Free Press Edition, N.Y., 1966.

Gelb, Michael, *Body Learning, An Introduction to the Alexander Technique*, Henry Holt, N.Y., 1987.

Gernet, Jacques, *Daily Life in China on the Eve of the Mongol Invasion 1250-1266*, Stanford Uni. Press, 1970.

Gernet, Jacques, *A History of Chinese Civilization*, trans. by J. R. Foster, Cambridge Uni. Press, 1982.

Gibb, H. A. R., *Mohammadanism*, Oxford Uni. Press, London & Oxford, 1971.

Goldsmith, Edward, *The Way: An Ecological World-view*, Shambhala, Boston, 1993.

Herrigel, Eugen, *Zen in the Art of Archery*, MacGraw Hill, 1964.
   A Classic!

Hoakham, Hilda, *A Short History of China*, Longman Green & Co., London and Harlow, 1969.

Hoover, Thomas, *Zen Culture*, Arkana, 1989.

Huanchu, Daoren, *Back To Beginnings, Reflections on the Tao*, trans. by Thomas Cleary, Shambhala, Boston and London, 1990.

Huang, Wen-Shan, *Fundamentals of Tai Chi Ch'uan*, South Sky Book, 1979.

I Ching, The Tao of Organization, tran. by Thomas Cleary, Shambhala, Boston and London, 1988.

The I Ching, tran. by James Legge, Second Adition, Dover Pub., New York.

The I Ching or Book of Changes, The Richard Wilhelm Translation, rendered into English by Gary F. Baynes, Vol. I, Routledge and Kegan Paul Ltd., 1951.

The Jerusalem Bible, Koren Pub., Jerusalem, 1983.

Jones, Frank Pierce, *Body Awareness in Action*, Schocken, N.Y., 1976.

Jou, Tsung Hwa, *The Tao of Tai-Chi Chuan: The Way to Rejuvenation*, Tai Chi Foundation, N.Y., 4th edition, 1981.
    An excellent source book for T'ai Chi.

Kaptchuk, Ted, *The Web That Has No Weaver*, Congdon and Weed, N.Y., 1983.

Laing, R. D., *The Divided Self*, Pelican Edition, 1965.

Lao Tzu, *Tao Te Ching*, trans. by Gia-Fu Feng and Jane English, Vintage Books, N.Y., 1972.

Lao Tzu, *Tao Te Ching, The Book of Meaning and Life*, trans. and comm. by Richard Wilhelm, trans. to English by H. G. Ostwald, Arkana, 1985.

Leggett, Trevor, *Zen and the Ways*, Shambhala, Boulder, 1978.

Leonard, George, *Mastery*, Dutton, N. Y., 1991.

Liang, T. T., *T'ai Chi Chuan for Health and Self Defence*, Redwing, 1974.
    The first book I read as a beginner. It helped enormously.

Lloyd, Dennis, *The Idea of Law*, Penguin, 1964.
A classic in its field.

Lowenthal, Wolfe, *There Are No Secrets*, North Atlantic Books, Berkeley, Calif., 1992.
An intimate look at Cheng Man Ch'ing from the perspective of a one of his students.

Mastering The Art Of War: Zhuge Liang's and Lui Ji's Commentaries on the Classic by Sun Tzu, trans. and edited by Thomas Cleary, Shambhala, Boston & Shaftesbury, 1989.

Needham, Joseph, *Science and Civilization* in China, Vols. 2, Cambridge Uni. Press, 1956.
Also a classic.

Pang, T. Y., *On Tai Chi Chuan*, Azalea Press, Bellingham, Wash., 1987.

Peck, M. Scott, *The Road Less Traveled, A New Psychology of Love, Traditional Values and Spiritual Grouth*, Rider, 1985.

Pelletier, Kenneth R., *Mind as Healer, Mind as Slayer, A Holistic approach to preventing stress disorders*, Delta, N. Y. 1977.

Plato, *Dialogue of Plato*, Pocket Library, N. Y., 1955.

Raz, Simcha, *A Tzaddik In Our Time*, trans. by Charles Wengrov, Feldheim, Jerusalem, N. Y., 1978

Rowley, George, *Principles of Chinese Painting*, Princeton Uni. Press, 1947.

Russell, Bertrand, *A History of Western Philosophy*, Touchstone, Simon and Schuster, 1945.

The Secret of the Golden Flower, trans. and explained by Richard Wilhelm, Harvest, 1962.

Secrets of Shaolin Temple Boxing, edited by Robert Smith,

Charles E. Tuttle, Rutland Vt. and Tokyo, 1981.

Siegel, Bernie S., M.D., *Love, Medicine and Miracles*, Perenial Library, Harper and Row, 1988.

Siou, Lilly, *Ch'i Kung*, Charles E. Tuttle, Rutland, Vt., 1975.

Smith, Robert W., *Chinese Boxing, Masters and Methods*, Kodansha International, Tokyo, New York, San Francisco, 1980.
 A classic on martial arts in Taiwan during the late fifties by a Westerner who visited and studied with many teachers there.

Stevens, John, *Abundant Peace, The Biography of Morihei Ueshiba, Founder of Akido*, Shambhala, Boston and London, 1987.

Sun Tzu, *The Art of War*, trans. by Thomas Cleary, Shambhala, Boston and Shaftsbury, 1988.
 Rich and insightful with pointers on life as well as push-hands.

Sunflower Splendor: Three Thousand Years of Chinese Poetry, edited by Wu-chi Liu and Irving Lo, Indiana Uni. Press, Bloomington, 1975.
 A stunning collection of Chinese poetry.

Suzuki, D. T., *The Awakening of Zen*, edited by Christmas Humphreys, Shambhala, Boston and London, 1987.
 Anything written by D. T. Suzuki, the man who almost single-handedly brought Zen to the west, is well worth reading.

Suzuki, D. T., *The Zen Doctrine of No Mind*, edited by Christmas Humphreys, Rider, 1969.

Suzuki, Shunryu, *Zen Mind, Beginner's Mind*, Weatherhill, New York & Tokyo, 1994.
 I find myself returning to this book for inspiration and clarity.

T'AI CHI (journal), Wayfarer pub., edited by Marvin Smallheiser, L.A., Calif.
 A bi-monthly journal that has served the T'ai Chi community

well for many years with informative and practical articles. It is also one of the best sources for ordering books on T'ai Chi. To write for a catalogue: Wayfarer Publications, P.O. Box 26156, Los Angeles, Calif. 90026.

Tai-chi Touchstones: Yang Family Secret Transmissions, trans. and compiled by Douglas Wile, Sweet Ch'i Press, 1983.
    Invaluable source of T'ai Chi commentary from the Yang family and others.

Thomas, Dylan, *The Collected Poems of Dylan Thomas*, New Directions, 1957.

Thompson, Lawrence G., *Chinese Religion*, 4th edition, Wadsworth pub.,1989.

Tobin, Michael S., *Psychosomatic Unity: The philosophy and psychology of Body-Mind Integration*. Unpublished doctoral thesis, Middlebury,Vt., 1979.

Taoist Tales, edited by Raymond Van Over, Meridian, 1984.

Veith, Ilza, *The Yellow Emperor's Classic of Internal Medicine*, Uni. of Calif. press, 1972.

Vitality, Energy, Spirit: A Taoist Sourcebook, trans. by Thomas Cleary, Shambhala, Boston and London, 1991.

Waysun Liao, *T'ai Chi Classics*, Shambhala, Boston and London, 1990.

Wei Tsuei, *Roots of Chinese Culture and Medicine*, Chinese Culture Books, Oakland, 1989.

Yang, C. K., *Religion in Chinese Society*, Uni. of Calif. Press, Berkeley and Los Angeles, 1961.
    A Classic in the field of Chinese religion.

Yang, Jwing-ming Dr., *Advanced Yang Style Tai Chi Chuan*, Vols 1 & 2, YMAA Publication Center, Jamaica Plains,

Mass., 1987.
  Dr. Yang's books are among the best.

Yang, Jwing-ming Dr., *The Root of Chinese Chi Kung: The Secrets of Chi Kung training*, YMAA Pub. Center, Jamaica Plains, Mass., 1989.

Zukov, Gary, *The Dancing Wu Li Masters: An Overview of the New Physics*, Flamingo, London, 1984.

INDEX

ORDER FORM

Name _____

Address _____

City _____ State or Country _____

Zip _____

❑ check ❑ money order or International Bank check (personal checks take 3 weeks to clear)

Please send me *Beyond the Closed Door* at **$19.95** per copy:

QUANTITY	PRICE	TOTAL

Add $5.00 for airmail (about two weeks from shipping date) and $2.50 for each additional copy or $3.00 by ship (two to three months) and $1.50 for each additional copy.

Make check(s) payable to Anne Lemieux.
Send to: The Almond Blossom Press
          P.O. Box 10600, Jerusalem, Israel.
          Fax: 972-2-933394

All checks must be in U.S. Dollars.

Mr. Breslow is available for workshops and lectures on T'ai Chi, Chinese culture and stress management techniques.
For information, write to the above address.

ABOUT THE AUTHOR

Arieh Lev Breslow has been teaching T'ai Chi for the past twenty years. He is the author of numerous articles on T'ai Chi, two of which are "T'ai Chi: The Cosmic Mobile" and "The Tao of Birthing." He is a graduate of the University of Nebraska in economics and the University of Wisconsin where he earned his MA in History. The last fourteen years he has been living in Jerusalem, Israel with his wife and three daughters where he founded the Jerusalem School of T'ai Chi Ch'uan.